PAUL AND THE PRISON EPISTLES

the Smart Guide to the Bible™ series

Kathy Collard Miller

Larry Richards, General Editor

THOMAS NELSON
Since 1798

NASHVILLE DALLAS MEXICO CITY RIO DE JANEIRO BEIJING

Paul and the Prison Epistles
The Bible Smart Guide™ Series
Copyright © 2008 by GRQ, Inc.

Published in Nashville, Tennessee, by Thomas Nelson. Thomas Nelson is a trademark of Thomas Nelson, Inc.

Thomas Nelson, Inc. titles may be purchased in bulk for educational, business, fundraising, or sales promotional use. For information, please e-mail SpecialMarkets@ThomasNelson.com.

General Editor: Larry Richards
Managing Editor: Michael Christopher
Scripture Editor: Deborah Wiseman
Assistant Editor: Amy Clark
Design: Diane Whisner

ISBN 10: 1-4185-1007-6
ISBN 13: 978-1-4185-1007-7

Printed in the United States of America
08 09 10 11 RRD 9 8 7 6 5 4 3 2 1

Introduction

Welcome to *Paul and the Prison Epistles*. This is another book in the exciting series that is a revolutionary commentary designed to uncomplicate the Bible. Within these pages you'll find interesting and practical ideas that go far beyond your typical Bible study or commentary. It has elements that bring many different concepts together into a wonderful whole that will make reading—and studying—the Bible fun and attractive.

To Gain Your Confidence

Within *Paul and the Prison Epistles—The Smart Guide to the Bible*™, you'll find a wealth of insights and information about the Bible, but written in a way that is practical and easy to understand. You don't need to know Greek to understand the three books that you'll be learning about—Ephesians, Philippians, and Colossians. The apostle Paul wrote these books originally as letters or epistles to people in three different areas of the Near East, and he didn't mean for it to be complicated. And in fact it wasn't complicated or unclear to them—just to us, because we don't understand all the background and customs of the day.

I've made every effort to keep it simple while still making it meaningful. I've uncomplicated the process by describing the background and explaining Paul's viewpoint. So, sit back and enjoy this unique adventure of *Paul and the Prison Epistles—The Smart Guide to the Bible*™ and see what Paul has written to you—from God!

So What's the Bible About, Anyway?

The Bible is a collection of sixty-six books written by many different people over a long period of time. Yet in spite of that, it has a common theme throughout about God's love and care of His created beings. In a sense, the Bible is God's love letter to you! And it must be a popular theme, because it is the best-selling book of all time—and it keeps on selling and selling and selling. People want to know about that love. No wonder it's so popular!

Why Study Ephesians, Philippians, and Colossians?

These three books of the New Testament—written after Jesus came to earth—are the letters the apostle Paul wrote to three different groups of people in the years after Jesus's death and resurrection. They are some of the most popular books in the Bible because they share practical instruction and tell of God's powerful grace and love. Paul definitely had love and grace on his heart when he wrote to his friends because he liberally sprinkled those words throughout his letters.

Paul's primary focus in his letter to the believers in the area of Ephesus (thus named Ephesians) is that Christians belong to a wonderful family and have a rich spiritual heritage. In his letter to the people at Philippi (and the letter is named Philippians), he speaks of how they can have joy in spite of unhappy circumstances. And in Paul's letter to the believers at Colossae (and that letter is titled Colossians), he shares about how people can believe the truth about Jesus and apply a personal relationship with Him to their everyday lives. Can you see now why these three books are so important?

I promise you'll find a rich treasure as you mine the depths of these pages...because God inspired Paul to write these books in order to share His love and to encourage each reader to live a fulfilled, abundant life.

Author! Author!

The apostle Paul wrote these three books. He was a Jewish man, a member of the Pharisee sect, and a hater of all things Christian until he met the resurrected Jesus as he was traveling to persecute Christians. Yes, you read that right. Paul originally didn't believe in Jesus. In fact, he thought that what he'd heard about Jesus being the Son of God was a lie, and he was determined to wipe out this new religion, Christianity. But after hearing a voice from heaven and seeing a bright light that blinded him, Paul became convinced that Jesus was real. Thereafter, he served Him.

The books of Ephesians, Philippians, and Colossians were written many years after Paul's encounter with Jesus. At the time of their writing, Paul was imprisoned because of his faith. You'll find it amazing to see the joy and trust in God that Paul wrote about under those circumstances. As a result, you'll learn to trust God even more and have a greater desire to be joyful regardless of your circumstances. Sounds great, doesn't it?

Then let's get started.

What's a Translation?

The Bible has been offered down through the ages in many different languages and translations. Translations are the different ways the Bible is brought into a particular language and culture. It doesn't change the meaning of the words, but since something can be described several different ways and still mean the same thing, translations give us a choice so that we can learn from whatever version applies best. For this series, I've chosen the New King James Version (NKJV) because it clearly expresses the original Greek version of the New Testament—where we find our three chosen books—in a contemporary way. At the same time, it remains true to the original intent of the writers—and ultimately God.

How to Use *Paul and the Prison Epistles—The Smart Guide to the Bible*™

- Sit down with this book and your Bible.
- Start in chapter 1 (Ephesians 1).
- As you work through each chapter, read the accompanying Bible verses from your Bible.
- Use the sidebars to give you a knowledge boost.
- Answer the Study Questions and review with the Chapter Wrap-Up.
- Then go on to the next chapter. It's that simple!

A Word About Words

As you read *Paul and the Prison Epistles—The Smart Guide to the Bible*, you'll notice some interchangeable words: *Scripture, Scriptures, Word, Word of God, God's Word*, etc. All of these terms mean the same thing and fall under the broad heading of "the Bible."

In most cases the phrase "the Scriptures" in the New Testament refers to the Old Testament. Peter indicated that the writings of the apostle Paul were quickly accepted in the early church as equal to "the rest of the Scriptures" (2 Peter 3:16 NKJV). Both Testaments consistently demonstrate the belief that is expressed in 2 Timothy 3:16 (NKJV). "All Scripture is given by inspiration of God" (NKJV).

One Final Tip

There's a wonderful promise given when we turn to the Bible for answers about life's questions. He promises that His Word will make a distinct difference in our lives, and that He is present whenever we read it.

As you read, pray, and open your heart to God, ask Him to speak to you. You will find your life enriched and changed forever.

About the Author

Kathy Collard Miller is the author of forty-nine books and is a popular women's conference speaker. Her most recent books are *Partly Cloudy with Scattered Worries* and another book in The Smart Guide to the Bible™ series, *Women of the Bible*. Her other books include *Why Do I Put So Much Pressure on Myself and Others*, *Through His Eyes*, and *Princess to Princess*.

Kathy has also published more than 145 articles in magazines such as *Today's Christian Woman*, and she has been on many television and radio programs, such as *The 700 Club*. She is a frequent speaker at women's retreats, conferences, and business events and also teaches parenting seminars and marriage seminars with her husband, Larry. She has spoken in thirty states and six foreign countries. Kathy lives in Indio, California, with her husband, Larry. Their two children are grown. When Kathy isn't at her desk writing, she enjoys golf and jogging.

About the General Editor

Dr. Larry Richards is a native of Michigan who now lives in Raleigh, North Carolina. He was converted to Christianity while in the Navy in the 1950s. Larry has taught and written Sunday school curriculum for every age group, from nursery through adult. He has published more than two hundred books that have been translated into twenty-six languages. His wife, Sue, is also an author. They both enjoy teaching Bible studies as well as fishing and playing golf.

Understanding the Bible Is Easy with These Tools

To understand God's Word you need easy-to-use study tools right where you need them—at your fingertips. The Smart Guide to the Bible™ series puts valuable resources adjacent to the text to save you both time and effort.

Every page features handy sidebars filled with icons and helpful information: cross references for additional insights, definitions of key words and concepts, brief commentaries from experts on the topic, points to ponder, evidence of God at work, the big picture of how passages fit into the context of the entire Bible, practical tips for applying biblical truths to every area of your life, and plenty of maps, charts, and illustrations. A wrap-up of each passage, combined with study questions, concludes each chapter.

These helpful tools show you what to watch for. Look them over to become familiar with them, and then turn to Chapter 1 with complete confidence: You are about to increase your knowledge of God's Word!

Study Helps

The thought-bubble icon alerts you to commentary you might find particularly thought-provoking, challenging, or encouraging. You'll want to take a moment to reflect on it and consider the implications for your life.

Don't miss this point! The exclamation-point icon draws your attention to a key point in the text and emphasizes important biblical truths and facts.

death on the cross
Colossians 1:21–22

Many see Boaz as a type of Jesus Christ. To win back what we human beings lost through sin and spiritual death, Jesus had to become human (i.e., he had to become a true kinsman), and he had to be willing to pay the penalty for our sins. With his <u>death on the cross</u>, Jesus paid the penalty and won freedom and eternal life for us.

The additional Bible verses add scriptural support for the passage you just read and help you better understand the <u>underlined text</u>. (Think of it as an instant reference resource!)

How does what you just read apply to your life? The heart icon indicates that you're about to find out! These practical tips speak to your mind, heart, body, and soul, and offer clear guidelines for living a righteous and joy-filled life, establishing priorities, maintaining healthy relationships, persevering through challenges, and more.

This icon reveals how God is truly all-knowing and all-powerful. The hourglass icon points to a specific example of the prediction of an event or the fulfillment of a prediction. See how some of what God has said would come to pass already has!

What are some of the great things God has done? The traffic-sign icon shows you how God has used miracles, special acts, promises, and covenants throughout history to draw people to him.

Does the story or event you just read about appear elsewhere in the Gospels? The cross icon points you to those instances where the same story appears in other Gospel locations—further proof of the accuracy and truth of Jesus' life, death, and resurrection.

Since God created marriage, there's no better person to turn to for advice. The double-ring icon points out biblical insights and tips for strengthening your marriage.

The Bible is filled with wisdom about raising a godly family and enjoying your spiritual family in Christ. The family icon gives you ideas for building up your home and helping your family grow close and strong.

Isle of Patmos
a small island in the Mediterranean Sea

something significant had occurred, he wrote down the substance of what he saw. This is the practice John followed when he recorded Revelation on the **Isle of Patmos.**

What does that word really mean, especially as it relates to this passage? Important, misunderstood, or infrequently used words are set in **bold type** in your text so you can immediately glance at the margin for definitions. This valuable feature lets you better understand the meaning of the entire passage without having to stop to check other references.

the big picture

Joshua
Led by Joshua, the Israelites crossed the Jordan River and invaded Canaan (see Illustration #8). In a series of military campaigns the Israelites defeated several coalition armies raised by the inhabitants of Canaan. With organized resistance put down, Joshua divided the land among the twelve Israelite

How does what you read fit in with the greater biblical story? The highlighted big picture summarizes the passage under discussion.

what others say

David Breese
Nothing is clearer in the Word of God than the fact that God wants us to understand himself and his working in the lives of men.[5]

It can be helpful to know what others say on the topic, and the highlighted quotation introduces another voice in the discussion. This resource enables you to read other opinions and perspectives.

Maps, charts, and illustrations pictorially represent ancient artifacts and show where and how stories and events took place. They enable you to better understand important empires, learn your way around villages and temples, see where major battles occurred, and follow the journeys of God's people. You'll find these graphics let you do more than study God's Word—they let you *experience* it.

Chapters at a Glance

PART TWO: Philippians

PART THREE: Colossians

Part One
EPHESIANS

Ephesians 1 Praise to God for Who We Are in Christ

Let's Get Started

When the **apostle** Paul wanted to communicate important information to the believers who resided in the town of **Ephesus**, he wrote a letter, even though at the time he was imprisoned in Rome—in his own home. Acts 28:30–31 tells us, "Then Paul dwelt two whole years in his own rented house, and received all who came to him, preaching the kingdom of God and teaching the things which concern the Lord Jesus Christ with all confidence, no one forbidding him" (NKJV). Because of his imprisonment, Paul couldn't visit the people he loved in Ephesus, but he could write them a letter. That's what he did—and through the centuries we have benefited.

The church at the city of Ephesus had been <u>founded</u> about seven years earlier by Paul on his homeward trip of his second missionary journey. On Paul's third missionary journey, he stopped and stayed at Ephesus for about three years—from the summer of AD 52 until the spring of AD 55. In Paul's letter, his heart was firmly rooted in wanting them to grow in their relationship with Christ.

Some very significant things happened when Paul stayed in Ephesus on his third missionary journey.

founded
Acts 18:19

apostle
one who walked with Jesus, called to ministry

Ephesus
city in Middle East

Events While Paul Was in Ephesus

Scripture in Acts	Event
20:31	Paul stayed in Ephesus for three years.
19:1–7	Paul baptized twelve followers of John the Baptist.
19:8–10	Reasoned with people in the synagogue for three months, then daily in the hall of Tyrannus for two years.
19:11–12	God healed people through Paul, even using his handkerchief and aprons at times.
19:13–16	Seven sons of a Jewish priest tried to use Paul's name to cast out a demon. The demon claimed to know Jesus and Paul but wouldn't obey the seven men.

go to

Tychicus
Ephesians 6:21

Events While Paul Was in Ephesus (cont'd)

Scripture in Acts	Event
19:17–20	Those who practiced magic were converted and burned their sorcery books.
19:21–41	Paul's reputation created a riot because Demetrius accused him of threatening to destroy Diana's temple.

A few years later, Paul was sent as a prisoner to Rome, where he wrote this letter to the believers living in Ephesus. At that point, Paul had been a Christian for nearly thirty years. The letter was carried to the Ephesus area by <u>Tychicus</u> on his way from Rome to Colosse.

Some scholars dispute the authorship of this letter as not being written by Paul. Here are their concerns and some answers.

Disputing Paul's Authorship of Ephesians

Reasons Paul didn't write Ephesians	Reasons Paul did write Ephesians
The wording, grammar, and doctrine of this letter are different from the other letters Paul wrote. Ninety words are unique and different from Paul's other letters.	As a brilliant teacher and writer, Paul could vary his style depending upon the topic he was addressing. Since this letter is regarded by most scholars as Paul's superior work in content and writing skills, Paul used a superior style to address grand ideas.
The language is more sophisticated.	True, except that fifty-five verses are identical in the two letters of Ephesians and Colossians.
Scholars don't think Paul wrote these letters.	Paul refers to himself twice in this letter (Ephesians 1:1; 3:1). Tychicus delivered both letters—to the Ephesians and to the Colossians, showing a common source (Colossians 4:7; Ephesians 6:21).
Since Paul's name isn't mentioned in all copies, some believe a disciple of Paul's wrote it.	If so, that person would have had to be more brilliant than Paul, and that is very doubtful.
The writer of Ephesians says, "after I heard of your faith in the Lord Jesus" (1:15 NKJV). Paul would have known personally of their faith—not just heard it.	If Paul intended that the letter be sent to many churches, he may have written a general statement that would apply to many churches, some of which he didn't know personally.

Scholars also dispute whether what we call "The Epistle to the Ephesians" was actually intended for the church in Ephesus. Since the words "To the saints who are in Ephesus" (Ephesians 1:1 NKJV) are not included in three early manuscripts, some say that it never

4 — The Smart Guide to the Bible

was to be sent there, since Paul was consistent in including the city that each of his other letters were sent to. That's why some commentators believe that this particular letter was intended to be circulated to the churches located in three cities in the Laodician valley: Ephesus, Laodicea, and Colosse. In fact, Paul writes in his letter to the Colossians, "Now when this epistle is read among you, see that it is read also in the church of the Laodiceans, and that you likewise read the epistle from Laodicea" (Colossians 4:16 NKJV). Some Bible researchers believe that Paul is referring to this letter (the one to the Ephesians) when he speaks of the epistle from Laodicea. This verse in Colossians also proves that these letters were passed around and enjoyed by several groups of people—not just the groups they were written for.

Marcion, who in the middle of the second century was the first person to put Paul's letters into a collection, called the letter to the Ephesians "The Letter to the Laodiceans." This gives us some insight that he, at least, as a part of the early church, regarded the Epistle to the Ephesians as the letter Paul referred to in Colossians 4:16. Later decisions within the Christian Church gave it the title "The Letter to the Ephesians."

A second reason commentators argue this letter wasn't originally for the Ephesian believers is that Paul hadn't mentioned the names of the people he had known and lived with in Ephesus for three years. His other letters to specific churches, such as the Philippian church, always included references to the people living there. We would certainly expect from Paul's living three years in Ephesus that he would mention his friends and give them greetings, as was his normal custom. Again, if this letter was supposed to be a general letter to several groups of people, that would explain why he didn't mention people by name. Some scholars—those who favor the letter being written to the Ephesians—maintain that since Paul knew so many people in Ephesus, he didn't mention anyone for fear of leaving someone out or making them feel bad.

Not knowing who a letter is intended for seems strange within our culture because the mail system uses a name and an address on the envelope. So all we have to do to know who a letter is for is look at the address. But that's not the way it worked in Paul's time. After the letter was written on papyri, it was rolled up and tied with a string. Then it was hand delivered, since mail service available within

abundant life
John 10:10

power in prayer
James 5:16

contentment
Philippians 4:11–12

body of Christ
church members

doctrine
principles of belief

the Roman culture could only be used by government and the military. Even if we still had the original papyri that held Paul's words, we wouldn't know who it was addressed to (other than what his opening remarks told us).

Paul's main goal in Ephesians was to communicate the importance of believers being a part of the **body of Christ** and how they could operate with their spiritual inheritance. A spiritual inheritance is all that a relationship with Christ offers. In this first chapter of Ephesians, Paul lists many of those: spiritual blessings, forgiveness, blamelessness, power, redemption, adoption, security, and acceptance, to name just a few. Other parts of the Bible name others: <u>abundant life</u>, <u>power in prayer</u>, <u>contentment</u>, and many others.

Also in this first chapter, he provided a significant **doctrine** for understanding the benefits of believing in Jesus. There are important advantages that every Christian can enjoy, but Paul knew that if the Ephesian Christians didn't recognize them, they couldn't live like the powerful believers God wanted them to be. So Paul sat down and wrote this important book of the Bible. As a result, he offers us the chance to recognize our own inheritance in Christ.

what others say

John White

Paul's letter to the Ephesians consists of a two-part prayer, boxed in theology, wrapped in exhortations, and tied with love. I have a feeling (not shared by commentators or New Testament scholars) that the prayer is the nodal point around which the whole letter turns. Paul's introduction leads up to the prayer. In the middle of the prayer he gets sidetracked, bemused by the wonder of the Christ about whom he speaks (Ephesians 1:20–23); but halfway through the letter he tries to get back to it (Ephesians 3:1), only to be sidetracked again. Not until Ephesians 3:14 does he finally settle down and finish telling the Ephesians how and what he is praying.[1]

Prolific Paul Penned This Prose

EPHESIANS 1:1 *Paul, an apostle of Jesus Christ by the will of God, to the saints who are in Ephesus, and faithful in Christ Jesus:* (NKJV)

Paul called himself an apostle even though he was not one of the original twelve disciples who walked with Jesus while He was on the earth. In the beginning, the word *apostle* referred to only those twelve disciples, because the word means "one <u>sent</u> with a special message or commission." But then Jesus <u>appeared</u> to Paul as he traveled on his way to persecute Christians; Paul then **converted** to believing in Jesus. Because the Son of God called him in a special way to serve Himself, Paul also qualified to be an apostle.

There is always hope for anyone to come to know Jesus as his or her Lord and Savior. Paul is affirmation of that truth. Of anyone, Paul could have been voted The Person Most Unlikely to Become a Christian. Here's why:

- He was a Jewish <u>Pharisee</u> who totally believed that he was righteous before God based on his spiritual heritage of **circumcision** and because his parents were in the Benjamin tribe.

- He **persecuted** the Christians of his day because he believed they taught false doctrine that turned people away from God. He forcefully had them brought to trial and then executed.

- He followed all the <u>rules</u> of his Jewish heritage and believed that he always obeyed God. Therefore, he didn't think he was spiritually separated from God.

Regardless of those things working against him, God designed for Paul to have an encounter with Jesus that would help open his eyes to the truth that Jesus was indeed God's Son and the Savior of the world—the very truths that Paul had killed others for believing.

The character of Jesus was revealed in the way He confronted Paul on his journey to Damascus with the intention of persecuting Christians, even killing them. The account is told in Acts: "As he journeyed he came near Damascus, and suddenly a light shone around him from heaven. Then he fell to the ground, and heard a voice saying to him, 'Saul, Saul, why are you persecuting Me?' And he said, 'Who are You, Lord?' Then the Lord said, 'I am Jesus, whom you are persecuting. It is hard for you to kick against the goads.' So he, trembling and astonished, said, 'Lord, what do You want me to do?' Then the Lord said to him, 'Arise and go into the city, and you will be told what you must do'" (Acts 9:3–6 NKJV). Jesus could have easily sent a bolt of lightning to pass judgment on this enemy of His believers. He could have angrily told Paul he was

go to

sent
John 13:16

appeared
Acts 9:3

converted
Acts 9:18

Pharisee
Philippians 3:5

circumcision
Philippians 3:5

persecuted
Acts 8:3; 9:2

rules
Philippians 3:6

converted
changed beliefs

circumcision
removal of outer skin of penis

persecuted
treated badly

wrong in what he was doing. But instead, He firmly but gently called out to him with a question. Jesus's patience and creativity were revealed and confirmed in His method of bringing a lost sheep of Israel to his knees in surrender.

When Paul called the Ephesian believers "saints," he was merely identifying them as believers in Jesus. Nothing special was required for them to call themselves that, nor for Paul to refer to them that way. The word *saint* comes from the Greek word *hágio*, meaning "set apart, sanctified, consecrated, or holy." This definition is referring to how "different" the person or item is that is called *hágio*. Every Christian is a "saint" because they have been cleansed of their sins through Jesus's death and therefore are considered by God holy and acceptable to Him. The word *saint* is used sixty-two times in the Bible and never refers to someone's earning the title. Paul's primary goal in this letter to believers is to help them see how to live out their spiritual role as saints.

key point

Usages of *Hágios* in the Bible as "Set Apart," "Holy," and "Different"

Scripture	Item or Person	How the Person or Item Is "Different"
Leviticus 21:6	Priests	They were set apart for a "called" position and purpose
Leviticus 27:30, 32	Tithe (a tenth portion of earnings)	Given to the priests for their personal use or the upkeep of the Temple
Exodus 26:33	Temple as the Holy Place	Used for specific, spiritual purposes
Exodus 19:6	Israel as a nation	God had chosen them specifically for His special purposes
Ephesians 1:1	Christians	Different from other people in their commitment to the Lord and the way they live

Today when people write a letter, they sign their name at the end. But when Paul wrote this letter and others to believers, it was the common practice to put the name of the writer at the beginning, along with a term that gave his or her qualifications for writing the letter. It makes good sense—readers immediately know whom the letter is from and why they should pay attention to it.

go to

position
Romans 6:8–12

removed
Romans 8:38–39

Saul
Acts 7:58

mission
Ephesians 2:10

ambassador
2 Corinthians 5:20

saved
having sins forgiven

grace
God's favor even
though a person
doesn't deserve it

what others say

Charles R. Swindoll

Let me suggest that we not think of saints as some exceptionally pious, almost superhuman group of people, but as real people like you and me, thoroughly human, garden-variety, sinful people **saved** by the **grace** of God. The original Greek word translated "saint" in English means "one who is set apart for God's use."[2]

J. Vernon McGee

A saint, my friend, is one who has trusted Christ and is set aside for the sole use of God. There are only two kinds of people today: the saints and the ain'ts. If you are a saint, then you are not an ain't. If you ain't an ain't, then you are a saint.[3]

If you've received Christ as your Savior, then you are a saint just like those Ephesian believers. You may not feel like a saint because in religious circles that word often connotes a person who is given special recognition by a religious group. But Paul called anyone who believed in Jesus a saint—meaning that in their position in Christ they were considered holy by God. <u>Position</u> in Christ refers to that place in God's perspective when we are acceptable to Him, not based on our performance or because we deserve it, but because Jesus's blood has cleansed us from our sins. Just as a baby is born into a family and has a place or position that isn't based on his level of performance, so a Christian has an unequaled place or position in Christ that cannot be <u>removed</u> from him. The word *in* also reminds us that we are constantly "in" God's presence, just as a plane is in the air and surrounded by the air. Of course, a Christian shouldn't misuse that gift by sinning intentionally, but instead desire to live in God's power and seek to sin as little as possible.

You're a saint in God's eyes if you know Jesus as your Lord and Savior.

Paul wrote "by the will of God." God called Paul, when he was still called <u>Saul</u>, to be a person specially assigned to God's purposes. Yet each and every Christian has that same distinction. Each of us is on a <u>mission</u> from God and called to that position as his <u>ambassador</u> "by the will of God." That doesn't refer only to those in full-time Christian service, but to everyone—from dentists to factory workers.

something to ponder

apply it

go to

choice
John 15:16

forgiveness
no longer held
accountable

Can't Have One Without the Other

EPHESIANS 1:2 *Grace to you and peace from God our Father and the Lord Jesus Christ. (NKJV)*

None of us enjoy being in a stressful relationship or situation where there is a feeling of tension or conflict. If we have an argument or disagreement, we want to make things right and happy again. Living in such peace and harmony is what Paul wrote about in his greeting.

Paul greeted the Ephesians with the two most wonderful desires for them that he could: grace and peace. In his day, Greek people began their letters with *Charis!*—the Greek word for "grace" or "rejoice!" Jews used the word *shalom* or *peace* in letters and for a verbal greeting.

Charis stands for grace that results in joy, pleasure, gratification, benefits, and beauty. The Greek word for "peace" refers to total well-being, harmony, peace of mind, and everything intended for a person's good. Who wouldn't want to be greeted with those two wishes for their day?

Since these were commonly used words, there may not have seemed anything special about them to most people at the time. But early teachers like Paul took those words and made them special by referring them to God's offered gifts of salvation and the benefits of living in God's power.

Paul recognized the important benefits Christians share by beginning his letter saying in effect, "Christians, you have grace and peace because you are believers in Jesus." There couldn't have been a better welcome to those about to read his letter.

what others say

Lloyd John Ogilvie

Don't miss this splendid word: *prevenient*. It means beforehand. When used about grace, it means "beforehand" love, acceptance that is given before we feel acceptable, **forgiveness** offered before we ask, and the Lord's <u>choice</u> of us before we even choose to respond.[4]

Philip Yancey

Paul harped on grace because he knew what could happen if we believe we have earned God's love. In the dark times, if perhaps we badly fail God, or if for no good reason we sim-

> ply feel unloved, we would stand on shaky ground. We would fear that God might stop loving us when He discovers the real truth about us.[5]

Grace and peace go together. When a person comes to know God because of His wonderful offer of forgiveness through Jesus's death on the cross, which is <u>grace</u>, that person then has peace—the <u>absence of hostility</u> between him and God. Plus, that grace and peace aren't just for the moment of salvation, but for the rest of their life. They are able to live in God's grace of receiving needed <u>forgiveness</u> when they fall into sin. Finally, they experience peace through knowing that salvation can never be taken away.

The people of the world are constantly striving for peace, which to them means an absence of war. People picket in order to bring an end to wars, and they pray for world peace. But there will never be total <u>peace</u> on our planet. There can be inner peace because God offers it as a result of knowing Jesus as Savior—which makes it impossible to be "at war" with God any longer. Inner peace is much more desirable than peace between nations. Furthermore, it is attainable; world peace is not.

Being a Beneficiary Is a Bountiful Benefit

EPHESIANS 1:3 ***Blessed be*** *the God and Father of our Lord Jesus Christ, who has blessed us with every spiritual blessing in the **heavenly places** in Christ,* (NKJV)

Verse 3 begins a very long sentence in the original Greek. There are no periods at the end of any verses between verse 3 and verse 14 in the Greek. Paul starts out talking about the spiritual blessings that Christians are blessed with, and then begins naming them through verse 14. That's a lot of blessings.

To bless someone means to reflect upon the good or great things they are or have done. Paul wants all believers to dwell upon how wonderful God is to Christians, just like a wonderful father gives to his children everything they need.

Paul uses the word *blessing* in two ways in a single verse: We're to bless God, and we're to acknowledge the blessings God has given us. Christians are blessed because they are the beneficiaries of <u>everything</u> they <u>need</u> to live in a godly fashion. Even though they are living on earth, on the inside—in their souls—they have everything they need.

grace
2 Corinthians 9:8

absence of hostility
Romans 5:1

forgiveness
1 John 1:9

peace
John 14:27

everything
2 Peter 1:3

need
Philippians 4:19

blessed be
acknowledging greatness

heavenly places
kingdoms

go to

devil
John 8:44;
Ephesians 2:1–3

advantages
Matthew 5:45

born again
John 3:3

Since we don't always live as we should, it might seem that we need to acquire more of our spiritual inheritance in order to live in God's power. But Paul stressed that everything has already been given to a Christian. It's not a matter of "will bless" or "sometimes blesses." It has already been done to the fullest—with "*every* spiritual blessing." We don't ever have to wonder whether we're missing out on something. It's all available; we just have to appropriate it by choosing to live in God's power.

Although God created every person, He isn't necessarily their spiritual "Father." Only those who have asked Jesus into their hearts can actually claim God as their Father. Jesus named another spiritual "father"—the <u>devil</u>. Everyone has one of two spiritual fathers: God or Satan. Even those who serve the devil through evil deeds are often blessed by God, but only with temporary, earthly <u>advantages</u>, not the spiritual blessings that Paul is writing about in this chapter. God's kindnesses to the unsaved are termed "common grace." For instance, every person has a God-given need to be loved; regardless of whether they believe in Jesus, they may enjoy having a loving spouse who meets most of their emotional needs. But only God can meet every emotional need.

Only a Father-child relationship with God, which the Bible says starts with being <u>born again</u>, can provide abundant life here on earth and eternal life after death. Abundant life doesn't mean never having problems. But when the inevitable problems occur, Paul says that every Christian has the ability to face them with grace because of his spiritual inheritance.

what others say

Theodore H. Epp

Becoming one with Christ is similar in meaning to what happens to copper and zinc when they are combined—they become an alloy known as brass which is neither copper nor zinc. In such a state, the copper is "made one with" zinc and the zinc is "made one with" copper so that together they constitute brass.[6]

Bill Hybels

When we have spent a few minutes praising God for who he is, our spirit is softened and our agenda changes. Those burning issues we were dying to bring to God's attention may seem less crucial. Our sense of desperation subsides as we focus on God's greatness, and we can truly say, "I am enjoying you, God; it is well with my soul." **Adoration purges** our spirit and prepares us to listen to God.[7]

William Barclay

In the Greek, the long passage from verses 3–14 is one sentence. It is so long and complicated because it represents not so much a reasoned statement as a lyrical song of praise. Paul's mind goes on and on, not because he is thinking in logical stages, but because gift after gift and wonder after wonder from God pass before his eyes.[8]

Life often becomes stressful or difficult, and we're tempted to respond in ways opposite to what God wants. We may want to become angry, try to control the reactions of other people, become bitter and resentful, or fret that something bad will happen to us. That isn't living as if we have every spiritual blessing. Instead, we can remind ourselves that God has made available the power we need to choose godly reactions. We can choose to be patient because we know anger doesn't accomplish God's will. We can relax and believe God will make changes in others. We can give up bitterness and instead forgive because we remember how much we've been forgiven by God. And we can refuse to worry because we know God will bring <u>good</u> from anything that happens to us—even unfortunate things.

In each and every stressful situation, the ability to respond like Jesus is already provided—that's the spiritual blessing Paul is talking about. We won't always do it perfectly, but <u>maturity</u> is when we grow stronger in our ability to live the way God wants us to.

<u>God Has Known You for a Very Long Time—Like Eternity</u>

EPHESIANS 1:4–6 *Just as He chose us in Him before the foundation of the world, that we should be **holy** and **without blame** before Him in love, having **predestined** us to adoption as sons by Jesus Christ to Himself, according to the good pleasure of His will, to the praise of the glory of His grace, by which He made us accepted in the Beloved.* (NKJV)

Before every person was even born, God knew all about them—even back before the world was created. God, who is <u>infinite</u> and who always <u>existed</u>, knew each person who would live on the earth,

apply it

go to

good
Romans 8:28

maturity
Hebrews 5:12–14

infinite
Psalm 102:25–27

existed
Psalm 90:2

adoration
worshipping

purges
cleanses

holy
without sin

without blame
not held accountable

predestined
known or chosen in advance

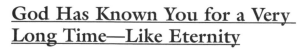

choose
1 Timothy 2:4;
Revelation 22:17

place
Romans 5:18

gift
Romans 5:17

even before He formed the earth. And He wanted every person to become His child. But because God wanted each person to <u>choose</u> that privilege, He gave mankind the freedom to make a decision about whether or not they would be saved from their sins. He longed for each person to desire to be a part of His family—but not be forced. And when a person makes that decision, they instantly become holy and blameless in His sight. That is possible only because they are forgiven of all their sins through Jesus's death in their <u>place</u> and considered holy and without blame. That's the grace Paul talked about in verse 2; he's talking about something that is available as a <u>gift</u>, not something earned.

When such a wonderful gift is understood as a fabulous opportunity, how can anyone not praise God for His incredible love? That's why Paul wrote that God's acceptance and adoption of men and women will bring praise to Him. His gracious love will be recognized and given the credit He deserves. God is not extending favor because we deserve it—if that were the case, then *we* should be praised. No, He is extending favor because *He* is wonderfully loving—and therefore, He should be declared great.

The spiritual concept of predestination that Paul writes about is a controversial one, and it has been for centuries. Although there are many variations in this controversy, there are three major belief systems:

1. *Calvinism or reformed theology:* This belief system purports that God in His sovereignty determines who becomes saved by grace and that there is no human free will involved because the depraved nature of man makes him unable to choose. As a result, a person cannot lose their salvation.

2. *Arminianism:* This theology was begun in the 1590s by Jacobus Arminius, who died in 1609. In a 1610 declaration called the Remonstrance, his followers determined that each person has a choice whether to accept or reject Christ. They also said that a person could lose their salvation.

3. *Harmonizing reason and faith:* In the late 1200s, a group of theologians explained predestination as God, knowing everything (sovereignty) and therefore predestining to salvation those whom He knew would choose to accept Christ (free will).

One way of viewing predestination is to think in terms of adopting a child. An adopted baby doesn't have any choice as to what family he will join. Instead, the mother and father choose that child because they love him; the child doesn't do anything to deserve it. He just lies there, not able to speak, walk, or feed himself. But the parents are thrilled that they now have him in their family. They want him to benefit from their name and all the wonderful things they plan to give him. Sometimes adopting human parents won't even have seen the child before meeting him at the adoption agency.

In Roman law, which the apostle Paul knew well as a Roman citizen, the adopted child had just as many benefits and privileges as a blood child, even if he had originally been a slave in the household. In addition, even a blood child had to be publicly declared as a son—a rite usually taking place when he was a teenager.

Prior to the public declaration, the adopted child was a slave; afterward, he was entitled to full privileges and responsibilities. Paul was trying to show his readers how strong their relationship with God was—based upon His choosing them even before they could love Him back. Spiritual adoption is God's way of saying we belong in the family of God.

Jesus is the Son of God and has always existed. He was the Creator of the world and God's right-hand man. Even before He created the universe, God knew humans would sin and planned for Jesus to come to earth to die for the sins of the world's people. From eternity past, Jesus knew the plan and cooperated with it.

key point

what others say

Charles Stanley

Freedom from **legalism** comes through accepting the truth about our favored position in the family of God. Those who have put their trust in Christ have been adopted into His family. There is no concept that speaks any clearer of acceptance than adoption. Whereas a pregnancy can come as a surprise, adoption is always something that is premeditated and planned.[9]

H. A. Ironside

There is no such thing taught in the Word of God as predestination to eternal condemnation. If men are lost, they are lost because they do not come to Christ. When men do come to Christ, they learn the wonderful secret that God has foreknown it all from eternity.[10]

Paul's comments should make us feel very secure because we realize that God's love has nothing to do with our performance. If He loved us and wanted us to be a part of His family even before we were born, then His love is rooted in His own character—not our good or bad behavior. God is <u>love</u>. God loves us now just as much as He loved us before He created the world, and His love can't be increased or decreased.

Bunches of Benefits Being "In Christ"

When we are "in Christ," Paul tells us we have an overflowing number of wonderful benefits to enjoy. He names several of them in these next six verses, but they aren't a complete list. He'll go on to report many others both here in this letter and others. But in this passage, he delights in encouraging believers by naming several advantages.

go to

love
1 John 4:8

redeemed
Romans 3:24

death
Genesis 2:16–17;
Romans 6:23

ransom
price to be released

redemption
something given in place of punishment

redeemed
bought back

There's a Price on Your Head and Jesus Paid the Ransom

EPHESIANS 1:7–10 *In Him we have **redemption** through His blood, the forgiveness of sins, according to the riches of His grace which He made to abound toward us in all wisdom and prudence, having made known to us the mystery of His will, according to His good pleasure which He purposed in Himself, that in the dispensation of the fullness of the times He might gather together in one all things in Christ, both which are in heaven and which are on earth—in Him.* (NKJV)

First, a Christian is **redeemed**. To be redeemed means to be set free from a penalty because a ransom has been paid. Since each of us was a prisoner of sin and our punishment was <u>death</u>, God sent Jesus to die in our place. His <u>blood</u> became the ransom that was enough to set us free because Jesus was without sin. If Jesus had been like any other man and had sinned, His death wouldn't have made a difference spiritually. But because Jesus was without sin, He could offer Himself as a sinless payment for sin. Only He could do that since only He was <u>without sin</u>. His blood is needed because God determined from the beginning, "For the life of the flesh is in the blood, and I have given it to you upon the altar to make **atonement** for your souls; for it is the blood that makes atonement for the soul" (Leviticus 17:11 NKJV).

Second, a Christian has the power to become wise and prudent far beyond human ability. When we begin to look at life and other people through God's eyes, we have spiritual insights and understanding that others may not have. Although the world system gives the impression that it offers wisdom through science and law, God's eternal wisdom sees things from a better vantage point.

Third, a Christian is forgiven. Paul stresses that because of God's grace, which He poured richly upon us, every single sin we have done, are doing, or will do was taken care of when Jesus died in our place. It was all future and covered by His gracious act of sacrifice.

Anytime you buy something, you have in a sense redeemed it; you have paid a price for that item to become yours. It is now your possession and you can do with it as you like. In the same way, God "<u>bought</u>" us from the possession of Satan and death with the high cost of Jesus's <u>blood</u> on the cross. After we are purchased, or "redeemed," we belong to God, and He can do anything He wants with us.

go to

blood
Hebrews 9:22

without sin
Hebrews 4:15

bought
1 Corinthians 7:23

blood
1 Peter 1:18–19

atonement
satisfaction

what others say

J. I. Packer and Carolyn Nystrom

The Bible gives us life stories of many persons whom God chose and called to his service. Again and again it takes time out to tell us of the weaknesses, moral lapses and spiritual failures in their lives. God's way with these folk is to change them as he uses them and to use them while he's remaking them.[11]

Billy Graham

For some people guilt is an excuse. They won't accept the forgiveness that is offered to them; it is so hard to believe. It

> seems too good to be true that God should let us go eternally
> scot-free from our sins—and yet that is the message that the
> **gospel** brings to us.[12]

We may feel so sinful at times that we think there isn't enough shed blood to cover our sin. But it's not a matter of enough blood; it's the act that made forgiveness possible. Regardless, even one drop of Jesus's blood was enough to make the forgiveness of every sin possible.

God's wisdom and understanding are always available, but we must empty ourselves of our own desires and perspectives in order to really hear what God has to say about something. That can be a challenge—one that requires selflessness and trust in God's viewpoint. Be careful to monitor your attitude.

No, It's Not a Whodunit Mystery

The mystery that Paul is talking about is not like a murder mystery, but is something that is known only to a certain group after previously being concealed from knowledge. Christians are that group of people who have come to know the formerly unknown fact of God's will: to reveal His Son as Savior and then eventually to unify the entire world and its people. The result: a new heaven and earth where Jesus is acknowledged as Lord and Master by everyone. That is what all of human history is flowing toward and when God's plan is finished, it will be "fulfilled."

Life seems chaotic and out of control at times, but remembering Paul's words can help us feel secure in God's ability to sort it all out. Most people who don't know God personally feel as if there is no purpose to life or to the existence of the universe. They don't see God's hand upon everything and how He began it all at Creation. But Christians know the truth, that God does have a purpose for His people. If God has the power to bring unity to the earth, then He certainly can empower us to deal with the confusing and stressful issues of life. He is powerful enough for it all, and He resides in His children to help them.

unify
John 17:20–23

new heaven and earth
Revelation 21:1

acknowledged
Hebrews 2:8

gospel
good news about
Jesus

Read Paul's Lips: You Are Chosen and Predestined

EPHESIANS 1:11–12 *In Him also we have obtained an inheritance, being predestined according to the purpose of Him who works all things according to the counsel of His will, that we who first trusted in Christ should be to the praise of His glory.* (NKJV)

This time, the word *chosen* refers to "being made heirs" or receiving an inheritance. An inheritance is a gift or something given because of having a relationship with someone else. You or I could receive the inheritance of a house or a car or some money because we are known and valued by a relative who died, having been designated in the will to receive something from the estate. In the same way, God has us as Christians written into His estate, and we are entitled to receive many wonderful things because of it. Many of them we receive now on earth, but there are even more benefits that we'll enjoy in heaven.

key point

All of this was how God planned it from the very beginning—through His purposes—and when we take advantage of it by living in God's power, we make others notice and hopefully they will praise God for it.

In these first two verses of this section, Paul's reference to "we" means the Jews. They were the first believers in Jesus—those who responded out of the synagogues where the gospel was first preached by converted Jews such as the disciples and Paul. In the following verses, Paul will address his readers who are Gentiles. Note that they are offered the same incredible gift of belief in Jesus.

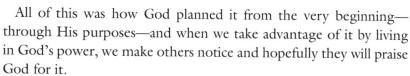

what others say

Joni Eareckson Tada

Praise the Lord. I don't mean that flippantly or superficially, and I'm not talking about a mechanical exercise either. I mean praise that is sincere, even if you have to grit your teeth and voice psalms of worship when your heart's not in it. Meaningful praise is sometimes praise you don't even feel. At least, not right away.[13]

Kay Arthur

You are not an accident! You are not useless. You are not worthless. You are not unredeemable. Your worth and purpose in this life do not depend on who you are, on what you have done, or on what has been done to you. Your worth and purpose do not depend on where you have been, even if you have been to the very precipice of hell.[14]

One of the powerful images of the importance of being chosen is communicated by a man or woman's choosing their spouse. Out of all the other people in the world—including other people they dated and maybe even liked—they choose this man or woman to live the rest of their life with. Talk about feeling special and important; no wonder we go into marriage on a high! *This person has chosen me above everyone else.* That's how God wants us to feel—that He has chosen each of us to enjoy His fellowship and the benefits of being His child.

Remember How Letters Used to Be Sealed with Wax?

> EPHESIANS 1:13–14 *In Him you also trusted, after you heard the word of truth, the gospel of your salvation; in whom also, having believed, you were sealed with the Holy Spirit of promise, who is the guarantee of our inheritance until the redemption of the purchased possession, to the praise of His glory.* (NKJV)

Now Paul writes, "you also trusted," and he is referring to the Gentiles of the Ephesian church. God never intended for the good news about Jesus to remain only with the Jews. His original plan was that Gentiles also would come into His forever family. In case the Gentiles should fear they aren't really a secure part of the plan, Paul talks about their being sealed by the Holy Spirit.

In Paul's day, a seal was a portable instrument used to stamp a document or other item. It had the power and authenticity of an actual signature, and no document was considered reliable unless it had a person's seal.

If you received a letter with the glued part partially open, you might wonder if anything was stolen or added to the letter. If it's an important document, you might even question whether it had been tampered with or altered. Because they didn't have gummed envelopes like we do today, the people in Paul's day needed a wax seal. The imprint in the wax of the sender's seal made it legitimate, since only the sender possessed that unique seal with his name or design.

When you became a Christian, God <u>sealed</u> you and gave you—whether you knew it or not—the Holy Spirit to be a deposit, a down payment. This is an indication of future blessings that God will give the believer in heaven.

Of course, the Holy Spirit also has the purpose of empowering you to live a holy life on earth, but His presence is much more than that. He also is God's assurance that you belong to Him and will receive the full inheritance that God has planned for every Christian. And this "<u>redemption</u>" is deliverance from all sin, even the ability to sin, when the believer arrives in heaven. If that isn't something to praise God about, what is?

sealed
2 Corinthians 1:22

redemption
Ephesians 4:30

ownership
2 Timothy 2:19

key point

---

what others say

J. Vernon McGee

Earnest money is the money that is put down as a down payment and pledge on a piece of property. It also means that you promise there is more money to follow. The Holy Spirit is our earnest money. He has been given as a pledge and token that there is more to follow in the way of spiritual blessings.[15]

The Holy Spirit gives us the assurance that we are:

• *Secure.* God doesn't break His covenant just as a seal shouldn't be broken before the right person receives it.

• *Authentic.* The design inlaid in the wax indicates that the person owning it used only one monogram tool. The Holy Spirit shows God's hand of <u>ownership</u>.

• *Approved.* A seal was used only after the owner verified the information within the letter or document as acceptable to him. God puts His seal of the Holy Spirit on each Christian because he or she is deemed "approved" and "acceptable" because his or her sins have been washed away by Jesus's blood.

- *Genuine.* A monogram tool's design was unique, owned by a single individual, impossible to be reproduced by another. In the same way, the Holy Spirit is unique and makes His genuine mark upon us that can't be imitated by another.

If you saw the movies *Toy Story* and *Toy Story 2*, you watched a great example of the Holy Spirit's "sealing" work. The mother of the son in the first movie had written the child's name, "Andy," on the bottom of the toy cowboy's boot as a way to identify it as Andy's possession. Then in the sequel, the cowboy is given a renewal job by the toy repair man, who paints over the name "Andy" on the cowboy's boot. Later in the movie, the toy is horrified to discover his owner's name is no longer there, and he wipes at the paint until the word *Andy* is again exposed. The identification had never been gone; it was just covered.

In the same way, you and I have the name "God's possession" written on our souls, and nothing can destroy that. At times the name is hard to see because of our sin, but once we ask forgiveness, the name shows clearly again. Let's make sure the words *God's possession* show all the time.

No Christian should think, *Well, I'm sealed and secure; therefore, I can sin all I want.* With salvation comes an implanted desire to please God. We won't take advantage of the Holy Spirit's power all the time, but we do have His power so that we can obey God more and more. Every Christian has the seal of the Holy Spirit upon them immediately at the time of salvation.

In other books of the Bible, other aspects of our inheritance in Christ are also mentioned.

Our Inheritance in Christ

Passage	Inheritance in Christ
Romans 3:24	We are **justified**.
Romans 8:1	We are not condemned.
Romans 8:2	We are set free from the power of sin and death.
1 Corinthians 1:2	We are **sanctified** and made acceptable to God because of Jesus.
1 Corinthians 1:30	We are **righteous** and holy because of Jesus in us.
1 Corinthians 15:22	At the resurrection, we will be made alive eternally.
2 Corinthians 5:17	We are a new creation.

Our Inheritance in Christ (cont'd)

Passage	Inheritance in Christ
2 Corinthians 5:21	We receive God's righteousness.
Galatians 3:28	We are one in Christ with other believers.
Colossians 1:28	We are perfect in God's sight.
Colossians 2:11	We are set free from our sinful nature.
2 Timothy 2:10	We will have eternal glory.

prayed
Romans 1:8;
1 Thessalonians 1:2;
2 Thessalonians 1:3

I've Been Praying for You from Day One

Now Paul begins to detail how he has been praying for this group of believers. His desires for them are what God wants for every part of His body, the church. Paul is praying God's will for them—the way God wants them to act and react.

Just as Ephesians 1:3–14 was one sentence in the original Greek, verses 15 through 23 are also a single sentence. Paul wants the Ephesians and every Christian to look at their inheritance in Christ as a whole—not divided up so that portions can be chosen. And in his prayer that encompasses verses 15 through 23, he intends for them to enjoy everything he mentions for their spiritual growth.

Persistently Pray Powerfully

EPHESIANS 1:15–16 *Therefore I also, after I heard of your faith in the Lord Jesus and your love for all the saints, do not cease to give thanks for you, making mention of you in my prayers:* (NKJV)

Paul knew how to pray. He mentions in most of his letters that he prayed for those he had led to the Lord or had influence upon. Whereas most of us often pray only when something bad might happen or has already happened, Paul remembers the faith and love of the Ephesian believers and gives thanks for them, along with praying for them.

John White

We cannot give thanks and remain the same. Our perspective changes as we open our minds to God through prayer. Hope is quickened. Is the person we pray for a difficult case? If so, are we perhaps focusing on the difficulties rather than on the God of difficulties, on what has not been done rather than on what has been done?[16]

apply it

Prayer is simply talking to God. It's a conversation with the almighty God of the Universe, believing that He hears and that He wants to speak to me and you. It's easy to talk to Him, but harder to hear, yet He tells us, "Call to Me, and I will answer you, and show you great and mighty things, which you do not know" (Jeremiah 33:3 NKJV).

Pray for "Aha!" Experiences

EPHESIANS 1:17 *that the God of our Lord Jesus Christ, the Father of glory, may give to you the spirit of wisdom and **revelation** in the knowledge of Him,* (NKJV)

Paul prays that each believer will have a spirit of <u>wisdom</u> and revelation of who God is. Although this does not refer specifically to the personal Spirit of God, we cannot receive true spiritual wisdom without the <u>Holy Spirit</u> being involved. Paul had just written to these believers about all the benefits and joys they have as Christians, but would they understand its significance? Only the Spirit could make its importance real to them. When they understood that, then they would really get to <u>know</u> God. Paul's desire was ultimately that every believer would know God better.

Without the spirit of wisdom and revelation that Paul mentions, a Christian can read their Bible and not receive anything from it. But with the Holy Spirit's input, a verse or passage can suddenly come alive and become very meaningful—even though he or she has read those verses many times before. Paul wanted the Ephesian believers to have many such "Aha!" experiences.

James 3:17 (NKJV) identifies God's wisdom as:

• pure

go to

wisdom
Proverbs 1:7

Holy Spirit
Isaiah 11:2

know
Philippians 3:10

revelation
insights only God
can give

- peaceable
- gentle
- willing to yield
- full of mercy and good fruits
- without partiality
- without hypocrisy

what others say

J. I. Packer

For some unfathomable reason, He wants me as His friend, and desires to be my friend, and has given His Son to die for me in order to realize this purpose. We cannot work these thoughts out here, but merely mentioning them is enough to show how much it means to know, not merely that we know God, but that He knows us.[17]

Beth Moore

Awareness is always the first step to freedom. This very awareness is exactly what motivated me in my late twenties to begin asking God to give me a heart to love Him and know Him more than anything in life.[18]

Paul wrote out his prayer for the believers that he cared about. He could have just said, "I pray for you," and left it at that. But instead, he detailed the different things he prayed. That way they could notice how God was doing those very things in their lives and be encouraged.

apply it

We can see the same benefit in those we pray for by writing out our prayers for others and letting them read what we've written. If you're e-mailing someone to say you'll pray for them, why not quickly type up the words you're saying to God on their behalf? Or write a letter telling them you are being faithful to pray as you said you would. It's bound to encourage them and you, for then they can report the difference your prayers have made.

Pray for 20/20 Spiritual Vision

EPHESIANS 1:18 *the eyes of your understanding being enlightened; that you may know what is the hope of His calling, what are the riches of the glory of His inheritance in the saints,* (NKJV)

hope
Colossians 1:5;
1 Thessalonians 1:3

maturity
Hebrews 6:1

fruit
Galatians 5:22–23

Paul wants these Christians to have spiritual eyes that see clearly the wonderful gifts of their salvation—all the things that Paul has been talking about. He's afraid that even though he mentioned so many glorious items in their spiritual "will," they won't live as if God makes a difference. But if they do understand and apply their spiritual inheritance as God's forever children, they will have <u>hope</u>. Hope is being assured of God's ability to help them live the way they really want to live: empowered by him for godliness and a growing knowledge of God's will. That's spiritual <u>maturity</u>. That hope also refers to a lack of fear about dying, knowing that death is just a transition toward receiving God's further inheritance in heaven.

Several translations use the word *heart* for "understanding," which can be defined as the center of one's personality. It's the idea of a person's total being. Paul wants their totality to be enlightened so that they can know all that is available to them.

what others say

Rick Warren

The Bible uses the word *heart* to describe the bundle of desires, hopes, interests, ambitions, dreams, and affections you have. Your heart represents the source of all your motivations—what you love to do and what you care about most.[19]

Without the Holy Spirit's enlightening, which Paul is praying for, each Christian could have nearsighted spiritual eyes, an inability to have vision for the future. Or they could have farsighted spiritual eyes—eyes that can't identify sin within their own lives. Or maybe they have spiritual glaucoma—eyes blinded so they live in the darkness of fear and worry, unable to trust God. But with 20/20 spiritual vision, a Christian sees clearly how God wants them to live and calls upon the indwelling Holy Spirit to obey and desire spiritual <u>fruit</u>. Wisdom is more than knowledge; it is the ability to apply knowledge for godly living.

No one's spiritual eyes can be enlightened without spending time reading and studying the Bible. Consistent study of God's Word, along with a Bible student's request for the Holy Spirit to teach them, will invariably result in spiritual growth—spiritual eyes opened and seeing clearly God's way of doing things. If someone says they don't understand the Bible, it's because they haven't searched it faithfully and allowed God to teach them. We must be willing to obey whatever we find there, in order for our eyes to see and understand.

Pray for Potent Power

go to

raised
John 21:14

seated
Colossians 3:1

right hand
Romans 8:34

head
1 Corinthians
15:24–28;
Ephesians 4:15

authority
Matthew 28:18

church
1 Corinthians 12:12

EPHESIANS 1:19–23 *and what is the exceeding greatness of His power toward us who believe, according to the working of His mighty power which He worked in Christ when He <u>raised</u> Him from the dead and <u>seated</u> Him at His <u>right hand</u> in the heavenly places, far above all principality and power and might and dominion, and every name that is named, not only in this age but also in that which is to come. And He put all things under His feet, and gave Him to be <u>head</u> over all things to the church, which is His body, the fullness of Him who fills all in all. (NKJV)*

Paul prays for these believers to know God to such an extent that they can utilize the very power that raised Jesus from the dead. Talk about a powerful example! There is nothing more powerful than bringing life back into a lifeless body—and especially three days after death. Doctors may be able to perform CPR to bring someone back from death immediately after they die, but no one can bring a three-day-old body back to life, yet that's exactly what God did for us by raising Jesus from the dead.

The "fullness" that Paul writes of refers to the church moving in God's power with spiritual gifts and abilities. And regardless of individual Christians' faults, or the oppression of the world upon the church, God's plan will be fulfilled because He has the power to do it all. And the Christian has that same power available to live a godly life.

Commentators believe that when Paul wrote, "principality and power and might and dominion, and every name that is named, not only in this age but also in that which is to come," he was referring to different levels of angels and demons in the heavenly spheres. Every single one of those beings will be brought under Jesus's <u>authority</u>.

Jesus also has complete authority over all believers. Each of us who is a believer in Jesus is a part of Christ's body, the <u>church</u>. He is the head, and we each participate in God's grand plan by fulfilling the role that He has designated. There is no favoritism by God toward any Christian who seems to have more exposure within the church, only His perfect plan for representing His love to a needy world.

There's nothing too hard for God. He has all the power—and more—that He needs to help us in any situation. Nothing is impossible with God. He can do anything He wants to fulfill His will. You are on a mission from God to accomplish His <u>plan</u> for you, and nothing will prevent that as long as you obey Him and call upon Him to help you.

Chapter Wrap-Up

- The apostle Paul wrote his letter to the Ephesian church while he was in prison in Rome. He wanted them to comprehend the wonderful grace that they enjoyed—along with knowing how to act like a Christian. (Ephesians 1:1–2)

- One of the spiritual mysteries is how God planned from the very beginning to send Jesus to die on the cross and to establish His church as the body of Christ. (Ephesians 1:3–12)

- Christians can know for sure that they will go to heaven because the Holy Spirit has been given to them as a pledge toward their future inheritance and their present one also. (Ephesians 1:13–14)

- Paul prays for the Christians at Ephesus that they will be aware of God's calling on their lives and the incredible power that He offers them as His children. (Ephesians 1:15–23)

plan
Psalm 33:11

Study Questions

1. Who wrote the book of Ephesians and what was his goal in writing it?

2. What significance is found in the fact that Ephesians 1:3–14 is one very long sentence?

3. How can Christians claim to be free of sin when they keep failing all the time?

4. What proof does a Christian have that he or she really belongs to God?

5. Along with praying for his friends, what is Paul always sure to mention to them?

Ephesians 2 Out with the Old and
in with the New

Chapter Highlights:
• **You Gentiles Were One of "Them"**
• **The Walls Come Tumbling Down**
• **Analogies for Believers**

Let's Get Started

What do you think would happen if you went up to the gates of the White House and asked for access to it and the Oval Office? You would probably be directed to the line of people waiting for tickets to tour the White House—but the Oval Office? No way! Very few Americans will ever see that—except in photos.

But I have a friend who is a Secret Service agent. I predict that someday when she's assigned to the White House, I will get to see parts of the White House *and* the Oval Office that are strictly off-limits to tourists. And I know what will happen. When I'm walking the halls with my friend and we encounter a guard, the guard will look at my friend, and then me, and nod and say, "If you're with her, you can go on."

This is similar to what Paul communicates in the second chapter of Ephesians. You and I have access to God's inner empowering life right now and in the future because we are indwelt and escorted by the Holy Spirit. When you and I are guided through the halls of heaven by the Holy Spirit, we'll be wearing Jesus's royal purple robe of righteousness that is stained with His blood, and each angel who guards the different doors that lead to the very throne of God will say, "If you're with Him, you can go on"—until we stand pure before our holy God.

Let's see how that personal relationship with God is lived out in our lives right now through Paul's telling us, "You're dead to sin and alive to God."

trespasses
wrong things done

sins
not obeying God

Here's the Past

EPHESIANS 2:1–3 *And you He made alive, who were dead in **trespasses** and **sins**, in which you once walked according to the course of this world, according to the prince of the power of the air, the spirit who now works in the sons of disobedience, among*

death
Romans 6:23

selfish desires
Romans 8:5

separate Himself
Ephesians 2:12

wrath
John 3:36

key point

whom also we all once conducted ourselves in the lusts of our flesh, fulfilling the desires of the flesh and of the mind, and were by nature children of wrath, just as the others. (NKJV)

Before a person meets Christ personally as Savior and Lord, he or she is dead in their sins—not physically, of course, but spiritually. Even if they considered themselves good people and in control of their lives, they were actually dead spiritually and controlled by Satan more than they realized. Just as a dead person can't communicate with the living, those who are dead spiritually have no communication with God. There's no relationship because sin causes a gap between God and unforgiven people. The Bible consistently identifies <u>death</u> as separation, not cessation of existence.

Paul isn't just pointing his finger at everyone else; he includes himself. He knows he was in the same boat and only wanted to fulfill his own <u>selfish desires</u> Because of that, God, who is completely holy, was obligated to <u>separate Himself</u> from Paul and everyone else who hasn't received His gracious gift of salvation. His <u>wrath</u> is justified because holiness must be angry toward the destructiveness of sin.

Trespasses (*paraptoma*) and sins (*hamarita*) are closely related words with slightly different meanings. In the Greek, *paraptoma* is a slip or a fall, like when someone falls away from following the right path. Therefore, a trespass is a slipping away from the truth. A sin, the word *hamarita*, is used in shooting at a target. When a person misses the target spiritually in not reaching God's high standards, he has sinned. Everyone is guilty of both, and Paul doesn't want anyone to think that somehow they could still be righteous through doing good or by doing one and not the other.

Often, people don't brand their own struggles as sin, preferring to focus on the sins of others. But in his letter to the Galatians, Paul gives us a broad list of identifiable sins: "Now the works of the flesh are evident, which are: adultery, fornication, uncleanness, lewdness, idolatry, sorcery, hatred, contentions, jealousies, outbursts of wrath, selfish ambitions, dissensions, heresies, envy, murders, drunkenness, revelries, and the like; of which I tell you beforehand, just as I also told you in time past, that those who practice such things will not inherit the kingdom of God" (Galatians 5:19–21 NKJV).

The Many Names of Satan

Paul knew that his readers would have no problem identifying Satan as the object of his words "the prince of the power of the air." These Christians believed that Satan and his evil spiritual forces inhabited the region between earth and sky. Satan is the head of those evil forces and is called many names.

go to

measure
Isaiah 64:6

Different Names for Satan

Scripture	Name
Revelation 12:10	accuser
Ephesians 4:27	devil
1 Peter 5:8	adversary
Revelation 9:11	angel of the bottomless pit
Revelation 9:11	Apollyon
Matthew 12:24	Beelzebub
Genesis 3:4; Revelation 20:2	serpent
Matthew 12:24	ruler of the demons
Matthew 13:19	wicked one

what others say

Patsy Clairmont

I know how it feels to receive merciful love, because I was a prodigal daughter. I ran away from home when I was sixteen. After a short time, I wanted to go home but feared my parents' reaction to my poor judgment. Finally, dejected, I returned. I can still see Mom in my mind's eye. She ran out the front door, down the driveway, and, with open arms and forgiving tears, embraced me. I was stunned at this undeserved show of love. It caused me to fill with sorrow for having brought my parents such anguish. I guess I thought after I ran that they would lock the door and throw away the key so I couldn't return. Instead, I learned their heart's door was always open to me.[1]

Some people like to point out that they do good things and are basically good people. They count the good things they do and believe that list overrides any bad they might do. Yet, a dead person is dead. There are no degrees of deadness. Spiritually speaking, a spiritually dead person is dead, not half dead because of their good deeds. Any amount of good deeds, no matter how many, can never <u>measure</u> up to God's total holiness. In order to be accepted before

holy
1 Peter 1:16

mercy
Titus 3:5

born again
John 3:3

forgiveness
1 John 1:9

God—without Christ—we would need to be totally <u>holy</u> like Him. It just doesn't happen, so that's why God made a provision for holiness, which is wearing the righteous robe of Jesus.

Here's the Present

> EPHESIANS 2:4–5 *But God, who is rich in mercy, because of His great love with which He loved us, even when we were dead in trespasses, made us alive together with Christ (by grace you have been saved),* (NKJV)

The single word *but* is arguably the most significant word in the English language. In any case, it's certainly significant here. Paul is drawing a contrast between the way those Christians were BC— "before Christ"—and AC—"after Christ." The difference in their spiritual lives was God's love and <u>mercy</u>, which offer freedom from sin. As a result, the new Christian is spiritually alive, having been "<u>born again</u>" spiritually, and is no longer separated from God's fellowship or from knowing His love.

The phrase *have been saved* is in the perfect tense, which expresses a "present permanent state as a result of a past action." In other words, because a Christian makes a onetime decision to receive Christ and be forgiven of all sins, he is permanently secure in eternity as a child of God; he is no longer condemned for his sins. That's grace—a gift of God's love because we don't deserve it. In verses 8 and 9, Paul will again talk about being saved by grace.

In the original Greek language, verse 4 reads, "But God . . ." Although we at times feel hopeless and helpless in our sins, we can depend upon the "But God . . ." of Scripture to give us hope.

In the New Testament, the word *mercy* means "undeserved kindness" toward sinners. God's great love and care about His created beings motivate Him to be merciful. That mercy and love offer sinners a chance to have a relationship with God. After salvation, that mercy extends to Christians on a daily basis even more opportunities to have a second chance through <u>forgiveness</u>. But the second chances aren't limited; they are always boundless.

born again
John 3:3

citizens
Philippians 3:20

seat
Revelation 3:21

what others say

David C. Needham and Larry Libby

Can you imagine what it's like to be loved by the Inventor of love? The one who dreamed it all up? God is the Inventor of father-daughter love, mother-son love, brother-brother love, parent-child love, husband-wife love, friend-to-friend love, even boy-to-dog love! He invented them all.

And the Inventor says, "I love *you*! Will you receive it?"[2]

Patrick Morley

We are saved by faith, not works. His approval of us isn't contingent upon our doing something to be good enough. He loves us because He made us. If your loved ones have withheld their approval, know that God works differently.[3]

something to ponder

Verses 1 through 7 of Ephesians 2 are another example of Paul's long sentences. Our versions today break it into shorter sentences so that it is easier to read and understand. But basically in the original, Paul had three verbs and three main points: "made alive with," "raised up with," and "seated with."

Here's the Future

EPHESIANS 2:6–7 *and raised us up together, and made us sit together in the heavenly places in Christ Jesus, that in the ages to come He might show the exceeding riches of His grace in His kindness toward us in Christ Jesus.* (NKJV)

Paul compares the raising of Christ with a Christian's spiritual raising from the dead through being born again. But that's not all. God also entitles them to become citizens of heaven, having a seat, a place where they belong, in heaven. And it's all because of that wonderful grace that Paul keeps mentioning over and over again. He just can't talk about it enough—it's just too incredible to think of a God who is willing to make it possible for a man or woman to be without sin in God's eyes.

All along, Paul is contrasting and comparing in these verses of chapter 2 between what happened to Jesus (mentioned in chapter 1) and what happens to Christians. The immense power God revealed in raising Jesus, He has used to do potent spiritual things in believers.

go to

raised spiritually
1 Corinthians
15:22–23

thinking
Colossians 3:1–3

confidence
Philippians 1:6

powerful
Philippians 4:13

worry
Philippians 4:6–7

transcendent
greater than we can
know

immanent
built in

omnipresent
present everywhere

What Happened to Jesus Compared to What Happens to Christians

Jesus	Christians
Jesus died physically (1:20).	Unbelievers are dead spiritually (2:1–3).
Christ was raised physically (1:20).	Believers are raised spiritually (2:5–6).
Christ is seated at God's right hand (1:20).	Believers will be seated with Christ in heaven (2:6).

All that God has done demonstrates to all of us His immense grace, which everyone will have to acknowledge in the future. In the eternal ages to come, each Christian will be like a displayed valuable item that shouts, "Look at what God did! I wasn't worth it, but God made it possible for me to be here and enjoy heaven."

Our spiritual life doesn't give us a license to sin on purpose. We have a responsibility to live as sinlessly as possible, with a desire to please God. Because of being born again spiritually, we have a whole new way of thinking and viewing life. Let's not belittle the importance of the price paid for our salvation.

> **what others say**
>
> ### Joni Eareckson Tada
>
> Faith assures us that heaven is **transcendent**. It is beyond the limits of our experience; it exists apart from our material universe. Heaven is also **immanent** in that it envelops all the celestial bodies, swirling galaxies, and the starry hosts. It we believe that God is **omnipresent**, then we can at least believe that what the Bible in Ephesians 2:6 calls the heavenly realms are omnipresent, as well. For where God is, the kingdom of heaven is.[4]

apply it

If God has demonstrated His fantastic power in raising Jesus from the dead, and the believer from spiritual death, then we can have every confidence that He is powerful enough to help us in day-to-day living. We don't have to worry or fear. Anxiety doesn't have to control us. Instead, we can believe that God will bring us through each trial and even bring good from it. As He promises in Romans 8:28, "And we know that all things work together for good to those who love God, to those who are the called according to His purpose" (NKJV).

How amazing that Paul could have such trust in God and such little fear, considering he was writing to the Ephesians while imprisoned, not knowing whether the trial that was to come would mean his life. These thoughts must have given him great peace and comfort in knowing that even his death would just put him on that heavenly seat beside his beloved Jesus.

It's All by Grace, Not Works

go to

faith
Romans 4:5

plan
Jeremiah 29:11

master potter
Isaiah 45:9

plan
Isaiah 64:8

EPHESIANS 2:8–10 *For by grace you have been saved through faith, and that not of yourselves; it is the gift of God, not of works, lest anyone should boast. For we are His workmanship, created in Christ Jesus for good works, which God prepared beforehand that we should walk in them.* (NKJV)

Paul doesn't want anyone to think that all the wonderful benefits he's been talking about are earned or deserved. It's a matter of applying Jesus's death to yourself and then trusting that God has done the rest—the raising, saving, and securing that Paul has been writing about. That's <u>faith</u>. It has nothing to do with being good enough to deserve or earn a place in heaven, because no one can be that good—that is, as good as God.

If someone could deserve it through earning it, then they would have the right to boast about it. But Paul says no one can rightly say they've done that. Instead, God does it by working within each person—shaping them just like a potter shapes the clay to create a work. "I created it. The pot didn't create itself. I did it!" God says of us. "This is My beloved creation, for whom I provided a means of deliverance from sin. I've designed it for My purposes, and I'll even provide the means to accomplish My <u>plan</u>."

Just as a clay pot doesn't tell the <u>master potter</u> what to make, a Christian doesn't tell Jesus how to use him for good works. God knows best, and He has a unique <u>plan</u> for each of His children. We just need to stop comparing His plan for us with the plan He has for others.

Paul uses the phrase "that we should walk in them." It's the idea that we walk down the path of the prepared good works God wants us to do by faith. We don't have to nervously look around or leave the path to find what He wants us to do to bring glory to Him. He

good works
Isaiah 25:1

Gentile
any person who is
not a Jew

will guide us as we walk with the belief that He already knows what He wants us to do. We just have to obey with confidence in His power to work within us.

what others say

Elisabeth Elliot

Salvation is a gift, purely a gift, forever a gift. It is grace and nothing else that obtains it for us. Discipline is not my claim on Christ, but the evidence of His claim on me. I do not "make" Him Lord; I acknowledge Him Lord.[5]

Charles Stanley

Note several things in that verse. First, you are God's workmanship. The word in the original Greek in which the verse was written literally means "a person of notable excellence." You may say, "Well, I don't look excellent," or "I don't do excellent things," or "I'm not excellent at anything." That's not what God says! He calls you a person of notable excellence because *He made you.* You need to see yourselves as God sees you—a prized example of His creation.[6]

God didn't save us from sin just to put us on a shelf. He saved us so that we can carry out a plan for the <u>good works</u> He has in mind. The good works don't save us, but they are the vehicle by which we exclaim, "God has made a difference in my life and I'm serving Him now. I'm doing the good works as a testimony of His work in my life, not as a means to gain His favor or to remove my sins." We are God's masterpiece, showing off His creative work of salvation in us.

apply it

<u>You Gentiles Were One of "Them"</u>

EPHESIANS 2:11–13 *Therefore remember that you, once **Gentile** in the flesh—who are called Uncircumcision by what is called the Circumcision made in the flesh by hands—that at that time you were without Christ, being aliens from the commonwealth of Israel and strangers from the covenants of promise, having no hope and without God in the world. But now in Christ Jesus you who once were far off have been brought near by the blood of Christ. (NKJV)*

Paul continues to show these Ephesian believers that they really don't have anything to boast about. In the previous verses, he says they can't boast about becoming saved—because it's all the result of

God's grace. Now, he points out to them that as Gentiles, they didn't even have a former history or relationship with **Jehovah** God like the Jews did. Jews consider anyone who is not a Jew to be a Gentile. During Paul's day, Jews had a very specific view of those who weren't **circumcised** like themselves; they called them the "Uncircumcision" with scorn. The division between them was so great that any Jew who married a Gentile was considered dead. A Jew couldn't even go into a Gentile home without being considered unclean

It was possible for a Gentile to become a part of the Jewish religion by being a "**proselyte**." Those who wanted to worship the Jewish Lord God were allowed to do so but never granted access to the main **Temple**. Instead, they were allowed to worship only within the Court of the Gentiles. Paul points out here that they were therefore "far off"—that is, far away from the main center of worship.

From a Jewish viewpoint, Gentiles were at a great disadvantage for five things, which Paul names here:

- Separate from Christ. They didn't look for a Messiah.

- Excluded from citizenship in Israel. They weren't Israelis, members of the nation of Israel.

- Foreigners of the **covenants** of the promise. They hadn't been given God's special covenants and couldn't benefit from them. The purpose of every covenant was to point to the coming Messiah and Savior.

- Without hope. They couldn't expect to be saved by the future Savior.

- Without God in the world. They didn't have a relationship with God that could give them the direction and purpose in life they needed.

The Jewish mind thought that the Messiah would come to deliver and save only Jews. They couldn't conceive that God would want to also save Gentiles. Yet God knew He would reach out to the Gentiles all along. Paul <u>preached</u> the good news of salvation through Jesus to the Gentiles, and though previously separated from God, they came to know Him as Savior.

Paul was referring to the different covenants that the Lord had made with His people, the Jews, over the centuries. There were basically four of them:

go to

circumcised
Genesis 17:10

proselyte
1 Kings 8:41–43;
Acts 13:43

covenants
Genesis 6:18

preached
Acts 13:46–49

Jehovah
Jewish term for God

circumcised
to cut off the foreskin of a male

proselyte
convert to Judiasm

Temple
place of worship

covenants
pacts made by God with groups of people

go to

sinners
Romans 3:23

free gift
Revelation 22:17

attitude
Romans 2:23–24

enmity
being an enemy

1. *Abrahamic:* Genesis 12:1–3; 15:18–21; 17:1–8

2. *Palestinian:* Deuteronomy 28–30

3. *Davidic:* 2 Samuel 7:16; Psalm 89:1–4

4. *New Covenant:* Jeremiah 31:31–34; Ezekiel 36:24–30

Each covenant promised benefits to the Israelites on the condition that they obey God's directions and laws.

---

what others say

Pam Farrel

It's glorious because God's power, ability, creativity and strength are there to help us walk the walk we are called to. God doesn't point to His place for us and say, "Good luck, hope you can pull it off!" No, God leads us to be usable by living the calling through us by His Spirit, and that pulls the pieces together. My life falls into place with more clarity, and less frustration, when I am relying on His power rather than my own.[7]

Christians need to be careful that we do not have an attitude of one-upmanship toward others like the Jews had toward the Gentiles. In God's eyes, every one of us is on equal ground: sinners in need of a Savior. And God offers every person who ever lived His free gift of acceptance and approval because He loves everyone.

The Walls Come Tumbling Down

EPHESIANS 2:14–17 *For He Himself is our peace, who has made both one, and has broken down the middle wall of separation, having abolished in His flesh the enmity, that is, the law of commandments contained in ordinances, so as to create in Himself one new man from the two, thus making peace, and that He might reconcile them both to God in one body through the cross, thereby putting to death the **enmity**. And He came and preached peace to you who were afar off and to those who were near. (NKJV)*

The Jews called Gentiles those "uncircumcised people," and the Gentiles were well aware of the Jews' critical attitude. Of course,

Gentiles didn't appreciate it. Therefore, the Gentiles responded with their own kind of prejudice and hate. In fact, the Greeks called anyone who wasn't a Greek "a barbarian." A wall of hostility separated them that no one seemed able or even wanted to destroy. Paul writes that only Jesus could do it—and He did. He brought peace between Christian Jews and Christian Gentiles by helping them see that they were no longer Jew and Gentile, but new creatures in Christ—a whole new group.

Gentiles and Jews who are saved were elevated to a new realm as one "new" man. Paul had two choices of Greek words when he wrote "new": *neos* or *kainos*. *Neos* is something that is newly created but is a replica of something else like it; *kainos* is a completely new item. Paul chose the Greek word *kainos* to indicate a new creation. No longer are believers <u>Jew or Gentile</u>. In God's eyes, they are only believers, and therefore brothers and sisters in Christ.

Jesus also created a new man by getting rid of the legalism as a requirement for acceptance by God. Jews and Gentiles no longer had to keep the thousands of laws created by the Pharisees in order to have peace with God and each other.

Paul uses two word pictures of the difference Jesus makes: Gentiles who were previously "afar off" and the "middle wall of separation." "Afar off . . . and to those who were near" refers to the custom of Gentiles who wished to convert to Judaism being said to be "brought near." The "middle wall of separation" refers to the wall in the Temple separating the court of the Gentiles from the court of the Israelites. Years ago, that wall was uncovered when the area was dug up. This inscription was found: "Let no Gentile, let no man of the nations, go beyond this wall on pain of death."

Paul would have known in a practical way the seriousness of that inscription and the emotional wall between Jews and Gentiles because he was <u>accused</u> of taking a Gentile into one of the inner courts. Paul had not actually taken his traveling companion, a Greek named <u>Trophimus</u>, into the court, but some tried to cause a riot and kill Paul with the false accusation.

go to

Jew or Gentile
Galatians 3:28

accused
Acts 21:28

Trophimus
Acts 21:29

Shalom
Jewish word for peace

what others say

Lloyd John Ogilvie

When Christ says, **"Shalom,"** he means it as more than a greeting. Peace is His life, His death, and His message com-

Prince of Peace
Isaiah 9:6

anxiety
John 14:27

bined. It touches a human life with forgiveness, acceptance, and freedom. When Christ comes to live in us, He resolves our fears, quiets the storms within us, and sets us at peace. Only then can we go about being peacemakers.[8]

Just think what would happen in the hostilities of the Middle East between Jew and Arab if everyone within those groups came to know Christ as their Savior. There would no longer be any reason to fight because they would suddenly all be on the same side, glorying God and wanting His agenda advanced, not their own. Unfortunately, this isn't likely to happen. But such a thought shows the impact Jesus can have if people let Him. The cross brings peace between different groups of people because we're all kneeling in submission before Jesus.

Jesus Christ is not just a peacemaker; He is peace Himself. For each attribute of God, God is totally that characteristic. In other words, when we say God is gracious, every part of God is gracious. He is grace through and through. The same is true of Jesus as the <u>Prince of Peace</u>. He doesn't just bring peace between warring parties; He *is* peace, through and through. There is no <u>anxiety</u>, fear, or uncertainty within Him. Never does Jesus stand up in heaven, wringing His hands, exclaiming, "Oh, no, I just don't know what I'm going to do about this situation that My child is in. This has caught Me completely by surprise." He is always prepared and knows everything from beginning to end. Paul wrote, "Jesus Christ is the same yesterday, today, and forever" (Hebrews 13:8 NKJV).

In contrast, you and I can be peaceful at times, but there are times when we feel anxious. We might feel peaceful one day and say, "I'm at peace." Yet the next moment, we might be filled with fear. As a peacemaker, we might have the opportunity to mediate between two people in conflict and be successful in bringing peace between them, but the next week we might fail in our attempt with another group. Therefore, we have peace and give peace at times, but it's not a total part of our character, like it is with Jesus. How wonderful it is that Jesus is total peace and His presence within us as Christians can help us more and more to experience peace and be peacemakers.

In His ministry as the Son of Man, Jesus brought God's perspective and peace into everyday life.

Jesus's Unique Works

Scripture	Jesus's Unique Work
Matthew 10:1	Using the talents and gifts of common men, rather than calling on the religious leaders to be His disciples.
Luke 2:32	Teaching that His ministry was also to Gentiles, not just to His own people by birth.
Matthew 27:55	Ministering to everyone, not just the "acceptable" people to the Jews of that time. He intentionally went to Samaria so that He could meet the needs of an outcast, a Samaritan woman.
Luke 8:1–3	Considering women equal with men, fellowshipping with them and using them in ministry.
Matthew 11:19; John 8:3–11	Offering equal love and concern for the outcasts of society, like the tax collectors and adulterers.

prophets
those who proclaim God's message through a special calling

cornerstone
used in building to line up correctly the walls

The Smashed Bricks Are Now Forming a Holy Temple!

EPHESIANS 2:18–22 *For through Him we both have access by one Spirit to the Father. Now, therefore, you are no longer strangers and foreigners, but fellow citizens with the saints and members of the household of God, having been built on the foundation of the apostles and **prophets**, Jesus Christ Himself being the chief **cornerstone**, in whom the whole building, being fitted together, grows into a holy temple in the Lord, in whom you also are being built together for a dwelling place of God in the Spirit. (NKJV)*

Since grace means that no one's efforts can make them acceptable to God for salvation, everyone—Jew or Gentile, slave or free, male or female, and black or white (or any other color)—needs Jesus's gift. And every person who accepts that gift has the same access to God the Father as everyone else. There are no steps or different levels of a platform before the throne of God where some can have a closer or higher standing with God. Somehow, we all will be considered equal in heaven, the undeserving who received God's mercy so that we can be standing there at all.

Then Paul creatively gives an additional metaphor to help his readers understand their oneness and unity in Christ with all believers. He contrasts being outside the fold (foreigners and aliens) with being members of God's family. The Greek word for foreigner is *xenos*, and for strangers it is *paroikos*. In Paul's day, the *xenos* and *paroikos* in any city were treated with disrespect and weren't accepted.

apostles and prophets
1 Corinthians 12:28

brings
Romans 8:26

foundation
1 Corinthians
3:10–11

But Paul says these people have become full citizens. It's as if a person comes into the United States on a visa from a foreign country and is identified by their green card as not American. Then, by going through the citizenship process, they stand before a judge, raise their hand, take an oath of loyalty, and recite the Pledge of Allegiance. They can tear up the green card because they are no longer foreigners—they are real citizens of the United States.

It is a complicated procedure to go through—classes and maybe even language studies. But with our citizenship into heaven, it's a very simple process: We simply receive Christ as Savior and suddenly become card-carrying members of God's forever family with all the benefits that includes. Plus, we are suddenly able, without taking any language classes, to speak the language of heaven: "Praise the Lord!"

Paul reminds his readers that what they believe is not some newfangled idea, but something that includes what the <u>apostles and prophets</u> had taught from the very beginning. They were the people, like the apostle Peter and the prophets Mark and Luke, who wrote and spoke the truth. They laid a foundation of truth for everyone else to build upon.

Paul refers to the three members of the Trinity in verse 18: God the Father, God the Son, and God the Holy Spirit. God the Son, Jesus, made the "access" possible by destroying the barrier between man and God. The Holy Spirit is the means whereby we have God's presence within us, and the Holy Spirit <u>brings</u> our concerns before God's throne.

what others say

J. I. Packer and Carolyn Nystrom

God doesn't always pick the nice men and the nice women. In fact, it's just the opposite. It is God's way to choose and to use flawed human material. God picks sinners; God saves sinners; God calls, equips, and uses sinners.[9]

Paul previously referred to a "body"; now here he uses the analogy of a building, which many of his readers would be familiar with. He points out the different aspects of a building: the foundation, the cornerstone, and the construction. The <u>foundation</u> of any building must be without cracks and faults because otherwise the whole building will crumble. The teachings of the apostles and prophets gave Christian doctrine that firm foundation.

Jesus is the cornerstone of Christianity. A cornerstone is essential to a building; in early building methods, the bricks were aligned based on where and how the cornerstone was placed. If the cornerstone was put in crooked, then the walls of whole building would be crooked. Without the cornerstone of Jesus's teaching and assured divinity, Christian believers could not know the truth.

temple
1 Corinthians
6:19–20

The construction on this living building continues; Paul uses the present tense to indicate that it's a work in progress. New believers are constantly being added, and the building (the body of Christ) continues to grow. It is like a building that never gets done, yet is being perfectly built for the Master's use. Paul also notes that this building is not haphazardly thrown together but carefully constructed with God's hand and influence upon it.

God's household is not a building but a group of people. Some people say, "I'm going to God's house"—meaning a church building. But in reality, God's house is within every believer because God dwells there through His Spirit. What makes it even better is that we are placed on the level of a "<u>temple</u>," a place of worship and of even greater significance than a house. We need to make sure that we keep our temple pure for God's use.

Analogies for Groups of Believers

Scripture uses several analogies for the church with specific purposes for each one. God wanted to stress that the church is:

Word Pictures Describing the Church

Scripture	Church Is:
1 Corinthians 12:12	Body; therefore it is a living organism and subject to the Head, Jesus Christ.
Revelation 19:7	Bride of Christ; therefore it is a loving relationship in which the caring Bridegroom provides for all the needs of the bride.
Ephesians 2:21–22	Building; therefore it represents a habitation, a temple for the Spirit of God to indwell.

Chapter Wrap-Up

- Every person is spiritually dead and controlled by Satan before they receive Christ as their Savior. While living a life without Christ, the lusts of their flesh are controlling them, and most of the time, they don't even realize it. (Ephesians 2:1–3)

- When a person recognizes that they need Jesus's love and forgiveness, they can ask Jesus into their heart, knowing that God's gracious gift of salvation is free. As a result, they become a child of God and can fulfill the specially designed plan that God wants for them. (Ephesians 2:4–10)

- Paul is writing the Gentiles to remind them that they were once considered strangers to God and reviled by Jews. He doesn't want them to feel prideful because they now know Jesus personally, unlike the Jews. (Ephesians 2:11–13)

- Jews and Gentiles who know Jesus as their Savior shouldn't have any division between them because they're all on the same side: Jesus's side. Jesus has made peace between them because He died for everyone. (Ephesians 2:14–17)

- All Christians have equal access to God because they are no longer foreigners separated from God. Because Jesus is the cornerstone of the body of Christ, every believer, like every brick that forms a wall, is of equal importance. (Ephesians 2:18–22)

Study Questions

1. Why is a person spiritually dead before he becomes a Christian?

2. What does it mean when a person is saved by grace?

3. Why did Jews have such a critical view of Gentiles?

4. What was the attitude Paul wanted Christian Jews and Christian Gentiles to have toward each other, and why?

5. How can every Christian—regardless of their nationality—have equal access to God?

Ephesians 3 More About Our Position in Christ

Let's Get Started

Everyone has experienced starting out talking about one thing and then shifting to another thought. That's exactly what happens with Paul in this third chapter of Ephesians. He starts out ready to say a prayer for the Ephesians, and then thinks of something brilliant—about how God's "mysterious" plan of salvation through Jesus unites Jews and Gentiles into one body. He referred to it briefly in the first chapter; now he's going to develop it and talk about how the church is a mystery recently revealed (at his point of time). From verses 2 through 13, Paul waxes authoritative on that subject. Then in verse 14 he goes back to his prayer for the Ephesian believers. Let's look at what has him so enthralled.

go to

Jerusalem
Acts 22–23

When You Have to Be in Chains, Choose Jesus as Your Captor

EPHESIANS 3:1 *For this reason I, Paul, the prisoner of Christ Jesus for you Gentiles—(NKJV)*

Paul is a great writer who uses transitions masterfully. He refers back to what he's been talking about: the reconciliation of the Jews and Gentiles into the body of Christ. He says that preaching this very message—all the way back to his days of preaching in Jerusalem—stirred up commotion, which led to his imprisonment. The Jews felt threatened and he was taken prisoner, ending up in Rome. People viewing his life would call him a political prisoner, but Paul did not consider himself a prisoner of Emperor Nero, the caesar, or ruler of the Roman world. He considered himself a prisoner of Jesus Christ—something that happened when Christ appeared to him in a bright light on the road to Damascus. Ever since then, he was captive to the living God, not man.

go to

under God's control
Jeremiah 29:11

good
Romans 8:28

dogs ate
1 Kings 21:23

Max Anders

He did not consider himself to be a prisoner of Rome. He considered himself a prisoner of Christ Jesus, because it was out of obedience to Jesus that he was a prisoner there; and he trusted completely in the sovereignty of God.[1]

William Barclay

When we are undergoing hardship, unpopularity, or material loss for the sake of Christian principles, we may regard ourselves either as victims or as the champions of Christ. Paul is our example; he regarded himself not as the prisoner of Nero but as the prisoner of Christ.[2]

apply it

How does each of us consider the circumstances of our lives? Do we see ourselves captives of bad luck or unhappy circumstances that create bitterness and resentment? Or do we look at every event in our lives as being under God's control and therefore usable by Him? Just as God brought good from Paul's imprisonment—he wrote several books of the Bible as letters during that time—God intends to bring good out of everything, even the unhappy things, in our lives.

Paul's Ministry Was Unique, and You Can Have One Too!

EPHESIANS 3:2 *if indeed you have heard of the dispensation of the grace of God which was given to me for you,* (NKJV)

Paul begins another of his famously long sentences here. This one starts in verse 2 and extends to verse 13. He just has so much good stuff to say that he doesn't want anyone to stop reading about it. And his very important message is that God wants everyone to experience God's grace—both Jew and Gentile alike—and be a part of the church.

Paul is amazed at how God has used him in such a unique ministry. When he was still a Pharisee, before he knew Christ personally as Savior and Lord, he wouldn't have given a single thought to wanting Gentiles to know God. The "uncircumcised" were disdainfully called "dogs" and considered worthless. In the Old Testament, dogs ate the evil queen Jezebel's dead body because of God's judgment. There wasn't a fate much worse than that. Paul's unique ministry calls for him to actually communicate the truth of eternal life available to those "dogs," the Gentiles. He definitely had a change of mind-set.

go to

vision of a sheet
Acts 10:11–16

warned
Leviticus 11:4–8

The Old Testament View of the Gentiles

Scripture	View
1 Chronicles 16:35	Wanted deliverance from the Gentiles.
Psalm 105:44	God gave the Gentile lands to His chosen people.
Psalm 106:35	The Gentile people were a bad influence.
Psalm 106:41	The Gentiles were a source of God's discipline.
Psalm 115:2	The Gentiles scoffed at the Jews serving God.
Psalm 117:1	The Gentiles should praise God.
Isaiah 11:10	In the end times, the Gentiles will seek God.
Isaiah 42:1	The Messiah will bring justice for the Gentiles.
Isaiah 60:5	The Gentiles' wealth will be used by the Jews.
Isaiah 60:12	Those who don't serve the Jews will be destroyed.

The word *dispensation* that Paul uses may seem vague to us, but Paul meant "stewardship." He was a steward, a caretaker responsible for the distribution and management of the wonderful message of grace that God had given him. He had every intention of managing it well.

> **what others say**
>
> **Lloyd John Ogilvie**
>
> Paul's phrase, "the stewardship of God's grace given to me for you," is a great motto for life's tough times. Everything that happens to us is not only for our own personal growth in grace but for our ministry to others.[3]

Paul's contemporary minister, the apostle Peter, had a different ministry or "stewardship." God called him to primarily minister to the Jews. Yet even Peter's heart had to change about reaching out to the Gentiles. God gave Peter a <u>vision of a sheet</u> lowering from heaven with "unclean" foods on it and told Peter to eat from it. Peter was shocked and he refused, believing that act would make him unclean as the Old Testament <u>warned</u>. But through God's vision, Peter realized that God did indeed want to reach out to make the gospel available to those who weren't Israelites. So Peter and Paul both had the same perspective: God wants to save all people of the world.

go to

Pentecost
Acts 2:1–13;
Exodus 23:16

tongues
Acts 2:6–8

homes
Acts 2:46

receive salvation
Isaiah 49:6

new idea
Romans 16:25

Pentecost
festival celebrated
fifty days after
Passover as a time
of feast

The Unrevealed Revelation

EPHESIANS 3:3–6 *how that by revelation He made known to me the mystery (as I have briefly written already, by which, when you read, you may understand my knowledge in the mystery of Christ), which in other ages was not made known to the sons of men, as it has now been revealed by the Spirit to His holy apostles and prophets: that the Gentiles should be fellow heirs, of the same body, and partakers of His promise in Christ through the gospel,* (NKJV)

Paul stresses again that God revealed to him the wonderful "mystery" of the believing Jews and Gentiles forming a church—the body of Christ. They are now on the same side, rather than enemies like in the past. The "revelation" of this new concept came to Paul when he encountered Jesus at conversion and then began to understand more and more of God's plan for salvation for everyone, not just Jews.

The formation of the church had begun at **Pentecost**, even before Paul was converted to Christ. At that point, the Spirit of God empowered believers in a special way through the speaking of different, unknown <u>tongues</u> as a way of bonding everyone together, causing many people to hear the message, and demonstrating God's amazing power. From that point on, believers began meeting in <u>homes</u> to boldly encourage each other and share with others. Before that, they were hiding in those homes, afraid of persecution. Apostles like Peter and James, who was Jesus's brother, were the first "apostles and prophets" and leaders of that early church who spoke the truth.

Although it was accepted knowledge in the Old Testament that Gentiles could <u>receive salvation</u>, the concept of the church was never referred to or disclosed in the Old Testament. Therefore, Paul said it was now being disclosed as a <u>new idea</u>. Paul wanted to make sure Gentiles understood the importance of their "membership" in the body of Christ.

what others say

Wellington Boone

The Lord is the Creator of race. There is no reason for whites in America, or any other culture anywhere in the world, to feel superior. None of us had anything to do with our coming into this world. It was God's idea.[4]

Hear, Hear! Hear About a Humble Heart!

EPHESIANS 3:7–9 *of which I became a minister according to the gift of the grace of God given to me by the effective working of His power. To me, who am less than the <u>least</u> of all the saints, this grace was given, that I should preach among the Gentiles the unsearchable riches of Christ, and to make all see what is the fellowship of the mystery, which from the beginning of the ages has been hidden in God who created all things through Jesus Christ;* (NKJV)

least
1 Corinthians 15:9;
1 Timothy 1:15

persecuting
Acts 8:3

unsearchable
Romans 11:33

Paul repeats his general message again of being an administrator of this mystery but reveals his attitude about this special calling and the gift of grace he received. We can hear his awestruck humility in having such an incredible opportunity to speak for this mystery. Yet, he credits God's power, not his own. When he wrote to the Christians at Rome, he declared, "For I will not dare to speak of any of those things which Christ has not accomplished through me, in word and deed, to make the Gentiles obedient" (Romans 15:18 NKJV). He knows that whatever fruit he sees from his efforts has nothing to do with him, other than his obedience. The inner working within changed lives is God's work—not his own. He humbly remembers that he is least of God's children because he intended to squelch the message by <u>persecuting</u> and putting Christians to death. He knows it was God's amazing grace that broke that deception and opened his eyes to the truth.

Because of that grace, he is very aware of the unsearchable riches of Christ—the fact that knowing Christ brings so many wonderful benefits both for temporal living and for eternity. He is awed by how he gets to take advantage of those gifts, even though he doesn't deserve any of it. And he gets to tell others how they can profit too. Paul is telling his readers that revelation and truth should make them humble, not puffed up.

The word <u>unsearchable</u> in Greek, *anexichníastos*, conveys the idea of "not capable of being traced by footprints." If someone were able to walk alongside the seashore and not make any footprints in the sand, they could not be searched for and found. In like manner, the full benefits of knowing Christ can never be completely searched for and found. And, even if some are discovered, there are many more.

go to

speak
2 Timothy 4:2

evangelization
sharing Christ with others

quotient
degree

manifold
numerous and various

what others say

Lloyd John Ogilvie

He knew he was a part of the Lord's strategy for the **evangelization** of the world and that his grace always would be sufficient in the difficulties he faced. In life's tough times, Paul focused on the privilege of grace rather than the problem which could have caused him grief.[5]

Paul was given a special gift to share the gospel of God's grace with a special group, the Gentiles. It would be more difficult to explain God's salvation to those who didn't know about Jehovah. But such a special gift isn't only for apostles like Paul; God wants every Christian to <u>speak</u> about the good news—and that includes you, regardless of whether you feel qualified or adequate. Although not every Christian will have the gift of evangelism, everyone can and should reflect God's power to others by living a godly life and giving Him the credit. Besides, every Christian can and should be an evangelist through his words and actions.

A huge part of humility is a spirit of gratitude. It's the mind-set that "I know I don't deserve this wonderful privilege, but I'm grateful God gave it to me." Paul was very grateful that he could speak of God's love and grace. He didn't begin to think he deserved to do that. He viewed it as a special task that God could have given anyone—but for which He chose Paul. A perspective of genuine gratitude acknowledges a person's unworthiness for the task and then credits God with any fruit that results. How's your "H.Q." (humility **quotient**)?

Here Come the Church

EPHESIANS 3:10–11 *to the intent that now the **manifold** wisdom of God might be made known by the church to the principalities and powers in the heavenly places, according to the eternal purpose which He accomplished in Christ Jesus our Lord,* (NKJV)

God's idea of having the Jews and Gentiles a part of one group, the church, shows His wisdom. We take for granted the brilliant concept of a church body, but God didn't have to do it that way. However, if He *hadn't*, each of us would be without the support we need, and Jews and Gentiles would still be at odds with each other—and what kind of demonstration of God's power is that? Obviously, not a good one.

And so God ingeniously created the unity of the body of Christ. As a result, <u>angels</u>—both good and bad—can point to it and say, "That shows how wise God really is!" Even evil angels headed by Satan have to admit the truth that God knows what He's doing, even if they won't surrender to His lordship.

Furthermore, this whole plan wasn't some last-minute idea where God said, "Oh, I just thought of something new! Let's build us a church!" No, He knew from the very beginning that He would develop it through the saving act of Jesus's death. God doesn't have any decisions up His sleeve that His eternal mind didn't know all along, even if they seem like surprises to us.

The word *manifold* in the Greek, *polupoíkilos*, refers to the beauty of an embroidered pattern or the variety of colors in flowers. It's defined as "assorted, multicolored, greatly diversified, plentiful in variety." Therefore, when Paul writes of the manifold wisdom of God, he is giving the visual word description of the creativity and varied hues of God's ability to do the right thing. And one of those is developing the concept of a church that includes former enemies.

go to

angels
Ephesians 6:12

anxiety
Philippians 4:6–7

variegated
multicolored

what others say

J. Vernon McGee

Another purpose of the mystery is revealed here. God's created intelligences are learning something of the wisdom of God through the church. They not only see the love of God displayed and lavished upon us, but the wisdom of God is revealed to His angels.[6]

Charles R. Swindoll

It is in the church, week after week, where we learn faithfulness. It is in the church where discipleship is carried out. It is in the church where accountability is modeled. It is in the church of Jesus Christ where we find the doctrinal roots that establish us in our faith.[7]

When we worry, we're really saying, "God must be surprised by my circumstances, and I'm not sure He knows how to handle this." Don't let <u>anxiety</u> steal your confidence in God's **variegated** wisdom. He has known from the beginning how to help you. All God's plans

apply it

go to

heavenly powers
1 Corinthians
15:24–26;
Colossians 1:16

redeeming
Hebrews 10:19

without fear
Hebrews 4:16

intermediary
go-between

are eternally known by Him from the beginning because He is sovereign (even while every man has a free will).

Don't Worry, Those Rulers and Authorities Can't Block Your Way to God

EPHESIANS 3:12 *in whom we have boldness and access with confidence through faith in Him.* (NKJV)

In Paul's day, the people believed that <u>heavenly powers</u> were angelic representatives of earthly rulers who could control access to God's throne. They felt afraid that they might not have God's ear and help. But Paul says that these believers actually do have power to approach God because those rulers and authorities don't have ultimate control—God does. And because each believer has been made holy in God's sight through Jesus's <u>redeeming</u> work, their sin won't block them from having God's ear also. They are clear to come before God <u>without fear</u> or hesitation. Yet at the same time, accessibility to God doesn't diminish His greatness and holiness. It's only through being redeemed and forgiven that we are entitled to approach Him.

Paul used the word *boldness* because it referred to the free speech every citizen in the Roman state had. They had the freedom to say whatever they wanted without fear of being arrested. In much the same way, you and I have complete freedom to tell God everything—without fear of being told God won't hear us. We don't even need someone to relay the message. We can approach God because Jesus is our **intermediary** who opens the door for our approach to God's throne and His attention.

what others say

Rick Warren

> The moment you were spiritually born into God's family, you were given some astounding birthday gifts: the family name, the family likeness, family privileges, family intimate access, and the family inheritance![8]

Most of us would feel hesitant about meeting the president of the United States or a powerful king of some country. But none of us, if we know Jesus as our Savior, need feel frightened or unsure of approaching God in prayer. Just the opposite: We can go before Him boldly. Hebrews 4:16 assures us, "Let us therefore come boldly to the throne of grace, that we may obtain mercy and find grace to help in time of need" (NKJV).

The next time you wonder whether God cares about your situation or whether you have the right to talk to Him, tell yourself, "I'm a prince (or princess), and I have every right to enter the palace where I'll meet with my Father, the King."

Because Jesus was a man in human form on earth and yet kept His God status, He <u>experienced</u> the problems and temptations that afflict every person on earth. Therefore, He compassionately ushers us into the throne room not as one who belittles our struggles but as one who is on our <u>side</u>. He urges us, "Yes, tell our Father what's bothering you. I guarantee He'll work on your behalf." Even more important, He says, "Come and confess your sins to our Father, and I will be your defense attorney—and I always win every case because your sin is cleansed by My blood, and My Father desires to forgive you."

go to

experienced
Hebrews 4:15

side
Romans 8:31

I'm in Prison Because of You, but Don't Feel Bad

EPHESIANS 3:13 *Therefore I ask that you do not lose heart at my tribulations for you, which is your glory. (NKJV)*

Paul considers it a privilege to have shared the gospel with the Ephesians. He's concerned that they could grow discouraged in their faith because of what happens to those like himself who preach Christ. But he wants them to know that even persecution brings glorious results. Having eternal life is worth the inconvenience and pain he is experiencing, and they should boldly speak of Jesus too.

A pregnant woman knows the pain she's going to experience in childbirth, yet she is willing to go through it because of her love for the child. When a child comprehends the pain his mother went through to give him life, he feels loved and important. Paul wants the believers for whom he has sacrificed freedom to feel the same way: loved and important.

When we have the right priorities of valuing heavenly objectives above the comfort and <u>temporal</u> happiness of earth, we are truly seeing life through God's eyes and won't be discouraged by anything bad that happens to us in this fleeting life. We should be willing to endure any hardship that will bring others to heaven. When we reach heaven, we'll look back at life's trials and consider them tiny inconveniences, not even worthy of conversation. We'll only want to talk about how wonderful Jesus is.

Okay, Now Back to Our Program . . . er, Prayer

Paul is the great "pray-er," and he gives us a wonderful example of a prayer that you and I can pray for ourselves and everyone we know. H. A. Ironside, former pastor of the Moody Memorial Church in Chicago, gave this outline for Paul's prayer;

- Verse 16: **endowment**: God has provided everything we need.
- Verse 16: **enduement**: God has given us the power we need.
- Verse 17: enthronement: God dwells within us.
- Verse 17: establishment: God roots and grounds us in Him.
- Verse 18: enlightenment: God gives us the ability to comprehend spiritual insights.
- Verse 19: enlargement: We can grow greater in our knowledge of God's love.
- Verse 19: enrichment: We become spiritually richer as we surrender to God more.[10]

temporal
2 Corinthians
4:16–18

endowment
gift

enduement
ability

Let's Pray Like Paul

EPHESIANS 3:14–15 *For this reason I bow my knees to the Father of our Lord Jesus Christ, from whom the whole family in heaven and earth is named,* (NKJV)

Paul finally takes a breath after finishing his thought about the mystery of the church. Because of the importance of how believers are unified as members of the body of Christ, he now wants to pray for them to live out that unity here on earth with love for each other. So he tells them he is kneeling in prayer. Some commentators believe that Paul was in this consecrated position of prayer as he dictated to his scribe. Some scholars believe he was even prostrate on the floor.

Regardless of Paul's physical position, he first reminds them that they are all part of God's family. Families should stick together, and he's going to tell them how to do that. Paul had already prayed for the Ephesians in <u>chapter 1</u>, when he emphasized that believers should know their inheritance in Christ. In this second prayer, he stresses how they should live out that inheritance.

go to

chapter 1
Ephesians 1:15–23

knelt
Luke 22:41;
Acts 9:40

---

what others say

Charles Haddon Spurgeon

We cannot all argue, but we can all pray; we cannot all be leaders, but we can all be pleaders; we cannot all be mighty in rhetoric, but we can all be prevalent in prayer. I would sooner see you eloquent with God than with men.[11]

Lloyd John Ogilvie

As a Hebrew, Paul usually prayed from a standing position. But he told the Christians that when he prayed for them he bowed his knees. "Bowing the knees" was a phrase used to express prostrating yourself. He wanted the Christians to know the deep earnestness of his prayers for them.[12]

Paul has chosen to mention that he <u>knelt</u> in prayer, which is one physical position for praying. The position of our body doesn't matter to God, but it can reflect our attitudes and feelings as we communicate with God. If someone is worshipping God, they may want to kneel or even lie prostrate on the ground to show their own unworthiness before such an awesome God. Some people raise their hands as they pray to represent their dependence upon God and their surrender to Him. At times, we may just sit quietly in God's presence with our heads bowed or lifted up. Standing is another way to honor God, just as we would honor a king by standing before him. The position of our body isn't as important to God as the heart attitude that accompanies it as we pray.

Paul could have addressed God in any number of ways because

apply it

God has many titles and characteristics. Because Paul is going to be praying about the Ephesians being loving members of the body of Christ, he uses the title "Father" to acknowledge God's ultimate control and example as the most loving member of any family. If any human father needs an example of great fatherhood, then the heavenly Father can be his example. If any person had a hurtful childhood because of a hurtful father, he can receive healing through knowing that his earthly father isn't like his heavenly Father, who is perfectly loving.

Been Working Out Your Spiritual Muscles?

Ephesians 3:16–17a *that He would grant you, according to the riches of His glory, to be strengthened with might through His Spirit in the inner man, that Christ may dwell in your hearts through faith;* *(NKJV)*

Here Paul arrived at the meat of his prayer. He wanted them to receive all of God's blessings, but in order to do so they must be strong with the Spirit's power. If a woman hadn't eaten for a long time and her stomach was empty, she might be physically unprepared to consume a heavy steak dinner. If she did, her stomach might grow upset or, if she was too weak, she couldn't eat at all. She would need a certain level of physical strength to enjoy that delicious steak dinner.

In a similar manner, Paul says that unless these believers are at a certain level of trust in God, they can't receive or be aware of God's riches—their inheritance in Christ. When they are walking in that inheritance, they have the ability to trust God and love others. That's allowing Christ to dwell in their hearts. Being spiritually strong is giving God <u>reign</u> and control within our hearts.

Paul used the Greek word *dwell*, or *katoikein*, with a very specific meaning. He wanted it to represent Jesus's "settling in" and "being at home"—not just as a guest who usually leaves after a period of time. Rather, Jesus is to dwell in our hearts as one <u>enthroned permanently</u>. Jesus is only at home in our hearts when He has His proper place: being in charge because He is Lord and truly knows best.

If you had a visitor to your home who was a plumber by trade and you suddenly had a problem with the faucet, would you not call upon that visitor to help solve the problem? We have a Dweller who

reign
John 15:5

enthroned permanently
Galatians 2:20

resides in our hearts who is an expert at everything. We should breathe a sigh of relief to think He wants to not only be available to consult but actually take over and make the running of our lives peaceful and calm in the midst of great difficulties. Who wouldn't want to make Him Lord and Master of their heart's domain?

go to

fullness
Colossians 1:19

what others say

Patsy Clairmont

When I'm flitting, fighting, and forging through life, I don't have the presence of mind or spirit to accept the balm He offers. But when I nail down my hypersandals in a quiet place and lean in to hear His voice and then respond accordingly, I often receive cheer and comfort. Not that I always get what I want from the Lord, but He meets me at my need. It may be only one word, but a word from Him is life, and it sustains me.[13]

Spiritual Weakness Versus Spiritual Strength

What exactly is spiritual strength? Consider this contrast and evaluate the strength of your heart.

Spiritual Weakness	Spiritual Strength
Focuses on the negative aspects of life	Focuses on God's blessings and the good of life (Philippians 4:8)
Can't trust God because He seems unable to help with life's problems	Trusts that God is in control and believes He wants the best for each person because He loves each one (1 John 4:8)
Filled with fear and worry	Has ability to turn fear into trust by believing God is strong enough to handle that situation (Philippians 4:6–7)
Concentrates on how others have hurt him and becomes bitter and resentful	Believes God even allows bad things for good results and therefore can forgive others for hurts (Ephesians 4:29, 31–32)
Feels too ashamed to ask God for forgiveness from his sins	Confidently asks God to forgive their sins believing God is a loving, forgiving God (Isaiah 43:25)
Can't obey God's commands in the Bible or the directions He gives	Obeys God's principles and desires to listen as He guides each day (Proverbs 4:11)

something to ponder

<u>There's a Fountain Flowing Deep and Wide</u>

EPHESIANS 3:17b–19 *that you, being rooted and grounded in love, may be able to comprehend with all the saints what is the width and length and depth and height—to know the love of Christ which passes knowledge; that you may be filled with all the <u>fullness</u> of God.* (NKJV)

go to

firmly
Psalm 1:3;
Hebrews 4:14

prodigal
Luke 15:11–32

perpetually
continually

unstintingly
generous

indispensable
essential

prodigal
disobedient

Paul uses a variety of verbal word pictures to uniquely refer to love.

- *Rooted:* <u>firmly</u> put into the ground so that nothing can dislodge it.
- *Grounded:* established like a building that is safe even during earthquakes.
- *Comprehend:* a mind that holds an idea firmly and securely.
- *Filled:* having every part of a person occupied.

When a person is filled with God's love, he is able to overflow with love toward others. If we don't feel loved by God, it's more difficult to pass it along to others. Paul desires for us to know God's unlimited love so that we will be able to completely allow Him to reign in our hearts as Lord and Master. Of course, that won't happen all the time, but it should be our goal.

---

what others say

Dallas Willard

So we must understand that God does not "love" us without liking us—through gritted teeth—as "Christian" love is sometimes thought to do. Rather, out of the eternal freshness of His **perpetually** self-renewed being, the heavenly Father cherishes the earth and each human being upon it. The fondness, the endearment, the **unstintingly** affectionate regard of God toward all His creatures is the natural outflow of what He is to the core—which we vainly try to capture with our tired but **indispensable** old word love.[14]

John White

Paul's third request indicates to me that to be rooted and grounded in love means to live a life in which all my thoughts and actions spring from an awareness of how much *God loves me*.[15]

Is That Your Final Answer?

Different commentators have different meanings of the words *width, length, depth,* and *height.* Here are some to consider:

- *Width* could represent Jesus's arms stretched wide to receive "whoever believes in Him" (John 3:15–16 NKJV). God doesn't want any person to be left out, but each one must make that decision himself.
- *Length* could symbolize how God will go to any length to bring the unbeliever and the **prodigal** back to Himself. He will do

anything necessary and will never give up until that person has made a final decision to reject Christ.

- *Depth* could point to how God's love is able to dig to the depths of a human's shame and sin and pull him out. No one can say their sin is unforgivable; God's love is deep enough to reach even them.

- *Height* could refer to the "heights" of God's love. He has unlimited creativity of designing wonderful purpose and plans for our fulfillment and future glorification.

what others say

Bruce H. Wilkinson

He knew that, until that issue was fully settled in their minds, they would never have faith in God's methods. The same is true for your life—if you believe His motive is grounded in love for you that nothing can change, the "Why?" question is settled and you can move into asking Him, "How, Lord?" And you will have confidence in His motives.[16]

Keep Those Logs Burning!

Paul encourages these Ephesian believers to work on these things side by side with other believers. Someone has used the illustration that a burning log will lose its flame when removed from the fire pit. Christians need each other because God designed it that way. Hebrews 10:24–25 exhorts us, "And let us consider one another in order to stir up love and good works, not forsaking the assembling of ourselves together, as is the manner of some, but exhorting one another, and so much the more as you see the Day approaching" (NKJV).

Know the Unknowable? Yes, Paul Says

In an interesting paradox, Paul encourages believers to know something that he says is unknowable. It goes beyond knowledge. God's love is greater than anyone's ability to comprehend it. Every Christian should make it his lifelong goal to seek to know more of God's love, though none of us will ever reach it. What a wonderful thing to focus on: God's love.

go to

stronger
1 Peter 4:12–13

good
Romans 8:28

doxology
prayer of praise to
God

Every Christian—all the saints—can know God's love. Yet, so many people are still unsure of God's love. Having wrong ideas about God and the way He works can contribute to doubting His love. Another common wrong assumption is feeling that a God of love would only allow good things to happen. Isaiah 45:7 tells us, "I form the light and create darkness, I make peace and create calamity; I, the LORD, do all these things" (NKJV). Yes, God does allow, and even create, unfortunate things. But His intention is to use the unfortunate things of life to make us <u>stronger</u> and to bring ultimate <u>good</u>.

What's a Doxology?

EPHESIANS 3:20–21 *Now to Him who is able to do exceedingly abundantly above all that we ask or think, according to the power that works in us, to Him be glory in the church by Christ Jesus to all generations, forever and ever. Amen. (NKJV)*

Paul closes his prayer with praise to God in what is called a **doxology**. Maybe he thought that the things he had prayed and the concept of unity between Jew and Gentile might seem too amazing for these Christians to believe. Could they really be filled with God's power to live as God wanted them to? Could there really be unity, love, and peace between two former groups of enemies? As if all that was too amazing for the Ephesians to understand, Paul closes by reflecting on God's greatness. He's subtly reminding them that all that he prayed and taught them is possible because God is a great enough God to pull it off. Why? Because God is capable of doing far more than any of them, or even Paul himself, could ask—or even imagine. And you know how we humans can imagine! The Empire State Building started as a dream. The Eiffel Tower started as a dream. Michelangelo's works each started as a dream. The most amazing projects, successes, and accomplishments started as dreams, but every single one is tiny and insignificant in comparison to what God can do.

what others say

Merrill F. Unger

In the applications of the word *glory* in Scripture, it is easy to trace the fundamental idea involved in it. Properly it is the

effulgence
brilliance

exercise and display of what constitutes the distinctive excellence of the subject of which it is spoken; thus, in *respect to God*, His glory is the manifestation of His divine attributes and perfections, or such a visible **effulgence** as indicates the possession and presence of these. In *respect to.man*, his glory is found in the things which discover his honorable state and character, such as wisdom, righteousness, superiority to passion, or that outward magnificence which is expressive of what, in the lower sphere, bespeaks the high position of its possessor.[17]

David C. Needham and Larry Libby

"Within us!" That's right! Paul was expecting God to do something that was far, far above what I would have ever thought of imagining, much less asking. And Paul's God is my God! Dare we dream that our lives would overflow with the fullness of God's love? Yes! This is not "the impossible dream." You and I have been joined to Someone who is more powerful than we have ever begun to imagine.[18]

Charles Stanley

If you ever catch a glimpse of how much God loves you, desires to be with you, and has prepared good things for you, you'll find yourself with confidence and inner assurance that can't be matched.[19]

Paul's outburst of praise was a result of his concentrated thoughts about the glorious things God was doing and wanted to do. You and I can have the same outburst of praise as we focus on God and His unlimited abilities to do great things through us. Praise is focusing on God's nature and attributes, whereas thanksgiving is focusing on what God does. The more we dwell upon who God is, the more we will want to praise Him. That in turn will build our confidence in God's ability to work through us and in us. Everything God wants to do through us and in us is by His Spirit's power. It cannot be of our own power or through our own efforts. We need to surrender to Him, believing by faith that He will do His will in us.

Chapter Wrap-Up

- Paul considers himself a steward and servant of God's grace—a grace he wants to give others. He knows that grace personally, but he acknowledges that he of all people didn't deserve to be a "dispenser" of God's grace because he persecuted the church. (Ephesians 3:1–2)

- In the past, God didn't reveal how He would make it possible for all people to be united within one group: the body of Christ. But once Jesus came and made redemption possible, that group became known. (Ephesians 3:3–9)

- Because God's creation of the church is so powerful, every being in heaven acknowledges God's wisdom and might in creating it. (Ephesians 3:10–13)

- Paul returns to praying for his readers. He prays that they will know God's riches and as a result be strengthened by the Holy Spirit, let Christ dwell in their hearts, and know more and more fully God's love. (Ephesians 3:14–19)

- Paul is so overcome with these amazing thoughts that he breaks into praise for God in what's called a doxology. (Ephesians 3:20–21)

Study Questions

1. Why is Paul so amazed at how God has used him?

2. What is the mystery that Paul is referring to?

3. Who should shake in their boots because God created the concept of the church?

4. What are some of the things Paul prayed for his readers?

5. How does Paul close his prayer for his readers?

Ephesians 4
First Unity and Then Holiness

Chapter Highlights:
* Get Ready to Rumble
* The Emperor Needs New Clothes
* The Emperor Should Wash His Mouth Out

Let's Get Started

No one enjoys a preacher who just talks theory and gives nothing practical. Sitting through a sermon like that makes us leave the church scratching our heads, muttering, "Okay, now how am I going to apply *that*?"

Paul doesn't want his readers to feel that way. So far in the first three chapters of Ephesians, Paul has given lots of theological and "up in the sky" information. He hasn't really been too practical. But hold on—he's about to begin pointing some fingers at behavioral issues and talk about living life the way God desires. The first three chapters talked about the church and its mission to reach others, bringing the Jews and the Gentiles together. Now Paul will give details about how a church—and each member—effectively represents Christ to reach others.

deportment
behavior

what others say

Lloyd Ogilvie

The author is placing before his readers and hearers the guidelines of Christian conduct and **deportment** in the church and the world. The foundation has been laid in a magnificent exposition of the theme, Christ-in-His-church; now the structure must be erected, with its complementary theme, the church-in-Christ, or more properly, Christ's church in its relations with society.[1]

Get Ready to Rumble

EPHESIANS 4:1 *I, therefore, the prisoner of the Lord, beseech you to walk worthy of the calling with which you were called,* (NKJV)

Paul never pulls any punches. As someone imprisoned for the sake of Jesus, he has undergone a real boxing match while living life God's way in the midst of very difficult circumstances. So he's reminding his readers, "I'm gonna tell you how to live now because I'm trying to live this way myself! We've been called to a wonderful inheritance in Christ, just like I told you, but now it's time to apply it to life. Here's how."

When Paul used the word *worthy*, he meant "equal weight." In other words, a person's knowledge of his inheritance and his obedience should be real in his life. One shouldn't be to the exclusion of the other; they are equally important.

what others say

J. I. Packer and Carolyn Nystrom

In spiritual life and ministry Paul's hope did for him what athletes hope training and lifting weights will do for them physically: It supplied strength and enhanced performance. So it should be with all of us.[2]

apply it

Paul is a wonderful example for encouraging people. As he "beseeches" them, you can hear his attitude of love and concern. He doesn't try to browbeat them into submission, but appeals to them as a patient fellow prisoner for Jesus.

Are You Ready? Be Humble

EPHESIANS 4:2–3 *with all lowliness and gentleness, with long-suffering, bearing with one another in love, endeavoring to keep the unity of the Spirit in the bond of peace.* (NKJV)

Lowliness, gentleness, and longsuffering! Paul couldn't have listed three more difficult assignments. Our natural tendency is to focus on ourselves, push others aside to get our own way, and then get upset if it doesn't happen. Paul is suggesting totally different behavior from our natural bent. Talk about radical! And to boot, he wants everyone to be unified—all desiring the same thing. That's taking it one more step that's really, *really* against our nature. Paul's readers may be scratching their heads and wondering if Paul has gone off his rocker. *Perhaps he's carrying this Christianity thing a little too far,* they may have thought. But Paul has every confidence that he is calling them to what God wants: godlike behavior.

Here Paul tells them to be humble or "lowly." After talking in the first three chapters about the incredible position in Christ they have, it's no wonder he has to remind them to be humble. Being so loved by God could easily make anyone feel special, unique, and . . . above everyone else. Yet, Paul says, "Even though you are special in God's eyes, don't consider yourself more important than anyone else."

When Paul wrote to the Romans, he used a similar theme in chapter 12 that gives a good definition of humility: "For I say, through the grace given to me, to everyone who is among you, not to think of himself more highly than he ought to think, but to think soberly, as God has dealt to each one a measure of faith" (Romans 12:3 NKJV). Paul says humility isn't thinking of yourself as worthless, nor is it thinking of yourself as more special than anyone else. It's simply looking at the talents God has given you and rejoicing in His use of them. Because none of us can take credit for how God uses us, we shouldn't get big heads. It's all to God's glory, not ours.

go to

oneness
John 17:21

Armed with that kind of humility, it'll be easier to follow through on Paul's other valued characteristics: gentleness and longsuffering, which is patience. Having a correct view of ourselves diminishes pride and makes it easier to value others and treat them with respect. Of course, the final result will be unity and <u>oneness</u> because then no one will think their way is the only way.

The fourth characteristic of the Christian reaching others for Christ is love. In Greek, there are four words for love. *Eros* refers to the love between men and women and includes sexual desire. *Philia* is the love of friends. *Storge* is love between family members. And *agape* is the kind of love that Paul is expressing here. It's the God kind of love, where someone wants the very best for another person—even if he has been hurt by that person. The first three are often expressed as feelings, but *agape* makes a choice to love with or without good feelings.

key point

The final quality of a healthy church member is peace, especially peace between Christian people. Paul says this comes through unity—every person wanting what God wants even if it's not what that individual wants.

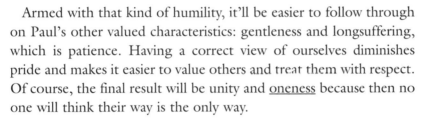

what others say

Ralph P. Martin

Yet unity does not mean a monochrome, deadpan uniformity, which might be the case if the church were a thing, an inert and static object. Rather, the church is an organism, pulsating with life and made up of living persons who are responsible for growth of character and personal development, according as they use the gifts that Christ has bestowed.[3]

Charles Stanley

How do we become humble? Think of someone you admire, maybe someone you have admired from a distance but have never met. Choose someone who in the broad scheme of things you would consider better than you. Okay? How would you treat this individual if he or she were the next person you were to come into contact with? Now, make a decision to treat the next person you come into contact with the way you would the one you consider better than you. That is the *attitude* of humility.[4]

In his letter to the Philippian believers, Paul would use Jesus as the ultimate example of humility. Paul admonished his readers, "Let nothing be done through selfish ambition or conceit, but in lowliness of mind let each esteem others better than himself. Let each of you look out not only for his own interests, but also for the interests of others. Let this mind be in you which was also in Christ Jesus, who, being in the form of God, did not consider it robbery to be equal with God, but made Himself of no reputation, taking the form of a bond-servant, and coming in the likeness of men. And being found in appearance as a man, He humbled Himself and became obedient to the point of death, even the death of the cross" (Philippians 2:3–8 NKJV). That's the ultimate of humility: to release the position of who you are and to submit to the will of another, even if it means the ultimate sacrifice.

When you think about it, unity is just about impossible without humility. A person who isn't humble focuses on himself and meeting his own needs. Does that bring unity and oneness within a group of people? I don't think so! Paul knows how important this is, and that's why he reminded them that he's a prisoner—talk about humbling. That has to be the ultimate test of humility. Paul offers himself as an example of how unity can be achieved: by focusing on others. Being humble isn't being worthless; rather, it's recognizing God's power within.

Paul Has a "One" Obsession

EPHESIANS 4:4–6 *There is one body and one Spirit, just as you were called in one hope of your calling; one Lord, one faith, one baptism; one God and Father of all, who is above all, and through all, and in you all. (NKJV)*

In case Paul hasn't yet stated his case strongly enough, he repeats himself, using the word *one* to convince everyone that none of them as believers are operating on their own. They are tied within a wonderful entity that includes all believers, which he calls the "<u>body</u>" of Christ. What an amazing **metaphor**. Picture your own body and imagine what would happen if your right leg decided to go to Cleveland and your left leg decided to go to Los Angeles. That's not unity! A body whose legs fight about the direction each is taking will not get anywhere.

Or think of the disease of cancer. Basically, cancer is one or more cells within the body doing their own thing. They are not working for the benefit of the body; they are killing good cells or crowding them out by multiplying their own brand of ideas beyond their assigned boundaries. Paul doesn't want the cancer of division to take over the body of Christ. To prevent that, he uses the word *one* to describe several concepts:

- *Body:* The entity that all believers belong to.
- *Spirit:* The Holy Spirit that entwines everyone together because He indwells all believers.
- *Hope:* Every believer shares the <u>expectation</u> that someday they will dwell with God in <u>heaven</u>.
- *Lord:* Jesus is the Head of the church, and there's no one else who will ever replace Him. Paul uses the Greek word *kyrios*, which had two usages at that time: master (as opposed to servant or slave) and the word used to refer to the Roman emperor.
- *Faith:* There's just one major way to express faith in God: trusting that He's the <u>Lord</u> and Savior and then letting Him be Lord! It could also refer to the body of Christian doctrine.
- *Baptism:* The act of water baptism is a demonstration that unites people because they've expressed their reborn nature that is shared by them all. It could also refer to the baptism of the Holy Spirit when He enters a new believer's life.
- *God and Father:* There is only one God, albeit expressed through the Trinity by the Father, Son, and Spirit. Paul says that God is above, through, and in. "Above" refers to His sovereignty. "Through" means involved throughout the world. And "in" means His omnipresence, or being present everywhere.

go to

body
1 Corinthians 12:4–6, 13

Spirit
1 Corinthians 12:4

expectation
1 Peter 1:3

heaven
Colossians 1:27

Lord
1 Corinthians 12:5

Father
John 1:12

metaphor
visual picture

baptism
being submerged quickly under water as a spiritual commitment to Christ

transformed
2 Corinthians 3:18

fellowship
1 Corinthians 12:2;
1 John 1:7

what others say

Louis T. Talbot

The third great truth which forms the ground of the unity is "The one hope of your calling." A Christian does not have a thousand hopes; he has only one. An unconverted person has multiplied hopes which are never realized. A believer has the "one hope" which he will realize in the coming of the Lord. This "hope" is called the "hope of your calling."

What is that "hope"? It is that someday we shall behold the face of the Lord Jesus Christ and shall be <u>transformed</u> into His image. All true believers are included.[5]

Robert Wall

Paul sees salvation as something Christians experience together. To enter the living Christ by faith is to experience intimate <u>fellowship</u> with Him and also with other believers.[6]

The pagan people of Paul's day believed in a whole pantheon of gods—Roman and Greek gods who were created and discarded at the whim of the people depending upon what they believed they needed. Most communities had a "patron god" whom they called upon to help them. But if a time came where the city wanted to give a more superior image to others, they would discard that god and claim a more important god as their helper. It definitely wasn't "one god fits all." Every god had its own weaknesses and strengths, and the Romans and Greeks regularly adopted gods from each other and were influenced by one another's beliefs. Christian Jews and Gentiles believed there was one God, and that was flying in the face of popular opinion.

Okay, We're One; but We're Also Diverse?

EPHESIANS 4:7–10 *But to each one of us grace was given according to the measure of Christ's gift. Therefore He says: "When He ascended on high, He led captivity captive, and gave gifts to men." (Now this, "He ascended"—what does it mean but that He also first descended into the lower parts of the earth? He who descended is also the One who ascended far above all the heavens, that He might fill all things.) (NKJV)*

Suddenly it's as if Paul skids to a stop in his thoughts. He wants to assure everyone that they are one and should act like it, but he now begins a section that lets them know it's okay to be diverse in the roles they take to serve God. In that regard, different isn't necessarily wrong. They are indeed one, but they aren't all the same in their service.

grace
Ephesians 3:2, 7–8

We can almost picture Paul teaching his theology in a classroom: "Okay, students," he calls as he raps his pointer, "now listen up. We're all one in Christ and a part of one big, happy family."

Then one of the smart-alecky kids sticks up his hand. "But Professor Paul, look at us. We're all so different and we all are doing different things for God. We don't look too 'one' to me!"

Some of the students look around and nod, and Paul agrees. "Yes, I see what you mean. So I need to clarify. We're all one in Christ, but He has given each and every one of us different gifts to use for His glory. That's good. Just think if we were all trying to do the same thing. We'd be stepping on each other's toes. So God intended for each of us to fulfill His plan in creative and different ways."

The students nod their agreement as they look around at the other students, thinking, *I wouldn't want to be like him, or do what God has called her to do. I like God's plan for me!*

When Paul uses the word *grace* in this instance, he doesn't mean the typical "God's riches at Christ's expense" kind of definition. He's thinking of "enablement": the <u>grace</u> or power to fulfill God's call upon a person's life.

> ### what others say
>
> ### Gigi Graham Tchividjian
>
> I know one father who says he cannot love his children unless they please him. His acceptance is based on their performance. How thankful I am that my heavenly Father's acceptance is based on love through the sacrifice of His Son, not on my track record.[7]

Paul used an analogy of something that was common in Roman and Greek experience. When a military general or person in authority was victorious in battle, he would reward those who helped him by giving them gifts. In other instances, the victor was given gifts by others or brought the spoils of the war back to his city. In a similar way, Jesus was victorious by delivering sinful men from the bondage of death. He takes redeemed people and gives them as gifts to the church.

Commentators believe that Paul is quoting and/or summarizing Psalm 68 when he says, "Therefore He says . . ." In other words, "God says in the Old Testament . . ." That psalm is a song about God's victories as a Father providing for His children. In it, God is the "victor" who delivers His children from various problems. Interestingly, the psalm actually says, "You [God] have received gifts among men" (68:18 NKJV). Paul words it, "And gave gifts to men."

Going Up? Or Going Down? Jesus Did Both

Commentators don't all agree on a meaning for "lower parts of the earth." It could relate to lower parts of the earth, or it could mean hell. But most believe it means Christ's burial in the grave, which set men and women free from the bondage of sin. After the three days He ascended into glory and has the joy of dispersing His gifts to His believers so that His plan can be fulfilled in all the earth.

Scholars also aren't certain what "ascended" and "led captivity" mean. Some believe it refers to taking Old Testament believers out of Paradise and presenting them in God's presence.

Other scholars believe these verses refer to Jesus's descending from heaven to become a man in flesh and then, after His resurrection, ascending into heaven again.

what others say

Louis T. Talbot

Until the cross, the Old Testament saints went to Paradise which was called by the Jews "Abraham's bosom," which was a part of Sheol, the place of the departed spirits, where they waited for the accomplishment of redemption.[8]

Variety Truly Is the Spice of Life

EPHESIANS 4:11–13 *And He Himself gave some to be apostles, some prophets, some evangelists, and some pastors and teachers, for the equipping of the saints for the work of ministry, for the edifying of the body of Christ, till we all come to the unity of the faith and of the knowledge of the Son of God, to a perfect man, to the measure of the stature of the fullness of Christ;* (NKJV)

Variety is the spice of the Christian life too. God understands that each of us needs to fulfill a unique calling, and He provides that challenge through a variety of roles: apostles, prophets, evangelists, pastors, and teachers. Paul had specific job descriptions in mind for each of those roles:

- *Apostles and prophets:* Those sent out with God's specific authority, like the original twelve disciples chosen by Jesus or those who gave God's messages in the Old Testament. In the early church, a <u>requirement</u> for being an apostle was to have actually seen Jesus and witnessed His resurrection. Today, these requirements are not considered necessary by some denominations who believe Christians still receive apostolic and prophetic giftings.

- *Evangelists:* These are today's missionaries who travel to spread the gospel.

- *Pastors and teachers:* Those who work within an individual church to guide and direct the spiritual growth of believers so that they, in turn, can serve God.

Even today, though, people disagree on the meanings of those words, depending upon their **denominational affiliation**.

Regardless, all of these abilities given to Christians are for a three-fold purpose:

- Equipping believers for the work of ministry. *Equip* is the Greek word *katartismon*, and its variations are referenced elsewhere in the New Testament to <u>mending nets</u> and <u>disciplining</u> an offending Christian. Therefore, it's the idea of restoring something to its original state or making it ready for its purpose—their ministry.

- Edifying the body of Christ. This is a word for "building up." Just as a building gets constructed, so the believer must grow in his maturity while living in God's power.

- Resulting in unity between believers, knowledge of Jesus, and continual progress toward perfection. The more this happens, the more Jesus's characteristics and nature will appear in all that His believers do.

God's gifts are not for someone's ego trip or the lifting up of the individual to receive praise, but for the good of the church and every believer.

requirement
1 Corinthians 9:1;
Acts 1:21–22

mending nets
Mark 1:19

disciplining
Galatians 6:1

denominational
church body

affiliation
connection

Charles Colson with Ellen Santilli Vaughn

But note the role Paul assigns to the pastor in the process of building the body. Contrary to popular impressions today, the pastor is not paid to do our work (service) for us. Pastors and teachers are to equip the saints—that's us—to serve, to build the body, to be the church in the world. Every layperson is to be equipped as a minister of the gospel.[9]

Charles R. Swindoll

In a healthy church one of the vital signs is an absence of favoritism, prejudice, and status. In any other earthly organization, when you draw together a number of human beings, you're going to have prejudice, emphasis on status, and a display of favoritism. But not in the body of Christ.[10]

key point

Paul didn't intend for this to be a complete list. In other portions of Scripture, he lists even more ways for God's children to bring God glory. In 1 Corinthians 12, he includes other roles in addition to the ones listed here: "And God has appointed these in the church: first apostles, second prophets, third teachers, after that miracles, then gifts of healings, helps, administrations, varieties of tongues" (1 Corinthians 12:28 NKJV). Then in his letter to the Romans, he gives additional opportunities: serving, teaching, being an encourager, contributing to the needs of others, leadership, and showing mercy (Romans 12:7–8).

Are these the only kinds of "job descriptions" that are of service to God? No, Paul wasn't saying that. But right now he's referring to roles within the church meant to encourage members of a congregation, like in Ephesus. Actually, anything that anyone does in God's power is His gifting, whether it's mothering, working in a factory, helping at a daycare, or selling life insurance. God has chosen every single one of His children to have ministry.

something to ponder

Even if you haven't been called to any of the roles that Paul mentions, you are still a believer who is given spiritual gifts by God. Most people begin to discover their unique gifting by responding to an invitation to serve in the area that they naturally enjoy. Then, as they develop their dependence on God's power within them, they can branch out into other areas where they have God's gifting but lack confidence.

Like Balloons Carried by the Wind

cavalier
arrogant

EPHESIANS 4:14 *that we should no longer be children, tossed to and fro and carried about with every wind of doctrine, by the trickery of men, in the cunning craftiness of deceitful plotting,* (NKJV)

If you tell a five-year-old that a giant ant is in the front yard eating up his Big Wheel, you can bet that he'll want to run outside and chase it away. But if you tell an adult the same thing, he'll look at you like your next stop should be the mental hospital. What's the difference? It's how each person thinks and the types of experiences they've had. The child is naive and believes just about everything, while the adult has developed discernment skills (hopefully!).

That's what Paul wants Christians to develop through the influence and instruction they receive within the body of Christ. Such Christians won't run outside naively when someone offers some new, supposedly Christian teaching that contradicts what Paul and others are teaching them. People are always proposing new ideas, and Paul doesn't want followers racing to the front yard without carefully considering whether such ideas are man-based or God-based. Some believers tend to think that everyone has pure motives, but Paul warns them and us that some are out to be deceptive, either through their own ignorance or by careful design.

what others say

R. C. Sproul

The first thing we must do is get the Word of God into our minds. That responsibility is ours, not God's. We are required to be diligent in our study of Scripture. We cannot reasonably expect the Spirit to give us the excellent sense of the Scripture in our hearts if we are unwilling to work to get it in our minds. A **cavalier** approach to Scripture will not do. The only "devotional" reading of God's Word that pleases Him is a devout *study* of His Word.[11]

Don't believe everything you hear. Even the things other Christians teach may not be accurate. Ask questions, seek godly counsel, and compare any new idea against the truth of Scripture.

go to

loving
1 Corinthians 13:1–3

study
2 Timothy 3:16–17

prayer
Acts 1:14

fellowship
Hebrews 10:25

memorization
Psalm 119:9, 11

1 . . . 2 . . . 3 . . . Stretch Those Spiritual Muscles

EPHESIANS 4:15–16 *but, speaking the truth in love, may grow up in all things into Him who is the head—Christ—from whom the whole body, joined and knit together by what every joint supplies, according to the effective working by which every part does its share, causes growth of the body for the edifying of itself in love. (NKJV)*

Another part of maturing is speaking the truth in a <u>loving</u> manner. Many of us have no trouble speaking the truth—at least our version of it! We can blurt out how wrong a false teacher is, we can correct the theology of someone who should know better, and we can lecture someone about the meaning of a verse. We've got truth on the tip of our tongue and on every taste bud. But Paul presents this challenge: Are we doing it in love? Do we really want the best for the other person, or do we just want to appear like a big man on campus who is experienced and knowledgeable? Is our tone one of compassion and patience, or is it irritated because this bozo should know better? If we can learn to speak the truth in love, we will help ourselves grow spiritually by making choices that strengthen our self-control.

Paul continues using his metaphor of the body of Christ by referring to Jesus as the "head." Growth and change comes from the head, Jesus, and it flows down into the ligaments. Maybe the ligaments represent the support that we each give within the framework of the church. Regardless, the growth comes from Jesus as each person cooperates with Him.

> **what others say**
>
> **William Barclay**
>
> The only thing which can keep the individual Christian solid in the faith and secure against persuasive arguments that lead people astray, the only thing which can keep the church healthy and efficient, is an intimate association with Jesus Christ, who is the head and the directing mind of the body.[12]

apply it

Few Christians actively choose to be spiritually stunted, but it can happen if a believer isn't faithful in growing strong spiritually through the basics of the Christian life: Bible <u>study</u>, <u>prayer</u>, <u>fellowship</u>, and Bible <u>memorization</u>. If you aren't growing, your spiritual muscles are atrophying.

Don't Have Spiritual Heart Disease

EPHESIANS 4:17–19 *This I say, therefore, and testify in the Lord, that you should no longer walk as the rest of the Gentiles walk, in the **futility** of their mind, having their understanding darkened, being alienated from the life of God, because of the ignorance that is in them, because of the blindness of their heart; who, being past feeling, have given themselves over to lewdness, to work all uncleanness with greediness. (NKJV)*

Paul wants every Christian to keep growing and moving forward in their faith, not returning to the way they lived before they knew Christ. A Gentile who doesn't know Jesus as Savior suffers, in effect, from spiritual heart disease. His spiritual arteries are hardening because he has been chewing on the wrong things and putting into his spiritual body that which gums up spiritual knowledge: all sorts of lewdness (immoral sensuality) and uncleanness (anything evil). Plus, it's all wrapped up in a gift bag of greed. But the "gift" doesn't equip or edify, which is Paul's goal for believers.

Paul doesn't want these Ephesian believers to return to that kind of "dark" thinking. To prevent this, he calls their attention to how such people really live: controlled by whatever pleases them that they think will meet their needs. Because they aren't satisfied, they keep trying to find something more. But immorality and sin never do satisfy. "Just remember *that*," Paul exhorts them.

The word *futility* means being without purpose or objectives, something worthless and vain. God created men's minds with the intent of their coming to know the ultimate revelation: a knowledge of Himself that would develop into living with God's purposes as their primary goal. Those who didn't know Jesus were missing out on that, and Paul didn't want any Christians to backtrack into their old lifestyle of living without God's enlightened mind-set.

Paul uses the word for blindness here in reference to the insensitivity of a spiritual heart—one that is "past feeling." This kind of heart is unable to receive spiritual input, just as a blind person cannot receive ocular impulses to the brain. In some translations, the word is translated "petrifying," which is certainly a graphic description. It's as if these unbelievers are hardened, calloused, and insensitive to anything spiritual. Paul doesn't want the Ephesian believers to become like that.

dark
1 Corinthians 2:14

immorality
1 Thessalonians 4:3

futility
emptiness

Paul reminds the Ephesian believers what unbelievers live like, and it's a useful reminder for us. We need to think about what it means to live without God's presence and guidance. If we reflect on the uncertainty of having no <u>assurance</u> of heaven, of making decisions by ourselves, and of how empty it is trying to find meaning in temporary things, we won't want to return to such a lifestyle. Instead, we can thank God for the love, joy, direction, and peace that we enjoy.

As we thank God, we should also remember how easy it is to allow our hearts to become hardened, even as Christians. When we repeatedly give in to the same sin, we become insensitive to the Holy Spirit's conviction. A hard heart doesn't happen overnight. It starts out soft, but little by little grows callous unless we regularly ask for forgiveness and repent of our sin.

The Emperor Needs Some New Clothes

assurance
1 John 5:11–13

sanctification
1 Thessalonians 5:23

unregenerate
not born again

EPHESIANS 4:20–24 *But you have not so learned Christ, if indeed you have heard Him and have been taught by Him, as the truth is in Jesus: that you put off, concerning your former conduct, the old man which grows corrupt according to the deceitful lusts, and be renewed in the spirit of your mind, and that you put on the new man which was created according to God, in true righteousness and holiness. (NKJV)*

Clothes are an important part of our lives. Most of us give careful consideration to what clothes we adorn our bodies with, but we need to give more thought to the "clothes" our souls wear; they too make a fashion statement. If our souls are "dressed down" in anger, worry, fear, sin, and sadness, we aren't a very good representation of the Lord. We won't even look any different from the Gentiles Paul refers to. But if we put on the clothing of godly choices, patience, and love, then our spiritual fashion will definitely receive admiring looks!

Every believer has spiritual clothes available to him; it's just a matter of choosing to wear them. We must make sure we're <u>looking</u> at life the way God does.

"And be renewed" is written in the present tense. By it, Paul meant, "Go on being renewed in the spirit of your mind." It's the idea of something already done and yet never completely reached, of needing the daily obedience of putting God in charge of our minds. Paul also put his words in the passive voice, indicating that it isn't something we accomplish, but which we allow to happen within us. It's God's job! We just <u>cooperate</u> and faithfully persevere.

go to

looking
Romans 12:1–2

cooperate
2 Corinthians 10:5

new man
2 Corinthians 5:17

what others say

F. B. Meyer

Put it on by faith. Do not try to build up Christlikeness by your repeated endeavors. Just assume it by faith. Believe it is yours. Reckon that it is so. Go out believing that Christ's likeness is on you, His beauty clothing you as a beautiful robe; and men shall increasingly realize that it is not you but Christ.[15]

Louis T. Talbot

Some people wonder why it is that they are so weak when temptation faces them and why they find themselves without sufficient strength to walk as they know they should as Christians. Why, they go for weeks, even months, without opening the Bible. What physical invalids we would be if we treated our bodies in the way that we treat our spirits![16]

It can be discouraging at times to remember that we have put on the "<u>new man</u>" but wonder if we're maturing. Are we really growing closer to God in righteousness and holiness? If we look at just one day, we might think not. It helps to look back over months and years to see how God is changing us. Chances are, there have been many good changes in you overall. You may be more patient (but still get irritated at times), or perhaps you are more consistent in having your quiet time (even though you sometimes miss it). The

changes
Philippians 1:6

money changers
Matthew 21:12

important thing is to look at the broad brushstrokes of change, not the minuscule steps of each day. As God works, those minuscule steps add up to big dividends. Don't give up! God is making the <u>changes</u> He wants. It's a good idea to ask yourself, "What clothing is my soul wearing today?"

The Emperor Should Put on Some Patience and Truth

> EPHESIANS 4:25–27 *Therefore, putting away lying, "Let each one of you speak truth with his neighbor," for we are members of one another. "Be angry, and do not sin": do not let the sun go down on your wrath, nor give place to the devil. (NKJV)*

The first "new clothes" Paul suggests are telling the truth and controlling anger. Talk about a challenge! Our words should speak the truth, yet without anger—just like Paul said earlier, "Speaking the truth in love." Why? Because we are related—members of one body, the body of Christ. If one member gets hurt, it hurts the whole body. Our witness is damaged and we hurt individuals with lies. There's really no "little white lie." Everything injures.

Anger is the opposite of love. Anger indicates I'm trying to control the situation (or another person), and things aren't going my way. Now, there is such a thing as "righteous anger," and that's the kind of anger Jesus had when He purged the temple of the <u>money changers</u>. That was anger against unrighteousness; it wasn't selfish. He was focused on God's reputation and the damages those people were doing to God's children. We can have that kind of anger, but it shouldn't go on and on. Otherwise, Satan can easily turn it into bitterness. We need to get over it quickly by taking righteous action or by surrendering our own desires.

Some commentators believe that the Greek word *diabolos*, translated "devil," can also be translated "slanderer." Certainly, giving in to gossip and lies about others is very damaging and is often the result of anger that isn't dealt with. Either way, Paul says, don't do it.

Anger at the beginning stage—the first flash of feeling—is neither right nor wrong. It's just a feeling. It's what we do with it that makes it right or wrong. If we initially feel angry or irritated and we strike out physically, that's wrong. But if we express our frustration or anger appropriately, then we aren't giving Satan an opportunity to turn it into sin.

Have you ever wondered why God would give us such a potentially destructive emotion like anger? Didn't He realize how dangerous that was? Of course, He knew the possibilities, but He originally intended for the energy that anger creates to propel us to do something about injustice, to right wrongs. We need to use it for that, and be careful when our anger causes us to selfishly want things our own way.

When you're angry, be angry at the behavior of the person who is sinning, not at them personally. Every person is valuable and should be loved; but if their behavior is sinful, we should seek to influence them to change. Be careful how you express your anger: Do it constructively.

apply it

The Emperor Should Get a Job

EPHESIANS 4:28 *Let him who stole steal no longer, but rather let him labor, working with his hands what is good, that he may have something to give him who has need.* (NKJV)

Hard work isn't often thought of as an important soul characteristic, but Paul sure values it here. He says to clothe your soul with honesty and purposeful living. In that culture thievery was wide-

blessed
Acts 20:35

spread, and some new believers may have been guilty of it. Evidently, Paul must have known that some of his readers were thieves, because he told them outright the right thing to do. It is interesting that Paul says they shouldn't steal so that they can give to others from their earnings. That's certainly a unique motivation. But it makes sense because when we help others, we fulfill Jesus's words that it's more <u>blessed</u> to give than to receive. And when we are blessed by giving, we will be more motivated to live righteously without stealing.

> **what others say**
>
> **Charles R. Swindoll**
>
> Coming back with a positive solution helps support the person who is already demoralized in his spirit. Paul is not only telling the thief that it is wrong to steal; he also tells him what to do about it. He says, "Go to work so that you learn the joys of giving, and then you'll not want to steal." Remember: Condemnation without hope crushes.[19]

Paul includes an exhortation to stop stealing in his listing of the "new man." Stealing and other acts of dishonesty are indicators that we don't really trust God. If we did, we would believe that He will provide—that we don't have to take something illegally. The "new man" trusts God to provide whatever finances are needed.

The Emperor Should Wash His Mouth Out

EPHESIANS 4:29–30 *Let no corrupt word proceed out of your mouth, but what is good for necessary edification, that it may impart grace to the hearers. And do not grieve the Holy Spirit of God, by whom you were sealed for the day of redemption.* (*NKJV*)

The spiritual clothes of Spirit-controlled talking are a strong indication that a person is wearing new garments. James, the brother of Jesus, wrote in his epistle, "Even so the tongue is a little member and boasts great things. See how great a forest a little fire kindles! And the tongue is a fire, a world of iniquity. The tongue is so set among our members that it defiles the whole body, and sets on fire the course of nature; and it is set on fire by hell" (James 3:5–6 NKJV). He goes on to say that if you can control your tongue, you can control just about anything.

Truly, words are powerful—either a weapon for evil or a tool for blessing. Paul doesn't want his readers to slash people to pieces with destructive words, but instead to build them up. In other words, say things that will make others feel encouraged to keep trying when they fail. Point out the positives, instead of concentrating on the negatives. Be grateful for whatever a person can give, even if it's not all that was expected.

If we wield that sword of unwholesome words, we make the Holy Spirit grieve or feel sorrow. He won't <u>leave</u> us because of it—we're eternally redeemed—but such inappropriate behavior will separate us from fellowship with God. That will prevent the Spirit from giving us the help we need.

The Greek word *saprós*, which Paul uses for "corrupts", means corrupt, putrid, or rotten. It's used by James in his <u>letter</u> to refer to the gold and silver of the rich that will perish. Words that are unwholesome make a person feel insecure and hopeless. Like a gopher that eats the roots of a plant and causes its demise, unhealthy words take the support out of a person's spiritual root system and make him fall over in despair.

go to

leave
Hebrews 13:5

letter
James 5:2–3

mentor
Titus 2:1–8

what others say

Carol Kent

When I pray about who God wants me to <u>mentor</u> intentionally, I ask that I would be able to look past the woman's current ministry position and past her education (or lack of it) and see her potential. Perhaps she doesn't look like it today, but she may be the next Henrietta Mears or Corrie ten Boom or Elisabeth Elliot. We need to ask God to give us lenses through which we can see the potential of the people around us, to quicken our mind and touch our spirits with discernment as we seek to invest time and training in helping someone else carry the message of Christ.[20]

Anne Graham Lotz

An unconfessed sin or resistance to His authority will block the "flow" of His life within us. If we do not deal with it, our spiritual lives become stagnant and we lose our attractiveness and usefulness to God. And we have nothing refreshing about us that would draw other people to Christ.[21]

apply it

Paul says to talk to people according to their needs. Don't take for granted that you know what is best for someone, that what you like or need is what someone else likes or needs. Be sure to ask, not assume.

The Emperor Should Be Forgiving

EPHESIANS 4:31–32 *Let all bitterness, wrath, anger, clamor, and evil speaking be put away from you, with all **malice**. And be kind to one another, tenderhearted, forgiving one another, even as God in Christ forgave you.* (NKJV)

We are supposed to take off the inner clothing of anger and replace it with the attractive and stylish demeanor of forgiveness. Paul is very thorough in naming every kind of anger. No one could excuse himself for any kind of destructive reaction. When Paul's advice to deal with anger swiftly isn't taken, it turns into more destructive kinds of anger—the kinds of anger that put people in bondage:

- Bitterness: allowing anger to fester and continue
- Wrath: quick responses of anger
- Anger: anger that has become a habit
- Clamor: loud talking
- Evil speaking: insults
- Malice: evil plans

The solution? <u>Kindness</u>, <u>tenderheartedness</u>, and <u>forgiveness</u>. forgiving others diminishes the hold that anger, bitterness, and destructive reactions have over a person. If a person remembers how much Jesus has forgiven him, he will be more willing to let go of his anger toward others.

go to

kindness
Galatians 5:22

tenderheartedness
James 5:11

forgiveness
Colossians 3:13

malice
ill will

what others say

Charles Stanley

Forgive! "That's impossible," you say. Oh really? Think about it; what makes it impossible? Really only one thing, your refusal to let go of the lie that somehow those who have wronged you owe you something. To forgive is simply to mentally release the offending party of any obligation.[22]

Anger and bitterness, or acting out through verbal abuse, never solves a problem or motivates other people to change. Proverbs 15:1 exhorts us, "A soft answer turns away wrath, but a harsh word stirs up anger" (NKJV). The next time you're tempted to be angry, don't give in to it. It won't help the situation.

Many people think their own bitterness is the way to take <u>revenge</u> on someone. It's tempting to think, *My anger is making that person miserable*. But most of the time, the one we intend to punish isn't even affected! He is just going along his own happy way. And guess what? *You're* the one who is miserable.

key point

Forgiveness is actually for our benefit, not theirs; they aren't distressed like we are. Releasing our anger and the need to return hurt will free us from frustration. Forgiveness doesn't mean giving someone permission to hurt us again, nor does it preclude their suffering any consequences for their wrong choices. But it does mean giving up thinking about revenge.

go to

revenge
Romans 12:19

Chapter Wrap-Up

- Paul is very invested in helping Christians act like part of a bigger group: the body of Christ. Yet because people within a group can become divisive, he exhorts them to be humble, gentle, and patient toward others. (Ephesians 4:1–6)

- Knowing that each member of the body of Christ is important, Paul explains that they have been given a diverse set of abilities so that everything that is needed will be taken care of. (Ephesians 4:7–16)

- Paul doesn't want his readers to return to the old way of thinking that excluded knowledge of and obedience to God, so he reminds them how unhappy they were before they knew Christ. (Ephesians 4:17–19)

- Now that these people know Christ, Paul wants them to live like it: renewed in their minds, putting on the new self, and responding to others without anger. (Ephesians 4:20–28)

- There are definite characteristics of a person who knows Christ: He speaks encouraging words, allows the Holy Spirit to be in charge, and forgives those who hurt him. (Ephesians 4:29–32)

Study Questions

1. What are the three difficult assignments Paul gives his readers, and how does each one encourage unity within the body of Christ?

2. How does Paul explain that Christians within the body of Christ are supposed to be unified and yet also diverse?

3. What does Paul remind his readers to remember about the way they used to live before knowing Christ?

4. What is the new way Paul wants the Ephesians to live?

5. What are some of the characteristics of a Christian who is wearing new soulful clothes?

Ephesians 5
Walking As Imitators of Christ

Let's Get Started

In many parts of the world, electricity is not readily available. Yet for those of us who have it at our fingertips, we take it for granted. We flick on the light switch and expect light. And if we were somehow deprived of that great blessing? We wouldn't be very happy.

In the same way, Christians should not take for granted the Holy Spirit's empowering us to live the way God wants us to. In addition, we need to constantly take advantage of His indwelling presence. If we don't, we're like a fool who walks into a darkened room and doesn't turn on the light. Paul has been telling his readers how to stop living in the dark and start living in God's power. In this fifth chapter he will focus on how to "walk in the light" as imitators of God. No, it's not easy, but with the light of the Spirit within us, we can do it. Let's see what Paul suggests.

go to

imitate
1 Corinthians 4:16

Don't Do What I Say—Without Watching What I Do

EPHESIANS 5:1–2 *Therefore be imitators of God as dear children. And walk in love, as Christ also has loved us and given Himself for us, an offering and a sacrifice to God for a sweet-smelling aroma.* (NKJV)

One of the joys of parenting is watching our children imitate us. We may pronounce a word a certain way, and soon our learning-to-talk toddler is repeating the word the same way. Or our teen answers the phone and our friends think it's us. We're thrilled by their parroting—that is, as long as the qualities they imitate are attractive and wholesome. If they're mimicking the bad ones, that's another story. Then we feel embarrassed.

God never feels embarrassed when we imitate Him because He has only good qualities. That's why Paul tells readers to imitate God. At other places in his writings, Paul says to <u>imitate</u> himself, but here he

go to

God is love
1 John 4:8

sacrificial
Romans 3:25

fragrance
2 Corinthians
2:15–16;
Philippians 4:18

sacrificed
John 3:16

encourages them to be just like God in the way they act and respond. As a perfect heavenly Father, God is the best possible model. And because <u>God is love</u>, Paul says we should do everything in love. Out of God's very essence of love, everything He does and says is based upon wanting the best for every person. If we duplicate that, we will live the way we should live—like Him.

Here Paul uses the imagery of imitation which was a very important concept for the Greeks. That's how orators practiced speaking. They imitated and rehearsed the speeches of the experts in oratory. Paul may have done that kind of study himself.

Paul describes God's ultimate act of love: the <u>sacrificial</u> death of Jesus for a sinful world. Jesus's offering was like a sweet <u>fragrance</u> around the throne of God, and our loving actions can bring the same result. Just imagine God's throne surrounded by a wonderful scent as the Father remarks, "There's that magnificent fragrance. My children are being like Me again. Wonderful!"

Jesus willingly <u>sacrificed</u> His sinless life for a sinful world in obedience to His Father and out of His own love and concern for every person on earth. Such sacrificial love is the ultimate gift. Paul seems to be suggesting: "If you're loving like God loves, you're willing to die for another person. Since you most likely won't be called upon to actually do that, it really shouldn't be too much to ask or expect that you put others first and try to meet their needs—even at the expense of your own."

> **what others say**
>
> **Nancy Leigh DeMoss**
>
> The call to holiness is a call to follow Christ. A pursuit of holiness that is not Christ-centered will soon be reduced to moralism, pharisaical self-righteousness, and futile self-effort. Such pseudo-holiness leads to bondage, rather than liberty; it is unattractive to the world and unacceptable to God. Only by fixing our eyes and our hope on Christ can we experience that authentic, warm, inviting holiness that He alone can produce in us.[1]

Jesus didn't deserve to die, yet He sacrificed His life. Most of us excuse our unwillingness to meet others' needs by focusing on how unworthy they are. By saying, "They treated me bad," or "They don't deserve anything good the way they act," we justify our actions. But that's not imitating God, who gave the ultimate gift to a world that didn't ask for it, didn't want it, largely still doesn't appreciate it, and is <u>unworthy</u> of such love. God calls upon us to love not because that person is worthy or deserves it, but because we are imitators of Him.

Be Careful, Little Tongue, What You Say

EPHESIANS 5:3–5 *But fornication and all uncleanness or covetousness, let it not even be named among you, as is fitting for saints; neither filthiness, nor foolish talking, nor coarse jesting, which are not fitting, but rather giving of thanks. For this you know, that no fornicator, unclean person, nor covetous man, who is an **idolater**, has any inheritance in the kingdom of Christ and God. (NKJV)*

True love, the kind that God exhibits (that we're supposed to be imitating, remember?), doesn't talk nasty or dirty. Love doesn't put down others by joking about them or embarrassing them with sexual references. Oh, sure, a group of people may laugh at a dirty joke, but to what degree is that laughter filled with embarrassment? Is the woman in the crowd wondering if somehow she is being thought of in the same way? Paul strongly urges his readers to refuse to say anything except that which is filled with good language and expresses gratitude. He's so strong in his opinion that he says people who speak inappropriately won't reach heaven's gates, because when we speak coarsely, we are "worshipping" the idol of selfishness—wanting to say what we want to say without respect for the ears and minds of our listeners.

These were strong words for people in a culture that didn't see anything wrong with immorality. It was expected that every husband would have a mistress. Plus, Ephesus was the center of the worship of the goddess <u>Diana</u>, also known as Artemis, the goddess of fertility. The image of her was a carved female form with many breasts. The festival of Diana included wild orgies and carousing. In other cities where Greeks were widespread, like Corinth, there were temples where prostitutes, called priestesses, were available. This was considered normal, a means of financial support for the temple. It was a belief system that didn't even consider immorality unusual or disturbing, and certainly something their gods approved of.

go to

unworthy
Romans 3:23

Diana
Acts 19:28

idolater
worshipper of idols

go to

merry heart
Proverbs 15:15

consecrated
devoted

assimilation
absorption

So Paul's declaration was a completely new way of thinking for this group of believers, and a new way to think about God Himself.

A true believer in Jesus won't want to talk like this. If he does, he will be convicted by his carelessness. Generally speaking, those who haven't been redeemed through the Spirit fall most often into telling off-color jokes and referring to immorality. But if we do fall into such patterns, we need to see how it dishonors God and certainly doesn't imitate Him.

Paul used words like *fornication*, *uncleanness*, and *covetousness* in reference to all kinds of sexual intimacy outside of heterosexual, monogamous marriage. It may seem strange that Paul used the word *covetousness* when referring to sexual activity, but in this context he's referring to desiring a person's body for selfish sexual gratification.

what others say

J. I. Packer

Holy in both biblical languages means separated and set apart for God, **consecrated** and made over to him. In its application to people, God's "holy ones" or "saints," the word implies both devotion and **assimilation**: devotion in the sense of living a life of service to God; assimilation in the sense of imitating, conforming to, and becoming like the God one serves.[2]

R. C. Sproul

It is not enough to know that God forbids adultery. Nor is it enough to be convinced that God forbids it. We may still fail to grasp how utterly offensive it is to God. We tend to make it a small deal where God sees it as a big deal.[3]

Good humor isn't what Paul is referring to by "foolish talking." The Bible says we should be happy, joyful, and have a <u>merry heart</u>. Clean jokes, riddles, and fun stories lift people's hearts. That's not what he's talking about. He's talking about selfish conversation that destroys others and tears down other people's self-image. It's referring to immorality as if it's appropriate. When such talk is at the cost of another person's value, Paul says, "Cut it out! Don't say it! Only say that which will build up others and makes them feel good."

If you fall into the pit at times by cursing, telling coarse jokes, or speaking of others' sexual sins, don't despair. There is forgiveness even for that. If you are a Christian, you haven't lost your salvation.

You are different from the people Paul is referring to because you are convicted of your sin. (Those rejecting God's salvation don't feel convicted after a long time of refusing His offer.) Instead of feeling hopeless about your failures, go to God and ask Him to <u>forgive</u> you. His blood was shed for everything, including sinful speaking. He wants to forgive and cleanse you even more than you want to confess. If God could forgive <u>King David</u> of <u>murder</u> and <u>adultery</u>, then He can forgive you for coarse language.

forgive
1 John 1:9

King David
Psalm 51:1–3

murder
2 Samuel 11:15

adultery
2 Samuel 11:4

light
Matthew 5:14

reach out
Luke 5:30–32

Don't Be Their Partner, Pardner

EPHESIANS 5:6–7 *Let no one deceive you with empty words, for because of these things the wrath of God comes upon the sons of disobedience. Therefore do not be partakers with them. (NKJV)*

If we have contact with people who talk like those Paul is speaking against, we must be very careful that we aren't influenced by them. Such coarseness can become common to us if we don't tell ourselves the truth: It is sin that will bring God's wrath upon unbelievers who talk like that. Paul isn't saying that Christians shouldn't have contact with unbelievers. After all, we're supposed to be <u>light</u> in a dark world. We should <u>reach out</u> to those who don't know God personally and be His imitators so that they see what they're missing. But even as we do that, we must shield ourselves from growing used to such sinfulness.

God does say, "Do not be unequally yoked together with unbelievers. For what fellowship has righteousness with lawlessness? And what communion has light with darkness?" (2 Corinthians 6:14 NKJV). In marriage and in business partnerships, it's best not to be yoked with unbelievers. If we do, we're aligning ourselves with people who don't have the same ultimate goal we do: God's glory and our own sanctification.

what others say

J. Vernon McGee

If you can sin and get by with it, you are not a child of God. Do you know why? Because God would have to condemn you with the world, which would mean that you are not saved. If you are a child of God and do these things, God will chasten you—He will take you to the woodshed right here and now.[4]

In our world today we are being deceived, subtly but surely, by the empty words of movies and other media, including advertising. The things that God hates that were mentioned in the previous verses are promoted and glorified as normal and expected among any group of sane people. In contrast, that which God loves—purity, love, faithfulness, and morality—are ridiculed. We must be careful lest our minds be turned from God's viewpoint; otherwise, we could be the subject of God's wrath as Paul states strongly in this verse.

Turn on the Lightbulb

EPHESIANS 5:8–10 *For you were once darkness, but now you are light in the Lord. Walk as children of light (for the fruit of the Spirit is in all goodness, righteousness, and truth), finding out what is acceptable to the Lord. (NKJV)*

What do you do when you walk into a darkened room? Fumble for the wall to turn on the light switch, of course. If you don't, you might jam your little toe on a table. And you won't be able to see the person you're talking to if you sit in the darkness.

Spiritually speaking, each of us walks in darkness until we receive the light of Christ in our lives. "BC" (before Christ), we walked along unsure that we were really pleasing God or doing the right thing. Problems would throw us into confusion, and at times we felt hopeless, trying to make ourselves into something good. Yet, what a difference when we surrendered our lives to God. As if we've found the light switch, we suddenly see everything differently. Now we know how to live in God's power. Now we know what God requires of us. Now we have understanding and wisdom to handle problems, and we're actually considered holy by God. What a relief!

Light and darkness. Paul uses this metaphor to make a heavy theological concept understandable to his readers. What more simple and comprehendable visual aid could he use to remind his readers that they were once without the knowledge of God, but now they experience God's goodness and guidance? No more fumbling in the dark, fearful you'll stub your toe. Of course, Paul and his readers didn't have electrical lamps, but they did have oil lamps.

Paul says that three main things characterize a life that doesn't involve a lot of spiritual toe stubbing:

- _**Goodness:**_ The ability to generously respond to other people with right motives and love.

- _**Righteousness:**_ The knowledge of the right way to act and behave; plus, in God's sight we have already achieved His righteousness.

- _**Truth:**_ Although the world is still confused by the "seek your own truth" and "you can become a god" philosophies, those who follow God have His perspective from a heavenly vantage point.

We can know we are pleasing God when we walk in those kinds of light.

goodness
Romans 15:14

righteousness
Philippians 1:11

truth
John 14:6

impatient
Philippians 1:6

progress
1 Timothy 4:15

excellence
1 Thessalonians 4:1

what others say

Pam Farrel

There are times when we can ponder, plan, and think out our actions and reactions, but this title of *children of the light* seems to lead us to the conclusion that when we are in Christ we *are* different. We have radically different reactions, even when there is no time to think, no time to wonder, no time to rationalize, and no time to write a flowchart or business chart.[5]

Although we're walking in the light, we won't do it perfectly. At times there will be shadows—and even blackouts! But God doesn't require perfection, just the desire to please Him and to walk in the available light and knowledge that He gives. He's not impatient with us; He knows we'll never be perfect on this earth. But He does want us to progress. In God's eyes, there's a difference between perfection and excellence. Perfection is unattainable and discouraging—it's the standard that we can never live up to. But striving for excellence is doing the best we can and giving God the credit for His empowering. To live in God's light is to obey His leading.

apply it

Stop Snoring and Switch on the Light

EPHESIANS 5:11–14 *And have no fellowship with the unfruitful works of darkness, but rather expose them. For it is shameful even to speak of those things which are done by them in secret. But all things that are exposed are made manifest by the light, for whatever makes manifest is light. Therefore He says: "Awake, you who sleep, arise from the dead, and Christ will give you light."* (NKJV)

go to

expose
Matthew 18:15–20;
Galatians 6:1

key point

When Paul gives the command to "expose *them*," he is referring to Christians—not unbelievers—who are not walking in the light. Unbelievers can only be "exposed" through the light of the Holy Spirit within their hearts as He convicts them. It's not a Christian's job to convict others. Paul wrote to the Christians at Corinth about how they were allowing a so-called Christian to fellowship with them even though that man was living in obvious sin. He wrote to them, "For what have I to do with judging those also who are outside? Do you not judge those who are inside? But those who are outside God judges. Therefore 'put away from yourselves the evil person'" (1 Corinthians 5:12–13 NKJV).

But Paul does want these Ephesian believers to <u>expose</u> Christians who aren't living in the light. Paul may have been thinking of a custom in the shops of the Middle East. If a buyer was considering a product, he might take the item out into the sunlight to better see any flaws. He would be exposing any problem in the light of the sun. Paul wants sin to be exposed in the same way—through the light of truth.

One of the best ways for believers to do that is by living righteous lives themselves. Then God can use that example to convict a believer who is living in sin. Without even saying a word (although sometimes words are needed), a Christian's light will reflect how the believer is living in darkness. That person will see their wrong choices for what they really are: destructive and causing them to be separated from Jesus's fellowship. In that case, the light of a Christian's godly living will make visible the way for the sinning believer to change.

Some people complain that the Bible isn't clear: "Why didn't God just write the Bible so that we can understand it?" But they fail to understand that it was written first for the people who were receiving the letters—and for them it was relevant. One example of that is the quote that Paul uses about sleepers awaking. Because he says, "Therefore He says," it might seem like he's quoting an Old Testament passage. There is no verse in the Bible like that, although verses like Isaiah 26:19; 51:17; 52:1; and 60:1 have some similar words.

Commentators believe that Paul was most likely quoting from a hymn of that time period. Commentators suggest several possibilities for the hymn's meaning.

- The song encouraged people to arise from the deadness of their wrong choices and as Christians be forgiven and experience Jesus's favor.

- It refers to a baptismal song when a new believer would emerge from the water a new person.

- It is calling forth the archangel with a trumpet sound in the last days when there will be a great awakening of people to receive Christ.

Quoting from a hymn would be like you or me writing a letter to a friend and describing God's gracious work in our lives. We might say something like, "It's just like that song, isn't it? 'Amazing grace, how sweet the sound.'" We would be referring to something current, but someone reading our letter hundreds of years from now might not be familiar with "Amazing Grace" and wonder what we were talking about.

go to

understanding
Philippians 3:15

counsel
Proverbs 15:22

what others say

Steve Farrar

The lure of adultery is that another woman will truly meet your needs. The lie of adultery is that no other woman on the face of the earth, no matter how alluring, interesting, or beautiful, has the capacity to fully meet the needs of another human being. That's why adultery is the ultimate hoax. It promises what it cannot deliver.[6]

Oswald Chambers

When God sends His inspiration, it comes to us with such miraculous power that we are able to "arise from the dead" and do the impossible. The remarkable thing about spiritual initiative is that the life and power comes after we "get up and get going." God does not give us overcoming life—He gives us life as we overcome.[7]

Because it's so easy to be deluded about our own sin and to rationalize our wrong choices, it's important to expose ourselves to the light of the scrutiny of other wise Christians. All of us have experienced a time when suddenly, as if a light of <u>understanding</u> were turned on in our brains, we recognized a behavior as wrong—though previously it had seemed right. By evaluating our lives in the light of godly Christians and applying Scripture, we can shed truth on our actions. We may still need to seek the <u>counsel</u> of wise people to get their perspectives on our choices. If we're willing to be honest and do this, we may prevent darkness from slipping into our lives.

apply it

narrow
Matthew 7:13

Another application of these verses is that when we keep a sin secret, it has control over us. But if we expose it by confessing it to others, we are released from the power of sin. We will most likely find it easier to forsake that wrong behavior.

Be Careful, Little Eyes, What You See

EPHESIANS 5:15–17 *See then that you walk circumspectly, not as fools but as wise, redeeming the time, because the days are evil. Therefore do not be unwise, but understand what the will of the Lord is.* (NKJV)

How does a soldier walk through a minefield? How does a dog owner walk through his backyard before the pet's mess is cleaned up? How does a person walk through the house in the middle of the night when everyone else is asleep? One word: *Carefully!* None of us want to step in such a way that will bring about an undesirable outcome. We watch how we tread carefully when we know that doing otherwise could bring unhappy consequences.

How much more we need to wisely live and walk as a Christian so that we please our heavenly Father and show others the light God has illumined within us. We never know who is watching us, wondering if our Christianity is real. We never know how we'll be tempted further if we succumb to the initial temptation. The days are still evil—there are temptations all around. We need to carefully watch how we're acting and reacting and always seek God's will in everything. If we do, we are wise. And if we don't, we are foolish.

what others say

F. B. Meyer

Gird up your flowing robes with dainty care, lest they be soiled by the filth of the street. Beware of any side paths that would lead your steps away from the <u>narrow</u> track. Watch and pray. Especially be careful to turn every moment of time into an opportunity of making progress in the Divine life.[8]

Charles R. Swindoll

Paul begins with an imperative, a strong command. Literally, the Greek terms convey the thought of continuing to take heed how accurately, how exactly, you conduct yourself. Here's the idea: "Keep on taking heed how accurately you are conducting your life!" He is pleading for some honest self-analysis. Painful, but needed.[9]

Jesus was always alert to every opportunity to do what the Father wanted Him to do. He said that He only did what God wanted Him to do. As He walked on this earth, He unselfishly <u>reached</u> out to help everyone because He loved each person. There are hurting people all around us, many who are caught up in sinful lives, who are looking for the light that will set them free. Like Jesus, we can be alert to what our Father is <u>doing</u> and obey His nudging to use every opportunity even though our world seems so hopeless.

Often when we think of talking to other people about Jesus at just the <u>right opportunity</u>, we feel intimidated and wonder if we'll say the wrong thing. Yet, Jesus promised us that we would be given insight and understanding to say the right thing. We don't need to feel panic; we can be confident. And besides, it's not our "right words" that will turn a person to God, but rather the Holy Spirit's work within their lives that draws each one to him.

Get Drunk on the Holy Spirit

> **EPHESIANS 5:18** *And do not be drunk with wine, in which is* **dissipation**; *but be filled with the Spirit,* (NKJV)

Paul had just commanded his readers to know God's will and to live wisely. Now he tells his readers exactly what that is: being filled with the Spirit. He draws the comparison that believers shouldn't be drunk on wine because that leads to excessiveness and being out of control. But he does want them to be "out of control" of themselves and let the Holy Spirit control them.

Comparisons Between Wine and the Holy Spirit's Indwelling

Wine	Holy Spirit
Controls the person without the person's permission	Controls with the person's permission
Leads to wrong choices and destruction	Leads to the <u>fruit</u> of the Spirit, right living, and <u>pleasing</u> God
Is a temporary emotional high ending in sudden lows and depression	Gives a lasting "high" that can be sustained with continued yielding to the Spirit's power
Is not able to provide the power a person wants and needs	Provides the ability to live the way a person really wants to live
Focuses selfishly on getting own needs met, unconcerned about the needs of others	Focuses primarily on being selfless, knowing God will meet a person's true needs.

reached
John 4:9–29

doing
John 5:19

right opportunity
Luke 12:11

fruit
Galatians 5:22–23

pleasing
2 Corinthians 5:9

dissipation
immoral cravings

indwelt
Colossians 3:16;
Romans 8:9;
Galatians 4:6

changed
Ephesians 1:13

It may seem unusual and even silly that Paul would contrast being filled with the Holy Spirit and being drunk with wine. But in his day, the people involved in the cult of Dionysus (also known as Bacchus), the god of wine and drunken orgies, believed that being drunk was a way to be inspired. It was only when they were drunk, they theorized, that they could sense Dionysus' will for them and thus obey him.

It may be that some of the Christians Paul is writing to were previously involved in that cult before their conversion to Christ. Maybe they still believed inspiration occurred when they'd had too much to drink. Paul was telling them that true inspiration comes only through the Holy Spirit.

what others say

Joyce Meyer

So often we make mountains out of molehills. We blow things up all out of proportion. We make major issues out of minor situations that are of no real importance whatsoever. We need to learn to adapt, to let things go, to quit allowing our souls to rule our lives. We need to learn to walk by the Spirit and not by the flesh.[10]

Neil T. Anderson

When you first became a Christian, you were like a small engine for a lawn mower. You could accomplish a needed task and fulfill a worthwhile purpose. However, your goal is to mature into a giant tractor, and accomplish even greater things. Even as you mature, never forget that neither the small engine nor the giant tractor can accomplish anything without the gasoline. The only time we can fulfill our purpose for being here is when we are filled with the Holy Spirit.[11]

When we receive Christ as our Savior, we are immediately <u>indwelt</u> by the Holy Spirit. That can never be <u>changed</u>. But each moment, we must surrender control to the Holy Spirit. That's the kind of "filling" Paul is referring to here: He uses the present passive imperative tense of the word *filled*, which means "keep on being filled." If you're allowing the Holy Spirit to control you, you are being filled by the Spirit.

Speak, Sing, Shout "Thank You," and Submit

destroy
Jeremiah 29:11

good
Romans 8:28

EPHESIANS 5:19–21 *speaking to one another in psalms and hymns and spiritual songs, singing and making melody in your heart to the Lord, giving thanks always for all things to God the Father in the name of our Lord Jesus Christ, submitting to one another in the fear of God. (NKJV)*

Paul desired for his readers not to just talk about their faith but to use music as a means of expressing their joy in knowing Jesus. When we're filled with the Spirit, we are able to have attitudes that the world just can't comprehend, like joyfulness, gratefulness, and willingly submitting ourselves to others. Regardless of the circumstances we're facing, we can be empowered to:

- focus on God when speaking to others,
- have joy and contentment because we trust in God's hand,
- actually thank Him for anything we're facing,
- and be selfless because we trust God to meet our needs.

The Greek word for *submission*, *hupotasso*, is a compound of two words: *hupo*, meaning "under," and *tasso*, meaning "to accomplish a task or to line up." It's a word used in military strategy to have troops arranged under a leader to work together on a march, in war, or on an activity.

> ### what others say
>
> **Max Anders**
>
> The principle is an attitude of mutual subjection, which is a mark of being filled with the Holy Spirit. It is simply a matter of fulfilling the golden rule: doing to others as we would have others do to us.[12]

How can we have an attitude of thanksgiving when life crashes down upon us? When bad things happen? When death threatens or illness causes great pain? How can we trust God when it seems like He's ignoring our plight? It's a matter of believing that our Lord God is sovereign and that His love is the filter through which every single incident in our lives passes through before it can reach us. He doesn't intend that unhappy circumstances will <u>destroy</u> us, but He desires for each situation to draw us closer to His loving heart. He promises to use it for our <u>good</u>. And in that moment when we

go to

Joseph
Genesis 37:28

meditating
Psalm 48:9

control
1 Chronicles
29:11–12

submit
1 Peter 3:1–6

key point

think we can't trust any longer, He will supply supernaturally the strength we need.

If we reflect upon the people in the Bible who went through great calamities and yet saw God's love reflected in their circumstances, our faith and trust will grow—and we'll be able to give thanks in everything. For instance, Joseph had many bad things happen to him, yet he credited God's goodness as using those unfortunate circumstances to bring about a good result. We can also reflect upon the times in our lives when God brought good out of regrettable situations. Meditating on Scripture and our own experiences will increase our trust. Then we'll be able to sing praises to God and even submit ourselves to others as if we were submitting ourselves to God. As we know, He's ultimately in control of everything that happens.

Joy and contentment are different from happiness. Happiness is something that happens to you, while contentment is something you choose. Happiness is the feeling you get when things are going well. It's fickle—it comes and goes—and is dependent upon those good things. Joy and contentment, on the other hand, are the result of choosing to trust God regardless of your circumstances. You can be crying on the outside but still experiencing joy and contentment in your heart.

Submit but Don't Be a Doormat

EPHESIANS 5:22–24 *Wives, submit to your own husbands, as to the Lord. For the husband is head of the wife, as also Christ is head of the church; and He is the Savior of the body. Therefore, just as the church is subject to Christ, so let the wives be to their own husbands in everything. (NKJV)*

As if Paul felt he'd been too general in telling his audience to be filled with the Spirit and submit to each other, he now tells them how to do that exactly. The toughest place to do that would be within the home, in the marriage relationship. He tackles the woman's attitudes first, but has every intention of addressing the husband also. We must divide Paul's writings into verses and deal with small groupings, but his instruction to wives and husbands need to be viewed as one big package, not little gifts from which we can choose which we like better and want to obey.

Continuing his theme on submission as a fruit of the Spirit, Paul tells wives to submit to their husbands. In the original Greek text, the word *submit* is not included, but it follows the thought of verse 21. When Paul says, "as to the Lord," he doesn't mean for a wife to submit in the same way that she would if her husband were literally God, but rather that her submission is part of her service *to* God. It's one of the ways she lives out her surrendered heart to God and shows her trust in Him.

equal
Galatians 3:28

Paul did not mean to convey the idea that a wife is a doormat, with no ideas, opinions, or motivations of her own. Paul views women and men as <u>equal</u> in their value and power in Christ. Yet, because there can't be two masters within a harmonious home, Paul says that ultimately the husband is the head of the family. Just as Christians are powerful entities within the body of Christ, Jesus is the Head and has ultimate power.

what others say

Kevin Leman

Wives, Ephesians 5:22–24 clearly shows that your relationship with your husband must be your greatest concern. In modern times, we are sold such a bill of goods by "experts" who tell us marriage is a 50-50 proposition. It has to be 100-100; we don't just go halfway but put our spouse's needs ahead of our own.[13]

Elizabeth George

Instead of taking care of their own faithfulness to their God-given assignment as wives, they take on the self-appointed role of playing "Holy Spirit" in their husbands' lives, pointing out their faults and shortcomings. These wives may even assume a "when . . . then" attitude. In their hearts (and maybe even verbally), they say, "*When* he does this or that, *then* I'll do this or that." They postpone obedience to their roles as wives and make it conditional to that of their husbands.[14]

Submission is lived out as a husband and wife share their goals and ideas with each other. When a decision must be made, each should give their opinion about the problem or situation. After dialogue back and forth, hopefully they will come to a satisfying conclusion for both of them. But if not—and if the decision can't wait—the husband must make the final decision.

Regardless of how much a wife doesn't agree with her husband's ultimate decision, her cheerful acceptance of it will rest upon how much she trusts God. If you are disgruntled by your husband's deci-

sacrifice
John 10:11, 15,
17–18

sions, then you don't believe God is ultimately in control of everything in your life.

Yet, a wife shouldn't submit to her husband's desires if he calls upon her to do something against Scripture or something that is wrong. Submission by a wife to her husband does not mean she should allow herself to be abused in any way. A husband is wrong if he uses these verses for anything harmful. If that is the case, his wife is not bound to cooperation. God doesn't want anyone to be harmed physically, emotionally, or in any other way, and His intention in this verse was not for a wife's hurt or destruction. If a wife is being abused, she should separate herself from her husband and get the support she needs to prevent the abuse from continuing.

How Do You Spell Love? S-A-C-R-I-F-I-C-E

EPHESIANS 5:25–27 *Husbands, love your wives, just as Christ also loved the church and gave Himself for her, that He might sanctify and cleanse her with the washing of water by the word, that He might present her to Himself a glorious church, not having spot or wrinkle or any such thing, but that she should be holy and without blemish.* (NKJV)

You could have heard the shock wave across the Roman-Greek world with Paul's statements. He was giving instruction to Gentile believers in Ephesus and across Asia Minor that went against everything the Roman and Greek men believed. Oh, sure, many of them might actually love their wives, but a husband would never "give himself up for her" when she was considered his property. Plus, any husband was totally justified to have mistresses and use prostitutes. There wasn't anything shameful about that; in fact, it was the norm. Plus, a man could divorce his wife anytime for any reason. Even the Jews were taught by some Jewish teachers that they could divorce their wives for merely displeasing them—for something as minor as serving a bad meal. Paul was commanding men to have a totally different mind-set—to give their wives lots of respect, something the wives hadn't enjoyed before.

Husbands are to love their wives by reflecting upon Jesus's example of unselfish <u>sacrifice</u> for the church, His believers. Jesus gave up His own life as a substitute for each person on the cross so that He could make each person who believes in Him holy and righteous in God's sight.

Although people today often point in disgust at the Bible's command for wives to submit themselves to their husbands, husbands may actually have the harder job. After all, sacrifice isn't exactly a pleasant task or an easy choice. The primary point Paul is making in giving these commands is that if each spouse in the marriage fulfills his God-given command, they will have a happy and satisfying marriage. And isn't it interesting that Paul writes more to instruct the husbands than the wives? Certainly he must have thought they needed more instruction and had the bigger challenge (and maybe would balk the most!).

go to

exceptions
Matthew 27:19;
Acts 16:14

what others say

Elisabeth Elliot

What an assignment. What an honor—for him to love her so, for her to be so loved. The husband is to pay honor to the wife's body specifically *because* it is weaker and because they are heirs together of (they share) the grace of life. Thus honor is understood to mean not only respect for superiority, but reverence under God for . . . "the one placed under."[15]

In Greek and Roman societies before the New Testament era, wives had been secluded within homes in the "women's quarters." They weren't allowed out in public, because women who were in public without male accompaniment were most likely slaves or prostitutes. If a wife did leave the home, it was only for important public events. The reason for this social pattern was to protect women from sexual temptation so they would stay faithful to their husbands.

strengthen your family

By the time Paul wrote his letters, a woman was allowed in public but shouldn't begrudge her husband's immoral affairs, and she should be faithful—not worshipping a different religion from his. Most of the time she was expected to lead an uneventful life, caring for the home and wielding little influence upon her husband and society. There were <u>exceptions</u> to that, of course, because some women were active in business and commerce.

The Influence of Women in the Early Church

The new churches that Paul was addressing were welcoming the service and ministry of women. The Bible speaks of many women who were participating in making the church effective. Some of them were:

Woman	Role	Scripture
Lydia	Church met at her house	Acts 16:14–15, 40

love
Matthew 19:19

The Influence of Women in the Early Church (cont'd)

Woman	Role	Scripture
Priscilla	Traveled as a missionary with Paul	Acts 18:2–3
Phoebe	Helper in the church	Romans 16:1–2
Mother of Rufus	Helper to Paul; he called her "mother"	Romans 16:13
Chloe	Church met in her home	1 Corinthians 1:11

If anyone says that women are denigrated within Christianity, they need only read with an open and honest mind the ideas expressed in the New Testament. Christianity has done more than anything else to lift up the importance and value of women in the world.

Now Here's How to Sacrifice Like Jesus Did

EPHESIANS 5:28–30 *So husbands ought to love their own wives as their own bodies; he who loves his wife loves himself. For no one ever hated his own flesh, but nourishes and cherishes it, just as the Lord does the church. For we are members of His body, of His flesh and of His bones. (NKJV)*

Paul has just given a spiritual concept of Jesus's sacrificial death. Now he tells his male readers how to apply it. If a man wants to know what sacrificial love is, he should just look at how he cares for himself. Whatever he does to <u>love</u> his own body, he should do for his wife. He should provide for her needs just as he does his own. That doesn't necessarily mean he should do exactly what he would for himself. A man and a woman have different needs because of gender and personality differences. But it means that just as he does whatever it is that meets his needs, he should do whatever it is that meets her unique needs—from her perspective.

what others say

Bruce H. Wilkinson

You can *choose* to love your wife, or choose not to love her. Agape love doesn't keep going by itself; it's a choice you make to love. So if you feel like you don't love your wife anymore, you can change your feelings by simply choosing to do so. Choose to love her. Decide that you will do so.[16]

Charles R. Swindoll

You don't give yourself to others or consider them valuable if you don't first of all consider yourself worthy. Our own inse-

"Nourishes and cherishes" are what every woman wants. A husband can do that by being sensitive to her feelings (women are really into feelings!). He can listen without interrupting, because most of the time she isn't just sharing a problem to get a solution; she also wants her husband to hear her heart and respect her feelings about the issue. Proverbs 18:13 has this specific advice for a husband: "He who answers a matter before he hears it, it is folly and shame to him" (NKJV). Men have trouble listening without trying to fix the problem because they are logical. But a wife's needs are more emotionally based, and she desires compassion through attention and conversation. If a husband will listen attentively to his wife, she will feel nourished and cherished.

It Takes Two to Tango

> EPHESIANS 5:31–32 *"For this reason a man shall leave his father and mother and be joined to his wife, and the two shall become one flesh." This is a great mystery, but I speak concerning Christ and the church.* (NKJV)

Paul now says why the husband and the wife should work to meet each other's needs through submission and love: because they are one flesh. Paul quotes from Genesis 2:24 to make his point: what affects one will affect the other. If one isn't happy in the marriage, it will be harder for the other to be satisfied. If the wife isn't treated with love, she won't be happy and won't be able to submit to her husband as well, and he could become unhappy without her respect. It really takes both of them working together to create the kind of marriage that God wanted from the beginning—which refers to both marriage and the marriage-like relationship between Jesus and His bride, the church.

Paul's comment about becoming one flesh was another groundbreaking command to these Gentile believers in Ephesus. Greek and Roman views of marriage had so disintegrated that it was common for husbands and wives to have multiple marriage partners.

Historians have found evidence of a wife who had twenty-one husbands and a husband who had over twenty wives. What a shock for Paul to say a husband and a wife were one flesh and shouldn't be pulled apart.

Many husbands and wives are afraid to take the first step of giving their spouse what they need, especially if there has been a lot of conflict or tension. A wife might think, *If I submit, he's going to take advantage of it.* Or a husband could think, *If I love her as myself, she'll never be satisfied and always want more and more.* Instead of making those "agape" kinds of choices, a husband and wife may withhold love and respect because they fear they will be taken advantage of.

But Jesus sacrificially gave His life for every single person even though not everyone would respond to His overture of love. He knew many would not believe in Him or accept His free gift of salvation, but He still willingly gave His life for all. If a spouse will remember Jesus's example, he can be empowered to give love without any guarantee of returned love. And chances are that building up the other person will put in motion a loving process, because what affects the spouse will rebound into love toward himself.

A Great Marriage Can Be Summarized in Two Words: *Love* and *Respect*

EPHESIANS 5:33 *Nevertheless let each one of you in particular so love his own wife as himself, and let the wife see that she respects her husband.* (NKJV)

In case his readers didn't get the point, Paul summarized all he said by using two little words: love and respect. Interestingly, Paul hadn't used the word *respect* before. He said a wife should submit to her husband. But when a wife submits to her husband, he feels respected, and that is one of his primary needs because it makes him feel significant.

Psychologists tell us that every person needs to feel significant and secure in order to have a healthy sense of well-being. Although both men and women need significance and security, each gender needs one of those more than the other. Men primarily need significance because they need to feel important and valuable. Women need security—which is to feel loved.

Chapter Wrap-Up

- Paul told his readers to be imitators of God. Since God is loving and holy, they should be loving toward others and resist giving in to unholy living like immorality, coarse language, and empty words. (Ephesians 5:1–5)

- Because a Christian walks in the light of truth about how the world should operate, it's silly for him to partner with an unbeliever who doesn't have the same goals for God's glory. Paul wanted his readers to walk as wise men who make wise choices so that other people will identify them as Christians. (Ephesians 5:6–17)

- Being drunk in order to get spiritual insights was something some people from a particular cult did. Paul contrasted that by saying for his readers to be drunk on the Holy Spirit—*not* wine. He would know they were indeed doing that if they were joyful, thankful, and submitting themselves to others. (Ephesians 5:18–21)

- In case someone doesn't know how to make submission work, especially in the most difficult area of relationships—marriage—Paul directed the wives to submit to their husbands. (Ephesians 5:22–24)

- A husband is supposed to live out submission in his marriage by loving his wife to the point of sacrificing himself for her. (Ephesians 5:25–33)

Study Questions

1. What is the most important way we can imitate God?

2. Why shouldn't a Christian become a partner to someone who isn't following God's commandments?

3. How can a Christian show they are "spiritually drunk" on the Spirit?

4. How does a wife live out her dependence on the Holy Spirit?

5. How does a husband live out his dependence on the Holy Spirit?

Ephesians 6
Strength in God's Power

Let's Get Started

Policemen wear bulletproof vests. Firemen wear specially made heat-resistant clothing. Construction workers wear hard hats. Chefs wear aprons. It just makes sense to be protected, whether you are in a dangerous line of work or simply trying to avoid getting dirty. It's absolutely essential to prevent harm or damage to our bodies.

Our souls need protection too. Because we have an enemy who shoots fiery darts, we need to protect ourselves from spiritual harm. We may not be the gladiator of the movies, but we can put on the spiritual armor that Paul describes in this last chapter of Ephesians. This theme of being Spirit-filled continues by first addressing children and slaves; then Paul gives a description of the tools necessary for making sure the Holy Spirit is in control of our lives. Are you ready to put on your armor? It isn't even heavy, so let's get dressed.

something to ponder

Kids Need to Be Spirit-Filled Too!

> **EPHESIANS 6:1–3** *Children, obey your parents in the Lord, for this is right. "Honor your father and mother," which is the first commandment with promise: "that it may be well with you and you may live long on the earth." (NKJV)*

As far as we know, Paul never had children. But inspired by the Holy Spirit of God, he knew not to leave the kids out of his exhortation to be filled with the Holy Spirit. Back in the previous chapter, Paul began his theme of being Spirit-filled by first addressing wives and husbands. He now extends that theme to include the little members of the family. Children can know whether they are Spirit-filled by obeying and honoring their parents. The Spirit always brings peace within a family when He is obeyed, and if children obey Him, they will experience God's promise of a long and good life.

That "promise" is a general observation, not a guarantee of a problem-free life. Generally speaking, children who have obedient attitudes toward their parents will grow up to have obedient attitudes toward God. That's because they will have developed self-control and self-discipline that will be transferred to their relationship with God. And obeying God does bring a good and peaceful life. That spiritually mature person will be able to deal constructively with trials and problems, regardless of bad things that might happen.

Some people have scratched their heads at Paul's comment of "the first commandment with promise." The sixth of the Ten Commandments is, "Honor your father and your mother, that your days may be long upon the land which the LORD your God is giving you" (Exodus 20:12 NKJV)—the commandment Paul referred to. But the second commandment also had a "promise" that if the people make a carved image, God will [visit] the iniquity of the fathers upon the children to the third and fourth generations," and if they don't, He will "[show] mercy to thousands" (Exodus 20:4–6 NKJV).

So what was he saying? Commentators aren't sure, but some suggest that instead of "first," he means the "primary thing that children need to learn," and with the command comes the promise of a good life. Also, some commentators have pointed out that the other commands promised something if they were not kept, but this one promises something if it is obeyed. Another idea is that "first" refers to the first commandment that children should memorize.

There is a difference between obedience and honor. Obedience is something that underage children give their parents. Once those children are adults and become independent, they will no longer *obey* their parents, but they will always give them honor. *Honor* is a respect and love for someone, regardless of the behavior of that person. Honor offers up love and attention even when they don't deserve it. Giving honor to a parent can take the forms of:

something to ponder

- Listening
- Helping around their home
- Taking them places when they are unable to get around on their own
- Including them in family activities
- Taking their wise advice into account

The basic rules of abuse still apply here also: An adult does not have to subject himself to abuse from a parent who continues to verbally tear him down or treat him in a demeaning way.

Don't Exasperate, Frustrate, or Berate

EPHESIANS 6:4 *And you, fathers, do not provoke your children to wrath, but bring them up in the training and admonition of the Lord. (NKJV)*

As if Paul can read his readers' minds, he thought of the command he'd just given the children and wondered if fathers might take advantage of such obedience. It would have been easy for men to do in that culture. Although there wasn't such a saying at that time, this one definitely applied in Roman and Greek civilizations: "Children should be seen and not heard." In those days, children were merely considered property under what was called *patria potestas,* "the father's power." At any point a child could be abused. Even if an adult son was highly regarded, the father had control over his life as long as the father was alive. He could have him killed at any time; fortunately, public opinion did limit such things from happening frequently.

key point

When a child was born, the baby was placed at the father's feet and he could decide whether the baby lived or died. Many children were drowned if the father's fancy proclaimed it. Or they might be taken to the Roman forum and left for anyone who might want a child: those who weren't able to become pregnant, those who would sell them as slaves, or those who would use them in brothels. Also, sickly or deformed babies were almost always killed. Just as Christianity elevated the status of women, it elevated the value of children.

Even though there was complete authority of the father over his family, most fathers were genuinely concerned for their children and were expected to teach their sons a trade and show them how to

opportunity
Deuteronomy 6:6–9

make a living. A writer of the Roman era believed that a good father showed his love by imposing structure over his children. Fathers were known to be stricter than mothers, so it's no wonder Paul didn't want his instructions to be misunderstood. He addressed the father, not the mother.

Interestingly, Jewish literature of that period said it was an obligation of parents to provide for their children and teach them a trade for the future. But parents were not supposed to play or laugh with their children, for fear of spoiling them. Maybe Paul had in mind his Jewish readers also.

Paul gives several guidelines for being a good parent. He says to:

- *Bring them up:* rear and nourish them by providing for their physical and spiritual needs.
- *Train them:* discipline them with consequences for poor behavior and rewards for right choices.
- *Admonish them in the Lord:* make God the center of all family relationships by directing everyone's attention to Him with every possible <u>opportunity</u>.

With all the varied beliefs of his readers, Paul wanted everyone to be the kind of parent they should be as Christians: not making their children frustrated with discipline that was too harsh, but instead intended to draw each child closer to God. Also, Paul doesn't say, "Fathers, do not provoke your *sons*," but gives instructions that include every child, male and female.

If provoked, a child can become angry if his father plays favorites, places conditions on giving love, or isn't humble enough to admit when he's wrong. A child has a natural desire and instinct for fairness, so parents—especially fathers—need to carefully treat each and every child with equal respect.

William Hendriksen suggests there are at least six ways a father can embitter his children:

1. Overprotection
2. Favoritism
3. Discouragement

4. Forgetting a child has ideas of his own and need not be an exact copy of his father

5. Neglect

6. Bitter words and physical cruelty[2]

go to

discipline
Hebrews 12:5–6

instruction
Proverbs 1:8

way
Proverbs 22:6

> **what others say**
>
> **Steve Farrar**
>
> The idea behind the word *exasperate* is "do not embitter." This complements perfectly the word used in Ephesians 6:4, translated "provoke them to anger." The meaning here is "to anger, to make angry, to bring one along to a deep seated anger." This kind of anger in children springs from continual and habitual unfair treatment. Wouldn't that kind of treatment make you angry? Of course it would.[3]

If a parent focuses only on making a child obey—even when it's commanded by Scripture—such insensitivity could cloud the child's view of God. He or she won't be drawn closer to God because he may see God only as a strict disciplinarian and not comprehend God's incredible love. We know that children often form their concept of God based on their parents, and especially their father. If the father is too harsh, God could be perceived as someone who is only interested in obedience and does not desire a relationship with the child. Paul is encouraging a balance of love and discipline that creates a good concept of God: a loving God who knows self-control and self-discipline are best for a long life. Paul recommended a balance of <u>discipline</u> and <u>instruction</u>, with the discipline being done with sensitivity to the needs of the child. Some children who are compliant don't need lots of discipline, and their gentle spirit can be wounded by harshness. Other children are strong-willed, and a parent must be stricter. Every parent should respond to their child according to the <u>way</u> God has made him.

something to ponder

Who Is Really Your Boss?

EPHESIANS 6:5–8 *Bondservants, be obedient to those who are your masters according to the flesh, with fear and trembling, in sincerity of heart, as to Christ; not with eyeservice, as menpleasers, but as bondservants of Christ, doing the will of God*

free
John 8:36

Bible
1 Corinthians 7:22

choose
1 Corinthians 7:21

from the heart, with goodwill doing service, as to the Lord, and not to men, knowing that whatever good anyone does, he will receive the same from the Lord, whether he is a slave or free. (NKJV)

The Spirit-filled life is for everyone, even slaves, or as Paul called them, bondservants. Every person in God's eyes is a person of equal worth and value, and for those who know Christ, every person is a brother and sister to other believers—whether they are <u>free</u> or slaves. And spiritually, everyone is free. The <u>Bible</u> does not condone or discourage slavery, for it was an acceptable part of life that even the slaves did not question. Of course, they would <u>choose</u> freedom if given the opportunity, but they did not think of slavery as immoral. In fact, some slaves purchased slaves for themselves, although all of them belonged to the father of the household. And indeed, slaves were considered a piece of property that the father could do anything with. Yet, within the Roman and Greek cultures, there were limits to the abuse that a master could give a slave.

In the midst of those cultural attitudes, Paul addressed slaves who are also Christians, and he tells them how to be Spirit-filled: through a genuine willingness to serve their masters as if they were serving their Savior and Lord, Jesus. Just like everyone else, God will reward them for their selflessness and give consequences for their selfishness. Paul was concerned about their motives: Are they serving just to look good and gain their freedom, or sincerely striving to do well for those in authority over them? Paul continued his original theme of "submitting to one another" that he began in Ephesians 5:21, which is the mark of a Spirit-filled Christian.

Slaves were an important part of Roman life. In the empire at the time Paul wrote his letter to the Ephesians, there were millions of slaves—by some estimates, sixty million. People of the Roman Empire believed work was beneath their dignity and so even the most important duties and positions were filled by slaves, including doctors, teachers, and even those working for the emperor like secretaries. It's obvious that the definition of a slave was different from our concept today. On the other hand, many slaves didn't enjoy positions of importance and were truly "enslaved" to their work and at the mercy of the whims of their owners—even to the point of the owner having them killed.

It was quite common for Roman slaves to become free, because the attitude toward slavery was that it was not a permanent condition, but something to be done toward achieving a better life. Slaves were motivated to do well because they knew they could become free, and they usually received wages that could be saved toward their future freedom. Often a slave was freed by the time he or she was thirty years old. A freed slave also became a Roman citizen. In AD 4, Caesar Augustus was so disturbed by the high rate of slaves becoming freed citizens that he made a law that no slave could be freed before age thirty and also dictated how many slaves would be freed each year.

elsewhere
Colossians 3:22–25;
1 Peter 2:18–21

respond
1 Corinthians 10:31

purview
understanding

what others say

Ralph P. Martin

Modern readers of these verses need to recall the historical circumstances of the first-century world and be on their guard lest they ask questions of New Testament writings that do not come within the **purview** of the authors. Slavery is a case in point. Otherwise we shall be amazed (and maybe scandalized) that the call here in Ephesians as <u>elsewhere</u> is one to obedience and not to revolt. The latter course would have been suicidal, given the power structures of Greco-Roman society.[4]

Paul's commands to slaves could be applied to any Christian employee. God always wants employees who claim to know Christ to treat and respond to their employers with respect and fear, genuinely desiring their good. When you are tempted to respond negatively toward your employer, ask yourself, "If it were Jesus standing here, how would I act?" However you <u>respond</u> to your employer, from God's viewpoint, you are responding to Christ. Although you may not always be able to please your boss, you can please your heavenly Master because He sees your heart and knows your intentions. Be an employee that acts with integrity, wisdom, and respect—even when your boss isn't looking.

<u>Pointing the Finger at the Masters</u>

EPHESIANS 6:9 *And you, masters, do the same things to them, giving up threatening, knowing that your own Master also is in heaven, and there is no partiality with Him.* (NKJV)

unjust
Colossians 4:1

Master
James 5:4

servant
Philippians 2:7

Lest any owners of the slaves that Paul just addressed are reading his letter and poking at their slaves, Paul points his finger at those who managed slaves: "Do the same things I told the slaves to do with you." They were not to be angry or <u>unjust</u> because they had their own <u>Master</u> in heaven who loves each person equally. It wouldn't do any good to try to be God's pal as a fellow master and say, "Well, Lord, you know how trying it is to make these slaves do what they should. Ya gotta intimidate them sometimes, right?" Acting as if you share a common experience wouldn't make God act favorably toward you. He knows every heart, and He's looking for that spirit who will obey and serve Him regardless of his circumstances, while treating every person with dignity and honor.

what others say

James S. Jeffers

The traditional expectations were that masters would take advantage of their power over their slaves, and that slaves would respond with deceptiveness and lack of zeal for their work. Masters are told in the New Testament to deal with their slaves in justice and fairness, knowing that God is their master, and to give up threatening their slaves.[5]

The example for every human employer is Jesus, who, although He was God and Master/Creator over the whole earth, chose to humble Himself and become a <u>servant</u>. Being a servant as an employer doesn't mean taking the backseat, for Jesus was still a leader even as a servant. But Jesus models treating people with dignity and love, along with showing concern for every person's needs. Employers should do the same.

Paul was involved in dealing with the issue of slavery through one particular situation when he led a slave named Onesimus to Christ. Onesimus had run away from his master, Philemon, who was also a Christian. Paul knew that Philemon could put Onesimus to death for running away. It was also common in that era to brand the letter *F* for the Greek word for "fugitive" on a runaway slave's forehead—if the owner didn't have him killed.

Paul wrote a letter to Philemon encouraging him to receive back Onesimus in a gentle way, even suggesting that Onesimus be freed so that he could return to serve Paul. That letter is our biblical book of Philemon, in which Paul wrote, "I appeal to you for my son

Onesimus, whom I have begotten while in my chains, who once was unprofitable to you, but now is profitable to you and to me. I am sending him back. You therefore receive him, that is, my own heart, whom I wished to keep with me, that on your behalf he might minister to me in my chains for the gospel. But without your consent I wanted to do nothing, that your good deed might not be by compulsion, as it were, but voluntary" (Philemon 10–14 NKJV).

The attitude that Paul encouraged Philemon to have toward his slave is one that God wants every employer to have: to be gentle, seeing each person as important and valuable.

go to

greater
1 John 4:4

Fight for the Right with the Light

EPHESIANS 6:10–12 *Finally, my brethren, be strong in the Lord and in the power of His might. Put on the whole armor of God, that you may be able to stand against the wiles of the devil. For we do not wrestle against flesh and blood, but against principalities, against powers, against the rulers of the darkness of this age, against spiritual hosts of wickedness in the heavenly places. (NKJV)*

You just had the greatest urge to repeat something negative you recently heard about Sally. Where did that come from? The next day, you find yourself watching television with a big bag of chocolate chip cookies on your lap, and you want to eat the whole bag. Just last week, you were fed up at work with Pete, who can't seem to complete his project—and it's going to reflect on you. You were about to put him in his place, when your spiritual eyes were opened to what was really happening.

In each of those situations, it's easy to think that life is just getting hectic, or people are annoying, or gossip is a good way to connect with people. Yet, those temptations aren't just happening by coincidence; they are schemes of someone who wants to destroy us: Satan.

Satan is alive and well, but he isn't greater than Jesus. Yet, he still tries to overwhelm us in different big and little ways to desire the wrong things. We can't see his influence, for it's a spiritual one; but our spiritual eyes can be opened to how he's attacking us. When we see what's really going on, we're better able to remain strong and resist any temptation that Satan schemes for our spiritual poverty.

impossible
Philippians 4:13

cursed
Genesis 3:14

Paul continued this theme by talking about being strong, which is also a sign of being Spirit-filled. In all of the circumstances just mentioned and in countless others, we do have the power of God to resist and do the right thing, the godly thing. At the time, it seems <u>impossible</u>, but Paul is convinced and wants to convince his readers that there is hope. The answer: putting on the armor of God.

what others say

Evelyn Christenson

Satan's power is limited by God's *permissive will*. Since Satan was <u>cursed</u> and doomed by God in the Garden of Eden, God has allowed Satan to have power on planet Earth—but it definitely is limited power. As a being created by God, everything Satan does must be allowed by the sovereign God, the Creator.[6]

Patsy Clairmont

Satan slips his rowboat into the waters of our lives. Then he waits for our moments of weakness, watches for our unmet needs, and lurks in the murky, unsettled issues of our lives. He carefully checks his tackle box and selects just the right bait. When he thinks the time is ideal, he casts his line and waits for as long as necessary for us to take the bait. Then he reels us in with hopes of having us for dinner, and not as his guests. Unlike the fishermen I've known who return the small fish to the water, Satan never throws any back. In fact, he seems to favor the little ones.[7]

Satan is something real. He was created by God as an angel, but chose to turn from God when he wanted to take God's place. He is called a "fallen angel" and along with other fallen angels, creates evil and tempts people in order to turn them from God or prevent them from knowing God personally. Here are some important facts about Satan and what Scripture reveals about him.

Important Facts About Satan

Passage	Scripture	Satan
Satan's Actions		
Mark 4:15	"And these are the ones by the wayside where the word is sown. When they hear, Satan comes immediately and takes away the word that was sown in their hearts" (NKJV).	wants to undo God's work
Job 2:4–5	"So Satan answered the LORD and said, 'Skin for skin! Yes, all that a man has he will give for his life. But stretch out Your hand now, and touch his bone and his flesh, and he will surely curse You to Your face!'" (NKJV).	tries to make men turn from God
John 13:2	"And supper being ended, the devil having already put it into the heart of Judas Iscariot, Simon's son, to betray Him" (NKJV).	creates havoc and evil
Luke 4:6–7	"And the devil said to Him, 'All this authority I will give You, and their glory; for this has been delivered to me, and I give it to whomever I wish. Therefore, if You will worship before me, all will be Yours'" (NKJV).	wants people to worship him instead of God
Satan's Character Makeup		
Revelation 12:9	"So the great dragon was cast out, that serpent of old, called the Devil and Satan, who deceives the whole world; he was cast to the earth, and his angels were cast out with him" (NKJV).	uses deception as his primary tool
Revelation 12:10	"Then I heard a loud voice saying in heaven, 'Now salvation, and strength, and the kingdom of our God, and the power of His Christ have come, for the accuser of our brethren, who accused them before our God day and night, has been cast down'" (NKJV).	accuses and tries to condemn people before God
1 Peter 5:8	"Be sober, be vigilant; because your adversary the devil walks about like a roaring lion, seeking whom he may devour" (NKJV).	is against everything good meant by God
Satan's Methods		
2 Corinthians 11:14–15	"And no wonder! For Satan himself transforms himself into an angel of light. Therefore it is no great thing if his ministers also transform themselves into ministers of righteousness, whose end will be according to their works" (NKJV).	disguises himself as someone good
Genesis 3:1–5	"Now the serpent was more cunning than any beast of the field which the LORD God had made. And he said to the woman, 'Has God indeed said, "You shall not eat of every tree of the garden"?' And the woman said to the serpent, 'We may eat the fruit of the trees of the garden; but of the fruit of the tree which is in the midst of the garden, God has said, "You shall not eat it, nor shall you touch it, lest you die."' Then the serpent said to the woman, 'You will not surely die. For God knows that in the day you eat of it your eyes will be opened, and you will be like God, knowing good and evil'" (NKJV).	casts doubt about God's methods and motives
Matthew 4:6	"And said to Him, 'If You are the Son of God, throw Yourself down. For it is written: "He shall give His angels charge over you," and, "In their hands they shall bear you up, lest you dash your foot against a stone"'" (NKJV).	misuses Scripture
2 Corinthians 2:11	"Lest Satan should take advantage of us; for we are not ignorant of his devices" (NKJV)	uses schemes

Daniel
Daniel 10:1–13

what others say

Neil T. Anderson

There is not a verse in the Bible where we are told to fear Satan. His strategy is to roar like a hungry lion, seeking someone to devour. But why does the lion roar? The roar is to paralyze his prey in fear.[8]

In the book of <u>Daniel</u>, Daniel is given insight into why an answer to prayer didn't arrive quickly. An angel says that Satan's demons had delayed him and it wasn't until he enlisted the help of Michael, God's archangel, that he was successful in bringing God's response to Daniel.

Stand! Don't Sit, Slouch, Sprint, or Stroll!

EPHESIANS 6:13 *Therefore take up the whole armor of God, that you may be able to withstand in the evil day, and having done all, to stand. (NKJV)*

Just imagine. You're in an army and your general has just given you the most awkward command: "Just stand there!" The enemy army is advancing, and you feel like you should run toward them with your spear drawn. Your general shouts again, "Stand where you are!" You must wonder if he knows what he's talking about. He surely must not have gone to West Point or the Air Force Academy. Aren't armies and soldiers supposed to advance, not stand still?

Paul continues his theme of the Spirit-filled Christian by telling us how to fight spiritually. Only a Christian who is controlled by the Holy Spirit will be able to stand strong after he or she puts on the spiritual armor of God. Paul will tell us shortly what the armor is, but right now he says twice: "Stand!" That must have sounded strange to his readers, just like it would to a soldier in the field. Soldiers are supposed to be active and aggressive, aren't they? Yet, Paul says it once and then again: "Stay put!"

In spiritual battle we need to stand our ground. We need to stay focused on the promises of God and the truth He has revealed to us through the Bible. Evil has a way of trying to knock us away from truth. If we lose our balance and don't stand firm, we stop thinking the truth and calling upon God's promises. Or we stumble because of temptation and selfishly want our own way. Paul says, "Stand where you are and focus on the truth."

We can stand firm by calling out the truth when we feel our spiritual foundation shaking as if an earthquake were under us. Just as Jesus spoke the truth of Scripture when He was being <u>tempted</u> by Satan, we must remember God's promises and repeat them back to Satan. He then must <u>flee</u> from us. Here are some ideas for doing that:

tempted
Matthew 4:1–11

flee
James 4:7

How to Stand Firm Against Satan's Tricks

Ground Shaking	Scripture Reference	Standing Firm in the Truth
Go ahead and tell that tidbit about Sally you heard.	"A perverse man sows strife, and a whisperer separates the best of friends" (Proverbs 16:28 NKJV).	I'm not going to say something about Sally until I ask her permission.
My wife must not love me. She's talking to another man.	"A sound heart is life to the body, but envy is rottenness to the bones" (Proverbs 14:30 NKJV).	I won't believe a lie about her, and I won't let envy make me jealous.
I'll take credit for Pete's work and make points with the boss.	"And whatever you do, do it heartily, as to the Lord and not to men" (Colossians 3:23 NKJV).	God wants me to be honest because He knows the truth and can give me favor with my boss if I do a good job.
I don't need to pray today; nothing really important is going on that I can't handle on my own.	"Continue earnestly in prayer, being vigilant in it with thanksgiving" (Colossians 4:2 NKJV).	I need the Lord for everything, big and small. I'm going to depend upon Him, not myself.
My husband can't do anything right. He never remembers my birthday or treats me respectfully.	"Do all things without complaining and disputing" (Philippians 2:14 NKJV).	My husband does many wonderful things for me, and I refuse to concentrate on his shortcomings.

At the time Paul wrote his letter, he was tied to a Roman soldier while in prison awaiting trial. He must have focused a lot on the armor the soldier was wearing, and that in turn must have inspired him to think of the different spiritual weapons and protection the Christian possessed. What wonderful things to write about!

Paul said to "take up" the armor. That verbal phrase is in the Greek imperative, which makes it an urgent command. It's something that we choose to do—not something done for us. God's protective armor is always available to us, but we need to put it on.

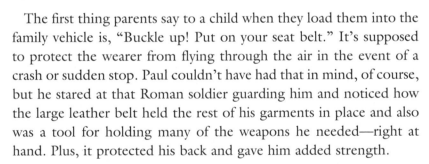

Paul said "in the evil day," not "*if* the evil day comes." Don't be surprised when bad things happen. Don't even try to avoid them (as if you could!) because God works in your character through each difficult situation.

The armor is made up of several different parts. We're told to put on the "full" armor of God. We must not be selective and only choose one or two parts. We must put it all on or we can't completely "stand."

Buckle Up!

EPHESIANS 6:14 *Stand therefore, having girded your waist with truth, having put on the breastplate of righteousness,* (NKJV)

go to

surprised
1 Peter 4:12

avoid
James 1:2

works
1 Peter 5:10

character
James 1:3–4

confusion
James 1:6

appropriating
taking advantage of

The first thing parents say to a child when they load them into the family vehicle is, "Buckle up! Put on your seat belt." It's supposed to protect the wearer from flying through the air in the event of a crash or sudden stop. Paul couldn't have had that in mind, of course, but he stared at that Roman soldier guarding him and noticed how the large leather belt held the rest of his garments in place and also was a tool for holding many of the weapons he needed—right at hand. Plus, it protected his back and gave him added strength.

Paul related that to the "belt" of truth—the Word of God, the Bible. If anything will protect us from "flying through the air" spiritually, it's holding fast—standing—on the truths of the Bible. We won't go off in a thousand different tangents of belief or confusion if we buckle up with the Bible. And our spiritual "backbone" will be strengthened to stand straight—to do the right thing!

After focusing on the belt, Paul wrote about the breastplate of righteousness. The breastplate of the Roman soldier was a metal piece that was molded to fit his chest. It guarded the most important organ of his body: the heart. He could not survive without that essential member of his body.

In like manner, a Christian can be protected from Satan's attacks by calling upon the <u>righteousness</u> available to him in Jesus's power. Every Christian has the power to live the way God wants him to live. When Satan throws the darts of doubt, selfishness, hate, or any other temptation at his heart, he can <u>call</u> upon God's breastplate of righteousness so that he can do the right thing, which will bring glory to God.

go to

righteousness
1 Corinthians 1:30

call
Romans 6:13

study
Ezra 7:10

meditating
Psalm 119:99

deeply
Psalm 119:9–11

> what others say
>
> ### Evelyn Christenson
>
> The metal breastplate was used to protect the front of a soldier, and even horses and elephants of war. It specifically covered the heart. It was like the bulletproof vest of today.[10]
>
> ### Bruce H. Wilkinson
>
> Lies keep us in bondage; they cause us to stop or to retreat. Truth frees us from that bondage; it causes us to start again, moving toward maturity. To believe a lie means that we do not believe the corresponding truth, because we behave according to what we believe. Our behavior is the outworking of our belief. That's why you cannot change your behavior while accepting the lie that caused you to behave in the first place.[11]

In order to "buckle up with the Bible," we must know it! We must <u>study</u> it and, ideally, memorize it so that we can call upon its truths whenever we need it. We won't always have time to do a study of a certain concept when a situation or temptation occurs; we must already have the truth buckled around our heart and mind so that we can snatch the spiritual weapons we need from it. Memorizing and <u>meditating</u> on its truths helps it to go <u>deeply</u> into our soul and spirit—and prepare us for anything we might face.

apply it

Sure Footing in a Shaky World

EPHESIANS 6:15 *and having shod your feet with the preparation of the gospel of peace;* (NKJV)

Roman soldiers wore thick-soled, hobnailed leather shoes that gave them sure footing even in the midst of battle because straps were tied around their ankles and shins. Since an enemy could easily bury sharp objects on the battlefield, a soldier's shoes were very important.

We need that same kind of security and sure footing. Satan loves to put sharp objects into our circumstances so that we will trip over them and easily lose our spiritual footing. The sharp objects can include: bad things that happen, doubts crossing our mind, people failing us, illness robbing our self-confidence, and our prayers seemingly not answered. We feel shaken and worried, and we wonder if God really is in control. But reflecting upon the reality of the gospel can give us sure footing again. Our peace will be restored. We must remember the facts that make the good news of salvation through Jesus real and relevant. When we do, we'll no longer feel like we're in the midst of a spiritual earthquake. We'll confidently say, "I know what I know what I know."

what others say

The Bible Knowledge Commentary

This verse does not speak of the spreading of the gospel, for Christians are pictured in vv. 10–16 as standing, not advancing. Instead this refers to a believer's stability or surefootedness from the gospel which gives him peace so he can stand in the battle.[12]

Watch Out! Incoming!

EPHESIANS 6:16 *above all, taking the shield of faith with which you will be able to quench all the fiery darts of the wicked one.* (NKJV)

While Paul was guarded by different Roman soldiers throughout every day, he must have noticed them propping their shields up against the wall. Although there were two kinds of shields used at that time, a large and a small, Paul refers to the large one, which is four feet long and two and a half feet wide. It was made of wood (often two layers glued together) and covered with linen and leather, which absorbed the fiery arrows shot by the enemy. In those days, arrows were often dipped in a flammable liquid or tar and set on fire before being shot at the enemy. Without the protection of his shield, a soldier would quickly be engulfed in flames.

That's exactly what Paul knew could happen to a Christian if he lowered his spiritual shield of faith while Satan is busy throwing arrows. The apostle John wrote in one of his letters about the main categories that these arrows can focus on, "For all that is in the world—the lust of the flesh, the lust of the eyes, and the pride of life—is not of the Father but is of the world" (1 John 2:16 NKJV). The flaming arrows are most often focused on:

go to

know
Ephesians 1:17

Eve
Genesis 3:5

- *Cravings for sin:* desiring sinful satisfaction
- *Lust of the eyes:* greedy and envious desires
- *Boasting of what he has and does:* pride that gives self credit for God's generous provision

Satan is an expert at throwing flaming arrows, especially when we've lowered our shield during times of weariness, depression, or anger. He's also good at disguising the arrows as thoughts that seem rational and truthful. But he is always only interested in our destruction, not our benefit.

> ### what others say
>
> **Evelyn Christenson**
>
> In Paul's day, the armies would shoot arrows with their tips wrapped in or filled with burning material (like a modern flame-thrower). They would shoot them from slack bows so that the speed would not put out the fire.
>
> So our shield of faith is designed by God to intercept and extinguish the fiery darts of Satan. His fiery darts are those temptations designed to cause us to sin, thus making us ineffective or completely useless in our spiritual battle against him.[13]

The shield of faith is powerful because it is based on trust: trust that God knows what He's doing in our lives and is dependable and trustworthy. We believe that when we <u>know</u> who God really is by dwelling upon His attributes and nature. Satan loves to make God appear unloving and unkind. Believing God doesn't want the best for us, especially because of His rules and laws (which seem too strict), takes away our trust and faith in His goodness. That was Satan's original flaming scud missile toward <u>Eve</u>. And she had her shield down and believed Satan's lie.

apply it

resist
1 Peter 5:9

father
John 8:44

grace
Titus 3:5

nothing
Romans 8:38–39

seal
Ephesians 1:13

Thessalonians
1 Thessalonians 5:8

When Satan catapults those flaming arrows at us, thoughts of temptation and wrong desires are not yet sin. If we put up our shield of faith and block them, we haven't allowed them to permeate our thinking and influence us, and therefore we haven't sinned. As we <u>resist</u> those thoughts, the arrows will splash against our shield and we'll be protected from believing the lies Satan has designed.

Don't Be Spiritually Brain-Dead

EPHESIANS 6:17 *And take the helmet of salvation, and the sword of the Spirit, which is the word of God; (NKJV)*

We saw how our hearts are guarded by the breastplate, and that's very important. If the heart is damaged, it is serious business. But there's another important part of our bodies: the brain! Our minds are essential for staying alive and being effective. A body can survive even when a brain is in a coma, but it sure isn't much of a life. It's also possible to be spiritually "brain-dead" or in a spiritual coma if we don't protect our minds from spiritual attack.

As Paul looked at the soldier's helmet, he knew that our spiritual minds are protected by the helmet of salvation. Satan loves to attack our minds with doubts, worries, and temptations. He makes us wonder after we've sinned, *Am I really saved? Maybe I've lost my salvation. God certainly can't continue to forgive me when I keep doing wrong things.* But those are Satan's lies. He's the <u>father</u> of lies. Having the assurance of our salvation will fend off those flaming arrows. We'll correct the lies he sends with the truth: that we are saved by God's <u>grace</u>—not our performance—and <u>nothing</u> can take God's <u>seal</u> of the Holy Spirit from us.

Some commentators believe, though, that it's not the assurance of our salvation that the helmet refers to, but the "hope of salvation" based on Paul's comment in his letter to the <u>Thessalonians</u>. In that case, it would refer to the future hope of eternity that we have and how we should live on this earth according to the spiritual value system of heaven.

Paul must have stared often at his guard's sword and wondered how that fits in with God's armor. And of course, he concluded that it represented God's holy and inspired words through Scripture. In the Roman soldier's arsenal of weaponry and protection, only the sword was an offensive implement of war. Everything else Paul talked about was defensive—protection for the soldier. Now, he refers to something that a Roman soldier and the Christian soldier can use actively, and it certainly is powerful. The "word" of God refers to several things: the Bible, God's messages within our hearts, and the words spoken by godly men and women.

go to

written
Matthew 4:4–10

parried
fought against

The Purposes and Description of the Word of God

Scripture	Purpose
Ephesians 5:26	Brings cleansing from sin
Romans 10:17	Offers the gospel message
1 John 2:5	Obedience to it shows a Christian's love for God
James 1:25	Convicts believers and unbelievers
Hebrews 4:12	Judges thoughts and attitudes
Description	
Psalm 19:7	Perfect
Psalm 19:8	Pure
Isaiah 55:11	Powerful and effective
1 Peter 1:25	Eternal
2 Peter 1:21	Inspired by God
Hebrews 4:12	Living and powerful

what others say

F. B. Meyer

There is no weapon so useful as the Spirit's sword, which is the Word of God. Our blessed Lord **parried** the devil's attacks by "It is <u>written</u>:" and we shall not improve on His method.[14]

Steve Farrar

We need both the right diet and the right exercise. Prayer and Scripture go together, and we are most effective when we have a good balance of the two. The man who studies the Bible without praying will develop a good mind with a cold heart. The man who prays without knowing Scripture will consistently pray outside the will of God, for that is where his will is revealed. This balance is critical to standing firm in spiritual battle.[15]

Although the Bible can be confusing and seem vague at times, and especially so when we first become Christians, God wants to reveal Himself through it. He promises, "If any of you lacks wisdom, let him ask of God, who gives to all liberally and without reproach, and

something to ponder

go to

wisdom
Psalm 111:11

time
1 Thessalonians
5:17–18

exhortation
command

it will be given to him" (James 1:5 NKJV). <u>Wisdom</u> comes from the Scriptures, and if we persist in seeking to understand the Bible, God will grant wisdom and insight.

Wave Your Spiritual Antennae

EPHESIANS 6:18–20 *praying always with all prayer and supplication in the Spirit, being watchful to this end with all perseverance and supplication for all the saints—and for me, that utterance may be given to me, that I may open my mouth boldly to make known the mystery of the gospel, for which I am an ambassador in chains; that in it I may speak boldly, as I ought to speak. (NKJV)*

We might read Paul's **exhortation** with a sinking feeling, thinking, *What? Does he expect me to be on my knees day and night? Pray all the time? You've got to be kidding!* We could easily reach this conclusion if we believe the only way to pray is by kneeling at the side of our bed, folding our hands, and using "thou's" and "thee's" in our prayers. But that isn't what Paul meant. Of course, God does want us to pray in a formal way, but we can pray at any <u>time</u>, using a variety of methods. When we can't take the time to get alone and be quiet, we can offer up those "arrow" prayers on the spur of the moment. We can say something as short as "Help, Lord!" Or we can pour out our feelings in a long-winded monologue. Just as a parent loves to hear his teenage child pour out her feelings and ask for advice, our heavenly Father loves for us to come to Him with our struggles, victories, praises, thanksgivings, and requests.

Paul encouraged believers to pray for others, but specifically asked for prayers for himself. He wanted to be effective for God's service by knowing what God wanted him to say in every situation. And he wanted to be bold and courageous in sharing the gospel message. He especially needed that courage because his life was constantly in danger from speaking about Jesus.

To be "alert in prayer," as Paul exhorted these believers, picture a Christian with spiritual antennae sprouting from his spirit and soul. Christians need to always be thinking of how they can pray about any problem or difficulty they are facing. They can also be alert to the ways they can thank and praise God. We should be waving our spiritual antennae so that we can be sensitive to God's leading to pray.

When Paul said to pray "in the Spirit," he meant that the Holy Spirit should guide and lead the way we pray. Ideally, we should discern what God's will is in a matter and then pray for that to occur. We won't always be able to immediately know what God wants, so we need to pray with an attitude of, "Lord, I surrender to whatever You want to do, even though I have my own preferences."

When asking for prayer support to be courageous and bold, Paul may have also been thinking of his upcoming trial, where he would have to defend himself against those who called him a **heretic**. In those days, Gentiles considered Christians a **sect** of the Jews, yet the Jews considered them heretics against Judaism. Paul would have to convince people at his trial that he represented a group of believers in God who were a separate entity from Judaism and not heretics. Such knowledge was like a "<u>mystery</u>" to those who didn't understand the claims of Christianity.

go to

mystery
Colossians 2:2–3

heretic
teacher of wrong ideas

sect
division

what others say

Warren Wiersbe

God enjoys answering our prayers. But He sometimes delays the answer to increase our faith and devotion and to accomplish His purposes at the right time. God's delays are not always God's denials.[16]

Bill Hybels

I write out my prayers every day; I have not been able to grow in my prayer life any other way. Experiment and see what works best for you. Try writing out your prayers once a week at first. If you find it helpful, do it more often. If it cramps your style and makes you uncomfortable, find another way that is more effective for you.[17]

Don't ever think that you're strong enough spiritually not to need the prayer support of others. Even though Paul is what we would call a "spiritual giant" because of his obedience and long service for God's glory, he is wise enough to know that he still needs prayer support. Every Christian, no matter who they are, needs the prayers of others. Paul didn't pray for God to have him removed from the chains. He prayed for courage in the midst of the chains.

something to ponder

go to

mentioned
Acts 20:4;
2 Timothy 4:12;
Titus 3:12

salutation
Romans 16:20;
Galatians 6:18;
Philippians 4:23;
Colossians 4:18

unequivocally
sincerely

Special Delivery

EPHESIANS 6:21–24 *But that you also may know my affairs and how I am doing, Tychicus, a beloved brother and faithful minister in the Lord, will make all things known to you; whom I have sent to you for this very purpose, that you may know our affairs, and that he may comfort your hearts. Peace to the brethren, and love with faith, from God the Father and the Lord Jesus Christ. Grace be with all those who love our Lord Jesus Christ in sincerity. Amen. (NKJV)*

Paul couldn't travel himself, so he sent his letter through his Christian friend Tychicus. Tychicus is <u>mentioned</u> several other places in Paul's writings and must have served with Paul over a period of time. Paul must have been very grateful for such a loving and faithful friend. Yet, even though Tychicus is so valuable to him as a support and help, he was willing to part with him for the good of the other believers. He was always thinking of the needs of others and wanted them to be helped by knowing how he, himself, was doing. Tychicus would not only carry the letter; he would give verbal testimony to Paul's good attitude and trust in the Lord.

Paul finally closed his letter by giving them the <u>salutation</u> about grace that he used for many of his other letters. He blessed them with peace, <u>love, faith,</u> and grace—all based on their knowledge of God and how Jesus loved others. He opened his letter talking about grace, and he closed it with the same emphasis. Truly, without grace, anything we do isn't being done in God's power.

what others say

Carol Kent

No one has ever loved us more completely or undeservedly than Jesus. When He lived on this earth, He didn't love some people and not others. He didn't love people because of how they treated Him or because of what they thought of Him. He loved everyone equally and **unequivocally**. Some people were surprised by His love, and others never even recognized His love. Certainly, none of us deserve His love.[18]

Chapter Wrap-Up

- Paul doesn't leave anyone out of his commands to be Spirit-filled—even the children. He reveals God's plan for the family even though his comments went against the current ideas of Roman-Greco society. (Ephesians 6:1–4)

- Slaves were generally known in the Roman-Greco culture to only serve their masters well when they were being observed. Paul wanted them as Christians to serve their masters cheerfully all the time because Jesus was really their boss—and they were serving their heavenly Lord. (Ephesians 6:5–9)

- Since Christians are in a spiritual battle, Paul wants his readers to use their heavenly armor to fight evil spiritual forces. He encourages them to use the belt of truth, breastplate of righteousness, shoes of peace, shield of faith, helmet of salvation, and sword of the Bible. (Ephesians 6:10–17)

- Even though Paul was a very strong Christian, he knew he desperately needed the support of others through prayer and communication. He asked others to pray for his boldness and encouraged them to pray for their Christian brothers and sisters. He concluded his epistle by blessing his readers with peace and love with faith. (Ephesians 6:18–24)

Study Questions

1. What is Paul's command to children so that they can be Spirit-filled, and what will be the benefit of following his command?

2. How should slaves act as Christians toward their masters?

3. In order to be Spirit-filled, what important resource do Christians have available to them and what are the different elements of it?

4. Should Christians ever feel like they don't need the prayer support of others? Why or why not?

Part Two
PHILIPPIANS

Philippians 1
Praise Even for Afflictions

Chapter Highlights:
- An Affectionate Reflecion
- My Chains Won't Strain My Faith
- Make Sure You All Pull Together

Let's Get Started

Ten years before Paul would write this letter, he visited the town of Philippi on his second missionary journey, around AD 52. Acts 16 tells us the whole story of his adventure there.

His first three converts represented every level of society. At the top was Lydia, who was Asian and a <u>seller of purple</u>. She was extremely rich because she sold one of the most expensive products of that time. "Purple" was a secretion from a certain shellfish's gland, which, when exposed to sunlight, became several shades of purple. The Phoenicians originally discovered it and had a corner on the market. It was a dye that was impossible to remove and produced cloth so expensive that only the highest members of society, such as kings and government officials, could afford it.

Paul's second convert represented the lowest of society—a demented Greek slave girl who was used by her masters to tell fortunes (Acts 16:16–18). There was quite a ruckus when Paul delivered her of her demon and her owners no longer could gain money from her lost fortune-telling skills. As a result Paul was thrown into prison, which led to his contact with his third convert: a jailer.

This jailer represents a working-class, middle-of-society kind of guy. He was a Roman citizen who was shocked when an earthquake threw off Paul's and his companions' shackles. When Paul and his friends didn't try to escape, which would have meant the jailer's death, this man received Christ and then introduced Paul to his own family for their salvation.

Even though Paul had amazingly quick results, he had to escape because of persecution. But the bond he'd formed with those people made them some of his favorite people, and they returned the fondness by sending financial support time after time.

While there, Paul had the privilege of leading a woman named <u>Lydia</u> and her family to a saving knowledge of Jesus. Paul first met

go to

seller of purple
Acts 16:14

Lydia
Acts 16:14

go to

imprisoned
Acts 16:23

earthquake
Acts 16:26

her by a river and shared the gospel with her. Then, while <u>impris-oned</u> for preaching the gospel, he was guarded by a man who was quite impressed that an <u>earthquake</u> caused Paul's chains to fall off—along with all the prisoners'. The guard immediately asked, "What can I do to be saved?" Now that was a question Paul loved to hear. He immediately led that jailer, and later that night his whole family, to Christ.

Those two households were the beginning of the church in the city of Philippi. The incredible ways that God worked to begin that church must have made Paul feel a particular joy about keeping in touch with those believers.

The Atmosphere in Philippi

And for the writing of this letter, his purposes are fourfold:

1. Express his gratitude for the financial support from the Philippians sent with Epaphroditus. (4:10, 15–18)

2. Encourage the Philippians to live in joy regardless of their circumstances. (1:12–26; 4:4–9)

3. Influence those who are in disagreement to become united. (2:2–4; 4:2–3)

4. Correct the wrong teachings of legalism. (3:1–19)

From those four points, we know that although the church in Philippi was doing very well, it was also experiencing disunity, a tendency to return to the letter of the law instead of depending upon grace, and a struggle to be joyful in the midst of difficult circumstances. To their credit, they continued to support Paul and be especially generous toward his ministry.

As with his letter to the Ephesians, Paul was in prison when he wrote this letter. Commentators don't agree on where Paul was imprisoned. Some say he was in Rome, others say Caesarea or even Ephesus. But if the majority who vote for Rome are accurate, then he would have written his letter about AD 61 or 62.

Regardless, one of Paul's main themes in this letter stems from his imprisonment. Even though he was in very difficult circumstances, he tells believers to rejoice—something he was able to do. Many people can tell other people to have joy while they're having few problems, but it's the truly godly person who can do it while they're having their own very difficult challenges. Paul was one of those people. Let's see what we can learn from him.

colony
Acts 16:12

The Problem of Philippians

Paul's writing through 3:1 seems to flow quite smoothly, and at that point he seems to be drawing to a close. He even says "finally." But then in 3:2, he begins a new thread of thought: Be careful of evil workers. Hey! Where did that come from? Paul then writes for two whole chapters on a seemingly different course.

Scholars and commentators have been curious about this for a long time. Many say, "Well, any of us could get a new thought. Maybe someone just arrived with news of how the Philippian church was doing. After all, remember, he's standing up, pacing, and dictating." Other scholars wonder if this "book" is actually the compilation of two different letters and that 3:2–4:3 is the second letter.

In spite of these possibilities, no New Testament scholar has ever doubted its genuineness. All commentators believe Philippians to be one of Paul's letters. Other letters aren't always so well accepted.

Paul picked Philippi as a place to preach because it was the commercial center of the ancient world. The city's name came from its founder, Philip, father of Alexander the Great. He began the city in 368 BC because it was a highly strategic site. It was the place where Antony defeated Brutus and Cassius, thus deciding the future of the Roman Empire. (Perhaps Cleopatra was there too!) Not long after, Philippi was designated a <u>colony</u>, which was formed by a group of about three hundred veteran Roman soldiers plus their wives and children. They brought with them their Roman culture and established the colony as a Roman outpost.

And they were proud of their Romanness! They made sure they were never assimilated into the culture surrounding them in other areas. The strategists of Rome created this concept of colonies as the means of controlling all the outlying areas under the thumb of their Roman government.

It certainly was effective. Even Paul and Silas's gospel message was resited because the Roman people countered, "But . . . we are Romans." In other words, "We don't want to believe in anything that isn't Roman by nature." No wonder Paul wrote to the Philippians that they were a colony of <u>heaven</u>. He wanted their allegiance to be with God, not their Roman roots.

How Are You?

PHILIPPIANS 1:1–2 *Paul and Timothy, bondservants of Jesus Christ, to all the **saints** in Christ Jesus who are in Philippi, with the **bishops** and **deacons**: Grace to you and peace from God our Father and the Lord Jesus Christ.* (NKJV)

Paul was motivated to send this letter because Epaphroditus (who may have been the pastor at Philippi) had brought some financial support to Paul from the believers at his church. This is Paul's thank-you letter, and he wants to bless them in return with grace and peace—his <u>common</u> greeting—for their help. (See commentary on Ephesians 1:2.)

The early teachers like Paul took those words and made a special meaning of them by referring them to God's offered gifts of salvation and the benefits of living in God's power. Paul took those two public salutations and turned them into a reminder of God's <u>grace</u> through Jesus that brings <u>peace</u> within the heart.

Paul calls himself and Timothy "bondservants" and identifies the Philippian believers as "saints." Saints, as explained in the Ephesian portion of this book (Ephesians 1:1), are those who believe in Jesus for salvation. It has nothing to do with their being sinless or achieving through works a special designation.

Elsewhere Paul uses this terminology to designate any and all who serve God as free bond-slaves—that is, as those who are free in Christ Jesus but have used that freedom to perform the duties of a slave (Galatians 5:13) in the service of God and of his people.

EXODUS 21:5–6 *"But if the servant plainly says, 'I love my master, my wife, and my children; I will not go out free,' "then his master shall bring him to the judges. He shall also bring him to the door, or to the doorpost, and his master shall pierce his ear with an awl; and he shall serve him forever"* (NKJV).

go to

Romans
Acts 16:20–21

heaven
Philippians 3:20

common
Romans 1:7;
1 Corinthians 1:3

grace
Romans 3:24

peace
John 16:33

saints
believers

bishops
pastors

deacons
church leaders

Very early in the formation of the church, God directed believers to choose certain mature Christians to take leadership. Those people were identified as <u>bishops</u> and were also known as overseers and <u>elders</u> and were primarily responsible for shepherding or <u>pastoring</u> a church. <u>Deacons</u> had special service responsibilities within the local church. God knows we can't operate as well as a part of the body of Christ without direction and guidance from those who are qualified.

Description of a Bondslave of Jesus

Old Testament Servant or Slave	Application for Christians	Scripture
Property of owner	Christians can't be owned by anyone else.	Romans 6:12–14
Obeys master	Obedience indicates servant-hood.	Romans 6:16
Purchased	Bought with the price of Christ's death.	1 Corinthians 6:20
Can gain freedom after six years of service	Serving Christ is a choice of the will, it is not forced, and is a commitment lasting forever.	Romans 6:12
In Old Testament, slavery was the lowest position of society	In God's kingdom, slavery to Christ indicates greatness.	Matthew 20:26–28
Out of love for master	Servanthood brings happiness.	Matthew 24:46
May or may not be promoted	Faithful service guaranteed to bring greater opportunities.	Matthew 25:21
Can only be judged by his master	Can only be judged by Jesus.	Romans 14:4

bishops
Titus 1:5–9;
1 Timothy 3:1–8

elders
Acts 14:23

pastoring
Acts 20:17, 28

deacons
Acts 6:1–7;
1 Timothy 3:8–13

Distance Makes the Heart Grow Fonder

PHILIPPIANS 1:3–5 *I thank my God upon every remembrance of you, always in every prayer of mine making request for you all with joy, for your fellowship in the gospel from the first day until now,* (NKJV)

help
2 Corinthians 11:9

joy
John 15:11

Paul's gratitude isn't based on an isolated incident of their financial and emotional partnership. Three other times they sent him <u>help</u>—twice when he was in Thessalonica and once when he was in Corinth. No wonder he had such fond opinions of them even though he hadn't seen them for ten years and was separated from them by eight hundred miles. But more than their financial support, he was concerned about their spiritual growth, and that's why he prayed for them and told them he was praying for them—and with <u>joy</u>, because he was full of confidence that God would answer his prayers.

what others say

Corrie ten Boom

Prayer is powerful. The devil smiles when we make plans. He laughs when we get too busy. But he trembles when we pray—especially when we pray together. Remember, though, that it is God who answers, and He always answers in a way that He knows is best for everyone.[2]

When we pray for others, we should pray with joy. When we pray for someone because they are in a difficult situation or possibly because they don't know Christ—and we desperately want them to—we might be tempted to be glum and unhappy. After all, God hasn't yet answered our prayers. We might doubt that He will. But praying with joy signifies that we trust God will do the right thing—even if it turns out not to be what we prayed for. If we're not praying with joy, we are indicating that we don't think God is powerful enough to make a difference in that person's life. Or we could easily think our concern isn't important enough to God for Him to answer. But praying with joy reveals our faith and confidence that God will respond.

And it's important to tell people that we are praying for them. If we pray and they don't know about it, they won't be as observant about God working in their lives. Even though Paul couldn't have known all the little and big things that were concerning the Philippians, he could pray for them anyway, because God knew!

When people think of you, do they rejoice and thank God for you? Make sure your life is something that makes people glad when they think of you.

When you contribute to the support—either financially or emotionally—of a person who is serving Christ as an occupation, you are a partner with them in their ministry. In a sense, you are right there helping them be successful and bring glory to God. Although we might feel helpless at times because we can't do all we'd like, any help we give is valuable and important—and we become colaborers with them for God's glory.

God Isn't Finished Yet

> PHILIPPIANS 1:6 *being confident of this very thing, that He who has begun a good work in you will complete it until the day of Jesus Christ;* (NKJV)

Paul is so sure of God's powerful hand upon his friends in Philippi that he could tell them he knew God would <u>continue</u> working in them until Jesus <u>came back</u> to get them. Of course, he didn't know when that would be, but even if they died, that would be their day of seeing Jesus face-to-face. The good work that God was doing included their salvation and their continued growth as Christians. God didn't ever plan to stop making them the quality people He wanted them to be.

Where Paul wrote "being confident," the Greek word *pépoitha*, we know from the tense that he was saying he'd already come to a proven certainty that God would work in them and that he was continuing to have that same assurance. So it was an already-established fact in his mind, and he kept on believing it. That's confidence!

Paul really stresses that it's God who is working in them. Everything that happens to them is not some coincidence, but God's hand so that God can "complete" the refining work on their <u>character</u> and their behavior.

This verse lets us know that we are not in charge of our spiritual growth; God is. At times, we might think that gritting our teeth and promising to act right will give us the results we want, but then we're doing it, not God! We must obey God, but not as if we're striving to make growth happen. It happens as we trust He is doing it, and since we'll have to wait our whole lifetime for the finishing touches, we'll have to learn to be patient.

go to

continue
Hebrews 7:25

came back
Acts 1:11;
1 Thessalonians
4:16–17

character
1 John 3:2

go to

conversion
John 3:3

predestined
Ephesians 1:5

conversion
being born again

predestined
predetermined

The Three Kinds of "Completeness" or "Perfection" That God Works in Us

Scripture	Kinds of "Perfection" or "Completeness"
Colossian 2:10	In our "position in Christ," we are already considered perfect in God's eyes.
1 Timothy 4:15	God is working a "perfect progress" while here on earth that never ends.
Philippians 3:20–21	When we reach heaven, we'll be perfect forever.

what others say

Jan Frank

Most of us struggle with waiting. If we have stepped out and done what we believe God has led us to do, we feel cheated or tricked when we don't receive what we think will be secured by our obedience. Americans have been conditioned to expect immediate gratification. We want to see the results in a timely fashion.[3]

Patrick Morley

Conversion does not take place in the blinking of an eye. Conversion occurs on a time line. Let's face it, if we knew everything about ourselves that God wanted to change, we would blow all our circuit-breakers. We couldn't handle knowing how God sees us all at once. We are converted to salvation in a moment of time, but our conversion to obedience is a lifelong process of daily surrender.[4]

God never gives up working on our spiritual growth.

The "work" that Paul knew God would do within them was to make them into the likeness of Jesus. Paul wrote in his letter to the Roman believers, "For whom He foreknew, He also **predestined** to be conformed to the image of His Son, that He might be the first-born among many brethren" (Romans 8:29 NKJV). God wants us to act like Jesus acted, and He allows circumstances in our lives that will challenge us to do that. Of course, we won't be formed into Jesus's exact likeness until we meet Him in heaven, but in the meantime, we're growing closer to Him.

Many people struggle with having to continue to work on becoming who God wants them to be in their character and their actions. It's discouraging to always be struggling. But if we don't continue to be challenged to grow, or if we could somehow "arrive" at a state of perfection on earth, we wouldn't need God's help. We might say, "Well, Lord, I have it all handled, so I really don't need you. Thanks anyway." But we should always be dependent upon Him. That's why we can actually look at our challenges as something <u>positive</u>: They cause us to grow closer to God.

go to

positive
James 1:2–3

disheartened
1 Corinthians 15:58

For the most part, we don't see spiritual growth day by day. If we're looking at it under a microscope, we're going to be disappointed. That could eventually cause us to give up or become <u>disheartened</u>. Growth happens over a long period of time—it's best to evaluate how far we've come through a long-range lens.

An Affectionate Reflection

> PHILIPPIANS 1:7–8 *just as it is right for me to think this of you all, because I have you in my heart, inasmuch as both in my chains and in the defense and confirmation of the gospel, you all are partakers with me of grace. For God is my witness, how greatly I long for you all with the affection of Jesus Christ. (NKJV)*

Paul doesn't hold anything back when he's speaking of his affection for friends. It's obvious that the intense affection Jesus has for these Philippian believers has been transferred into Paul's heart, and he's not afraid to speak of it. As though it might sound a little too passionate, Paul seems to defend his affection for them. And one of the reasons he gives for feeling that deep tenderness is because they have supported him and actually gone through difficulties with him.

> **what others say**
>
> **Kay Arthur**
>
> Pray through Philippians 1, substituting your circumstances for Paul's. Make his desire yours. Practice having his mindset, and claim the joy that will be yours. And know this: Your life shall then have a greater eternal impact.[5]

Some commentators believe that Paul is referring to a time when he was in chains while in Philippi. If that's correct, maybe some of his fellow believers were in chains alongside him. They had shared a common difficult situation and that always molds hearts together. There's nothing like sitting side by side in a dungeon with chains on to inspire talk about your soul.

Many men have trouble expressing their feelings and affection for others, especially in their families and for their wives—but Paul doesn't. God wants you to declare and demonstrate your love for others because they really need it. If you don't, you may find yourself very alone. Expressing that affection through your feelings lets others know how much you value them.

apply it

If you want to grow closer to someone, just go through a difficult situation with them. Even sharing a joy can bring greater friendship. Sometimes we back away from friends when they go through hard times, but they need the support we can give. And if we're brave enough to walk through their trials with them, our hearts will be bonded even more tightly together.

Abound More and More

PHILIPPIANS 1:9–11 *And this I pray, that your love may abound still more and more in knowledge and all discernment, that you may approve the things that are excellent, that you may be sincere and without offense till the day of Christ, being filled with the fruits of righteousness which are by Jesus Christ, to the glory and praise of God. (NKJV)*

Paul already mentioned that he prayed for these special people. Now he tells them what he prays. Paul's eloquence is inspired by the Holy Spirit as he prays the things God must desire for all Christians, that:

- Their love grows more and more through a "love with actions" kind of love. It should be a love that is based in knowledge of God and insights in how to live God's way. It's easy to tell someone "I love you," but abounding love based in God's kind of love is more than mere feelings; it's love that wants the best for another person.

- They know the best way to respond to situations and thus be without sin when Jesus returns or they leave this earth in death. The word *approve* (*dokimazein*) was used for testing metals for genuineness. For you and me, it would apply to testing an action—before you do it—to see if it meets up to God's standards. Paul wants each Philippian to stop and evaluate how they are going to act when faced with a joyful or difficult circumstance.

- The result of such testing will be sincerity or purity, *elikrinos*, from which commentators take two possible origins for the Greek word. The first is being able to stand the test of being exposed to light and found faultless. The other means being spun around as if through a sieve until every defilement is filtered out.

- They live in such a way that it's obvious they depend upon God. Paul refers to the fruit of righteousness here, but in his letter to the Galatians he defined that fruit: love, joy, peace, longsuffering, kindness, goodness, faithfulness, gentleness, and self-control (Galatians 5:22–23). Those are the very characteristics of God Himself. If someone has God living inside them, they will more and more exhibit those kinds of reactions as they grow stronger in Him.

> **what others say**
>
> **Oswald Chambers**
>
> Can God keep me from stumbling this second? Yes. Can He keep me from sin this second? Yes. Well, that is the whole of life. You cannot live more than a second at a time. If God can keep you blameless this second, He can do it the next.[6]

Don't say you'll pray for someone unless you intend to do it and actually do it. They're depending upon you and need your support. Keep your promise!

My Chains Won't Strain My Faith

PHILIPPIANS 1:12–14 *But I want you to know, brethren, that the things which happened to me have actually turned out for the furtherance of the gospel, so that it has become evident to the whole palace guard, and to all the rest, that my chains are in Christ; and most of the brethren in the Lord, having become confident by my chains, are much more bold to speak the word without fear. (NKJV)*

Just think of something dreadful that you wouldn't want to encounter. And just imagine that if it happened, it would seem to prevent you from doing the most important thing in the world to you. That's what Paul faced. Besides death, being chained to a guard twenty-four hours a day had to be a dreadful experience because it prevented him from doing the thing he loved best—spreading the

something to ponder

gospel. When it first happened, he may have wondered, *How in the world can God use this for good? How can I fulfill the great responsibility that God has given me? It just doesn't make sense.* Little did Paul know in the beginning when he was confined that God intended to use that difficulty for many people's benefit—including ours, through the centuries. Without Paul's imprisonment, he might not have written so many letters. Then his contemporaries and those who have read them down through the years wouldn't have drawn closer to God.

In these verses, Paul is expressing his conclusion that the results of his imprisonment were a "good" that he never could have imagined: the effect on the guards and Christians who were encouraged to be bolder in their witness for Christ. But he never could have anticipated the greater good of all of us readers benefiting from his words. Plus, it seems that there were people in Caesar's court (the palace guard of whom many were members of the royal family) and even family members who believed in Jesus—right under Nero's nose (Philippians 4:22). So Paul was encouraged by them also.

Since Paul was most likely under house arrest, the Roman soldiers came and went when it was their turn to watch over Paul. They were like Paul's own "hostages," since they had no recourse but to observe Paul's gracious attitude and hear him challenge them about faith in Christ. Then they returned to their barracks or their own homes and must have exclaimed, "Let me tell you what that religious nut Paul said today!" But God used it to get the word out—and that's all that concerned Paul.

what others say

Billy Graham

When you bake a cake, you put in raw flour, baking powder, soda, bitter chocolate, shortening, etc., none of which taste very good in themselves, but which work together to make a delicious cake. And so with our sins and our mistakes—although they are not good in themselves, if we commit them in honest, simple faith to the Lord, He will work them out His own way and in His own time make something of them for our good and His glory.[7]

Paul's comments may have been prompted by some messages he received from the Philippians saying they thought he might be discouraged by his bondage. Some commentators believe that the

Philippians hadn't heard from him for several years, and then when they did hear he was in chains, they were concerned and figured he would be troubled. He wants them to know that's the farthest thing from the truth: he's actually encouraged to see God using it in such powerful ways.

Everything we encounter, even chains, can be used by God.

What are you facing that you have concluded can't be used for your good or God's glory? When you begin to doubt that God is in control, remember Paul and his confinement. God creatively used it for a far-flung glory that Paul couldn't even imagine. God may be intending to do the same thing with your trial or problem. Don't waver from believing God knows best. Surrender to His will for you even if it doesn't make sense to you.

It must have been a huge encouragement to Paul to see other Christians growing bolder in talking about Jesus because of his own courage. You may be going through a difficult time and think no one is watching, but your faith in God and your steadfast surrender may actually be encouraging someone to be stronger in their faith. Don't belittle God's ability to use you even when you don't know it. Stand firm and be assured that He uses everything for good.

Although we know that Jesus knew the purposes of His crucifixion and death, He still struggled with surrendering to God's plan. But His cooperation brought salvation and benefit for many. Jesus is an example for us when we struggle with accepting God's plan—especially when He wants to use dilemmas and difficulties. When we surrender, God brings great things.

Just Do It!

PHILIPPIANS 1:15–18a *Some indeed preach Christ even from envy and strife, and some also from goodwill: The former preach Christ from selfish ambition, not sincerely, supposing to add affliction to my chains; but the latter out of love, knowing that I am appointed for the defense of the gospel. What then? Only that in every way, whether in pretense or in truth, Christ is preached; (NKJV)*

good
Romans 8:28

struggled
Luke 22:42–44

plan
Isaiah 55:8–9

Paul couldn't have been more selfless. He was willing to do anything to see Jesus lifted up so that people could come to know His wonderful gift of salvation. People could say anything about Paul—

tests
1 Thessalonians 2:4

envious
Proverbs 14:30

maligning
bad-mouthing

he didn't care; he actually rejoiced in it. People could preach with wrong motives—Paul just wanted Jesus talked about. He so trusted God that he didn't have to control what people said. He believed that God would use words about Jesus—even if they weren't spoken by him. All he cared about was that the truth be made known, even if something injurious was said about himself. That's selflessness! That's wanting the best for God's mission. Oh, that every Christian wanted Jesus spoken of by any means—and not get the credit themselves.

> ### what others say
>
> #### Charles R. Swindoll
> I have a strong word to all who are given to public criticism of other ministries. Watch yourself! Rather than being discerning, you may have become too narrow and rigid! Learn from Paul. Even ministries that may employ a few deceptive motives, even churches that you choose not to attend, Paul said, in effect, "I rejoice that at least Christ is proclaimed."[8]
>
> #### Kay Arthur
> Oh, dear child of God, whatever you are enduring now—or whatever comes your way in the future—it is not without purpose in the sovereignty of God. If you will let Christ be your life and if you will have a submissive mind toward God, you will have joy. And your joy, in spite of imprisonment, will be used by God to reach others.[9]

The believers who were preaching Christ from a wrong motive may have been presenting the same gospel but **maligning** Paul's name in the process. Maybe they picked out little differences between their theologies and made a big deal out of it, saying Paul's beliefs were incorrect. We don't know for sure exactly what they were preaching, but from Paul's perspective it really didn't make any difference—just as long as Jesus was lifted up.

We need to evaluate our own motives for representing Christ. Sometimes it may seem that speaking of Jesus could actually bring some rewards or benefits. Some people may see it as a way of making money or being lifted up as spiritual. God <u>tests</u> the hearts of everyone. What will He find in yours?

We need not to be jealous or <u>envious</u> of the opportunities God gives others and not us. Maybe you're a writer and you would like to be published like another author. Or maybe you're a speaker and would have liked to speak at a conference where someone else is speaking. You could be a pastor looking for a church to guide, but someone else got the "call" to pastor the church you'd been considering. In times like that, we need to remember that we're "one for all and all for one" in the <u>body of Christ</u>. Each person is given unique assignments by God, and we need to respect His decisions.

body of Christ
1 Corinthians
12:12–30

I've Got That Joy, Joy, Joy, Joy Down in My Heart

PHILIPPIANS 1:18b–20 *and in this I rejoice, yes, and will rejoice. For I know that this will turn out for my deliverance through your prayer and the supply of the Spirit of Jesus Christ, according to my earnest expectation and hope that in nothing I shall be ashamed, but with all boldness, as always, so now also Christ will be magnified in my body, whether by life or by death.* (NKJV)

Paul wrote about his deliverance but at the time didn't know what kind of deliverance that might be. There were three possibilities:

- His death by execution for being found guilty of his accused crime

- Vindication and freedom after testifying in court

- Freedom gained before testifying

The possibility of Paul's death was very real because Nero was on the throne and he was famous for killing Christians. Tradition says that Paul was held under house arrest for two years—the maximum amount of time that a prisoner could be held. Most commentators don't believe there's evidence that he did actually testify in court, so he may have been released. They also believe that he continued to travel and preach the gospel. He is also credited with writing his second letter to Timothy (2 Timothy) later during a second imprisonment in Rome. Eventually, Paul was executed for his faith—we do know that for sure, just not exactly when.

But Paul didn't know at the time he wrote to the Philippians what would actually happen. If he ended up testifying about his faith in Christ before a hostile judge and jury, he wanted to be bold and not shrink from the opportunity. Even if it meant his conviction and execution, he wanted to stay true to Jesus. And indeed, his death was a

Holy Spirit's
Matthew 10:19–20

very real possibility. In the face of that conceivable reality, he is surprisingly calm and unworried. He credits a lot of that to the Philippians' prayers for the <u>Holy Spirit's</u> strength. Their support meant so much to him because he didn't want his commitment to Christ and sharing the gospel to be diminished in any way. In everything Paul did and said, he wanted Jesus glorified—no matter what it took.

The word *magnified* is also translated "exalted" or "glorified." We can get a better understanding of this word if we think of how a microscope or telescope makes something bigger to the eye. If it's more readily visible, we are more prone to pay attention to it. That's the idea Paul wanted to convey. He wanted Jesus to be "magnified" or enlarged in the view of others. He wanted them to think of Jesus for salvation and for their needs. As that happened, Jesus would be glorified.

what others say

Earl Palmer

The word *help* in this sentence . . . originally meant "to lead a chorus," then "to pay the expenses for training a chorus," and by the time Paul wrote it had come to mean simply "to defray the expenses of something," "to provide," "to supply in abundance," "to choreograph."

This original root meaning of the word provides us with a marvelous and appropriate image for the work of the Holy Spirit in relation to our work of prayer. We can see the Holy Spirit as choreographing human prayer and His own work to make them work together in favor of this man who is imprisoned in Rome.[10]

There are many references to the words *glory* and *glorifying God* in the Bible. One of the main purposes of our lives as instructed in Scripture is to give glory to God.

Giving Glory to God

Why we should glorify God	How we are to give Him glory
God's marvelous deeds (1 Chronicles 16:24)	Requesting that God reveal His glory (Exodus 33:18–23)
God's deliverance (Psalm 50:15)	Confessing sin (Joshua 7:19–20)
God's love and faithfulness (Psalm 115:1)	Praise (Psalm 66:2)

Giving Glory to God (cont'd)

Why we should glorify God	How we are to give Him glory
What God has done (Isaiah 25:1–3)	Singing (Psalm 69:30)
God does everything right (Daniel 4:37)	Giving thanks (Psalm 69:30)
God's mercy in spreading the gospel message to the Gentiles (Romans 15:9)	Speaking of God's marvelous deeds to others (Psalm 96:3)
God will make believers kings and priests (Revelation 1:6)	Rejoicing in God (Psalm 105:3)
God created everything (Revelation 4:11)	Christian unity (Romans 15:5–6)
Jesus died on the cross (Revelation 5:12)	Accepting others (Romans 15:7)
God will judge righteously (Revelation 14:7; 19:1–2)	Living good lives (1 Peter 2:12)

Between a Rock and a Hard Place

PHILIPPIANS 1:21–24 *For to me, to live is Christ, and to die is gain. But if I live on in the flesh, this will mean fruit from my labor; yet what I shall choose I cannot tell. For I am hard-pressed between the two, having a desire to depart and be with Christ, which is far better. Nevertheless to remain in the flesh is more needful for you.* (NKJV)

Paul's purpose for life is his Lord Jesus Christ. Everything he does is motivated in seeing Christ exalted and glorified. Although Paul would prefer to see Jesus face-to-face in heaven and leave behind all the hardships he continually faces, he is content to keep living so that other believers are encouraged to continue growing spiritually. Paul continues to reveal his selflessness. He's always thinking of the good of others, not himself.

Paul considers two wonderful options: while he is alive he lives for Christ, and after he dies he'll gain from being in Jesus's presence. Paul is saying from his eternal perspective that life is worth it! Heaven is worth more, but life is worth it. Wouldn't we love to have two good things to choose from every time we made a decision? What joy! Paul's use of the Greek word *senechomai* for "hard-pressed" might remind us of the saying "caught between a rock and a hard place." It describes a person walking or riding between two walls of rocks, unable to turn around. Paul is equally drawn to two great things, and he doesn't want to "turn" from either one.

As Paul is looking forward to being in Jesus's presence, he gives us the first of four explanations of who Jesus is to him.

Who Jesus Is, According to Philippians

Scripture in Philippians	Paul Says Jesus Is:
1:21 For to me, to live is Christ, and to die is gain. (NKJV)	Jesus is everything to Paul, and nothing is more important to him than Jesus. His very life revolves around Jesus.
2:5–7 Let this mind be in you which was also in Christ Jesus, who, being in the form of God, did not consider it robbery to be equal with God, but made Himself of no reputation, taking the form of a bondservant, and coming in the likeness of men. (NKJV)	The model for humility. Even though Jesus is God in human form, Jesus did not claim that but humbled Himself to fulfill God's purpose, even to the point of a misunderstood death. Paul wants to be like that, and he wants the Philippians to be like that.
3:20–21 For our citizenship is in heaven, from which we also eagerly wait for the Savior, the Lord Jesus Christ, who will transform our lowly body that it may be conformed to His glorious body, according to the working by which He is able even to subdue all things to Himself. (NKJV)	The One who will transform every believer (whether alive or dead at Christ's appearing) into their glorious state of having their eternal body in heaven.
4:13 I can do all things through Christ who strengthens me. (NKJV)	The One who provides the power for everything God wants to do through him.

Paul's use of the word *depart* should be a source of comfort to believers, especially those who fear the departure of their spirits from their bodies. The Greek word is *analuein* and has several meanings:

- pulling up camp by loosening the tent ropes and moving on
- setting sail by pulling up the anchor and loosening the mooring ropes
- solving problems by having all the uncertainties and cares of life left behind
- setting free a prisoner from prison, his chains loosened and released
- unyoking oxen and releasing them from the burden of work

No wonder Paul could have the eternal perspective of wanting to go to heaven. How we long to enjoy such freedoms described in those visual word pictures.

go to

rewards
1 Samuel 26:23

Lloyd John Ogilvie

We cannot live—really—until we come to grips with death. Paul's statement to the Philippians about death was based on the previous phrase about life. He had died to himself and his own willful design for his life long before he made this statement in prison. Death was not an ending for him but the beginning of the next phase of eternal life which had begun when he turned his life over to Christ.[11]

When we aren't facing death, it's easy to be flippant and say, "Oh, sure, I'm looking forward to dying. I'll be with Jesus and heaven will be great." But I can only imagine that if I were indeed facing imminent death, in my own power I would be frightened. I trust the Lord would give me the peace I needed, but it must be scary to face such an unknown, even as a Christian. We can be encouraged by Paul's example.

If you're not ready to give up this life, you're not ready to really live. Having a grand purpose like Paul had gives true meaning to life. For those who don't know and serve Christ, this present life is the only thing they have to look forward to. Even though they may strive to accomplish great things and be successful (by the world's standards) they will never reach true satisfaction and long-term purpose. How much better it is to be a Christian and serve a mighty God who is worthy to be glorified and will give eternal <u>rewards</u>.

key point

If You're Happy, Then I'm Happy

PHILIPPIANS 1:25–26 *And being confident of this, I know that I shall remain and continue with you all for your progress and joy of faith, that your rejoicing for me may be more abundant in Jesus Christ by my coming to you again. (NKJV)*

Of course, Paul can't really choose whether he'll live or die. Yet this process of acting as if he could choose has freed him from being held hostage by the fear of death. *If* he were indeed able to decide, he would prefer to choose life on earth, because it'll mean benefit for the Philippians and every other Christian whom he contacts. Even though Paul would be thrilled to see Jesus and experience the joys of heaven, his fixed vision on the spiritual sees the needs on earth. He gladly sacrifices his own spiritual well-being to produce greater fruit—the Philippians' progress and joy in the faith—on earth to God's glory.

Paul used the word for *continue*, or *paramenein*, which gives the impression of waiting beside a person ready to help. Paul reminds me of a parent standing beside a toddler who is learning to walk, ever ready to offer a hand so that the child can learn to walk alone and then run. Paul wants his Philippian friends to succeed in their Christian lives, and he'll do just about anything to make it happen.

In time, of course, Paul also got his other option: a heavenly welcome into Jesus's very presence. With God as our Lord and Master, we can have both: fruitful lives now lived in the power of the Spirit and eternal joy in Jesus's presence. That's a win-win situation! But it's all dependent on choosing Jesus as our life now. We need to allow Jesus to walk closer to us so that more and more of our earthly vision is enhanced by Jesus's glorious presence.

Make Sure You All Pull Together

PHILIPPIANS 1:27–28 *Only let your conduct be worthy of the gospel of Christ, so that whether I come and see you or am absent, I may hear of your affairs, that you stand fast in one spirit, with one mind striving together for the faith of the gospel, and not in any way terrified by your adversaries, which is to them a proof of perdition, but to you of salvation, and that from God.* (NKJV)

Paul uses several analogies in these verses. First, he appealed to the Philippians' loyalty as citizens of Rome in a Roman colony by using the word *politeuesthai* for "conduct." The Greek word referred to obeying the rules applying to citizens—in other words, being a good citizen! The Philippians enjoyed Roman privileges, giving them a spirit of oneness and victory based on the strength of being citizens of the most powerful kingdom on earth. Thus, Paul says, "Live in such a way that demonstrates your loyalty to God's kingdom. Trust in the victory God guarantees you as citizens of heaven while living on earth."

go to

flee
James 4:7

Second, Paul continues with another analogy of an athletic team. "Contending" or "striving" is the translation of a Greek word used for athletic contests. In English, our words *athlete* and *athletics* come from it. Paul is referring to athletic contests where teams work together toward victory. He wants the believers to be unified in working toward a common goal: seeing Jesus glorified and the gospel preached.

They won't do that if they are "terrified," the Greek word *ptyromai*, of the enemy Satan or those who oppose Christianity. When a Christian isn't afraid when faced by opposition, he demonstrates to an unbeliever his strength in his faith, which unnerves the opponent. Plus, such power forces Satan to <u>flee</u> when he is resisted.

what others say

Earl Palmer

During the summer of 1987 I taught a summer school class on Philippians at Regent College in Vancouver, B.C. During one of the morning sessions we discussed this word, and during the coffee break a young man from Calgary sought me out because this word *ptyromai* had caught his attention. He was a rancher who worked with horses, and he told me that those who handle horses know all about *ptyromai* because it describes a horse that is "spooked" by something. He told me of races that are held in Calgary which test this very quality in horses as they run through a designed course that contains various jumps, obstacles, and bridge crossings that ordinarily startle horses. The challenge of the race is to find the rider and the horse that are least easily spooked.[13]

If you and I have a spirit of victory that makes us focus on the overall needs of our Christian "team," we aren't going to be *ptyromai* by the schemes of the evil one. One of his favorite schemes is to make us fall back into selfishness. When we don't fall back into our natural form of selfishness, it shows that we truly are walking in God's power—and that brings glory to God. Plus, we are encouraged in our Christian walk to know we're pleasing God. We are more convinced in those moments that the Lord is real, our salvation is secure, and God will have victory over evil in this world.

apply it

go to

suffer
1 Peter 4:12–13

A spirit of victory empowers selflessness. When Christians are fighting Satan's evil plan, putting aside their own agenda, and not fighting among themselves, their enemies will understand they're on a losing team. Then Christians will be stronger in defending their own opinion. We'll be more convinced we're fighting on the winning side and more eager to cooperate with each other. We won't be afraid as we face our opponents, whether they are unbelievers wanting to block our sharing of the gospel or satanic forces oppressing those we love.

I've often seen football or hockey players fighting a member of the opposite team, but I've never seen two members on the same side fighting each other. Because they are unified toward their desire for victory, their focus is on defeating the other team, not tearing down their own team. Let's not fight within our Christian ranks.

You Can Rejoice in Suffering

PHILIPPIANS 1:29–30 *For to you it has been granted on behalf of Christ, not only to believe in Him, but also to suffer for His sake, having the same conflict which you saw in me and now hear is in me.* (NKJV)

If you were to take a survey that asked, "Would you like to invite suffering into your life?" chances are no one would say yes. No one volunteers for difficulty, and no one wants to suffer. However, Paul says that suffering is something all Christians will experience, just as he did. Sometimes the spirit of victory that Paul is advocating is subdued when we believe the lie that our Christian life should bring only good experiences and feelings. Most of us came to know Christ because we "want to live life without worry or fear" or we "want to be happy and Jesus seems to offer happiness." But once we know Christ and we still struggle, we shouldn't allow the surprise of it to take away the joy Paul wants us to have. Paul says to his readers, "You will <u>suffer</u>. I suffer. Don't expect anything else." And of course, he wants that suffering to represent and glorify Christ—the purpose of everything he's written in this chapter.

go to

refined
1 Peter 5:10

stronger
James 1:2–4

only results
Job 8:1–4

surprised
1 Peter 4:12

key point

what others say

Joseph Stowell

As we race toward the close of the twentieth century, most of the emphasis in Christianity is on becoming happier here, healed here, more blessed here, and more fulfilled here. Worship must excite our spirits, sermons must entertain and enthrall our minds, music must penetrate and propel us. And our counseling must make us feel better about ourselves and strengthen our human bond of friendship and family. While this may be nice and necessary, without heaven in clear view our Christianity fails to have a heavenward compulsion pulling us closer to God, closer to eternity, closer to home. It tends to become instead self-serving entertainment or a therapeutic center. A heavenless church seeks to satisfy longings and needs here rather than serving and sacrificing here with a view to satisfaction there.[14]

There are benefits of suffering. Here are some to consider:

• Our character is <u>refined</u>.

• We grow <u>stronger</u> as we depend upon God more faithfully.

• God is glorified through our ability to handle the suffering in His power.

• Those who claim to know Christ but don't are forced to evaluate their lack of commitment.

• Our fellow Christians are encouraged and inspired to trust God more.

• We long for heaven's joys even more and are willing to give up the false comforts of earth.

Some people think that suffering <u>only results</u> from being sinful. As a result, Christians who believe this way constantly feel defeated because they think their difficulties mean they've sinned. But problems come regardless of our spiritual purity or lack of it. That doesn't mean we should give up our goal of living a righteous life, but it does mean we shouldn't be surprised or discouraged by trials.

Chapter Wrap-Up

- Paul had a special place in his heart for the believers in Philippi, and he wanted them to know he loved them and prayed for them. He assured them that he knew God was working in them and that he desired for their love to grow and for them to seek to do the things that were excellent. (Philippians 1:1–11)

- The most important thing to Paul was that Jesus's love and free gift of salvation be made known to everyone—even at his expense. Paul didn't care what motives were behind people's preaching about Jesus; he just wanted Jesus lifted up. (Philippians 1:12–18)

- Paul was really torn between wanting to join Jesus in heaven and staying on earth to continue his ministry. He saw advantages and blessings in both. Although he really couldn't pick his death, he decided that staying on earth would benefit his fellow Christians more, so he was willing to sacrifice his own heavenly joy to stay with them. (Philippians 1:19–26)

- All Christians experience strife; it shouldn't surprise them. If they will not be overwhelmed and instead stay unified with other believers, the enemies of the gospel will see that they will not be victorious in defeating Christians. (Philippians 1:27–30)

Study Questions

1. What was Paul confident of and what did he pray for the Philippians?

2. Why didn't it bother Paul that some people preached about Jesus even from the wrong motive?

3. Why did Paul decide he'd rather stay here on earth than join Jesus in heaven?

4. How could believers show their enemies that they would be victorious in the Christian life?

Philippians 2
Be Humble and Don't Grumble

Chapter Highlights:
• No Man Is an Island
• Beam Me Down
• But I Thought I Was Saved by Grace
• Here's Timothy!

Let's Get Started

Paul wants his readers to be united, and he carries through with his theme by giving them several ways to do that: by being humble and selfless. How? He first lists Jesus as the ultimate example. Then he points to himself, Timothy, and Epaphroditus as examples of those who are living selflessly, who offer a pattern for harmonious relationships.

Sprinkled among Paul's examples are wonderful insights for unity: seeing the benefits, seeing others as better than yourself, and refraining from grumbling and complaining. Paul never lacks practical and inspirational ideas for his themes. We'll be challenged by his exhortation. Let's see what he says in order for us to accomplish God's goal for us.

strength
Ecclesiastes 4:12

No Man Is an Island or a Continent

PHILIPPIANS 2:1 *Therefore if there is any consolation in Christ, if any comfort of love, if any fellowship of the Spirit, if any affection and mercy,* (NKJV)

Paul is going to be encouraging his readers to be selfless (or like-minded), so he begins setting the stage by continuing his thought from the end of chapter 1. He says, in effect, "I've called you to spiritual unity with other believers, and now I'm going to tell you why you can have that unity. Then I'll tell you to be selfless." He lists four reasons for being unified and says that if they will carry those out, he will be filled with joy. Those four reasons are:

• *Consolation or encouragement from being united in Christ.* There are <u>strength</u> and encouragement in numbers. Paul wants them to see the advantages of being unified, of being a part of the body of Christ. When we are selfless and looking out for the needs of others, it's much easier to be like-minded. Having the common purpose of seeing God glorified helps take away our need to stand out or get our own way. God wants you to be unified with your brothers and sisters in Christ.

96% 40

go to

indwells
1 Corinthians 6:19

servant
Mark 10:43–45

God empower thru the Holy Spirit

- *Comfort from God's love.* If everyone in a group knows that their master or leader loves them equally, they don't have to contend with each other for his attention. Knowing God loves every member of the body of Christ should diminish disunity between them: They don't have to compete for God's love. They can be secure and comforted by that thought.

- *Fellowship of the Holy Spirit.* Since the Holy Spirit <u>indwells</u> every believer, there doesn't need to be competition. They are united by His presence within each one, for they have a common motivation inspired by God's Spirit. Paul says there are lots of reasons to be unified, but it's primarily wrapped in the gift of the presence of the Holy Spirit, who never draws attention to Himself. Although of equal importance within the Trinity, and yet a distinct element, He always seeks to have the Father God elevated so that people will praise him. No wonder the Spirit seeks to encourage unity within each of us—He's an expert at it!

- *Affection and Mercy.* The Spirit is the "common denominator" within every Christian and if we let Him, He will give a desire for unity by developing caring attitudes toward others.

All these things are impossible for a person to do without God's help. But when God calls His children to any behavior, He empowers them to carry it out.

If we don't understand the meaning of Paul's use of the word *if*, we might think he's saying it's only a possibility. In his perspective, it's not a possibility; it's a certainty. He's not saying, "Consider whether you have encouragement, comfort, affection, and mercy." He's actually saying, "Since you have" or "In light of" those things available to you, you can be unified and have the same purposes for God's glory.

> ### what others say
>
> **Henry T. Blackaby and Claude V. King**
>
> Some would define a <u>servant</u> like this: "A servant is one who finds out what his master wants him to do, and then he does it." The human concept of a servant is that a servant goes to the master and says, "Master, what do you want me to do?" The master tells him, and the servant goes off by *himself* and does it. That is not the biblical concept of a *servant* of God. Being a servant of God is different from being a servant of a human master. A servant of a human master works for his master. God, however, works *through* his servants.[1]

Paul stresses the importance of fellowship with other Christians, but at times, we can begin to believe we should be "Lone Ranger Christians." The fact is, though, we <u>need</u> each other. Fellowship, or the Greek word *koinonia*, can be translated "<u>partnership</u>." We are all partners with each other in the <u>body of Christ</u>; each is connected with the success of the others. Yet, Paul will clarify in a bit that none of us is not more important than another. We're neither an island nor a continent.

Don't Go to the Wizard of Oz for the Same Brain

PHILIPPIANS 2:2 *fulfill my joy by being like-minded, having the same love, being of one accord, of one mind.* (NKJV)

unity not uniformity

After mentioning the reasons for their unity in verse 1, he declares the results of their unity:

- *Like-mindedness:* thinking the same way. Each person will see life from God's perspective rather than from an earthly perspective

- *Love:* each believer will want whatever is best for their brother or sister in Christ

- *Of One Accord:* not disagreeing. Being willing to <u>change</u> their own ideas if they are wrong in their thinking

- *Of One Mind:* wanting the same thing: God's purposes to be revealed and fulfilled.

Paul is not suggesting that there will never be disagreements or differences of opinion. Unity and uniformity aren't the same thing. With unity, we regard others as being on the same side instead of being enemies; we have the same goals. But with uniformity, no one is different. That's not what Paul wants from his readers.

what others say

J. Vernon McGee

To be of one accord does not mean you have to be a duplicate. You don't have to be a Xerox copy of someone else, nor do you have to be a "yes man." It does mean that believers should seek a common ground of agreement. You can disagree on minor points of doctrine and still be "of one accord."[2]

need
Hebrews 10:25

body of Christ
1 Corinthians
12:12–27

love
John 13:34–35

change
Philippians 3:15

ambitious
Galatians 5:20

good
Galatians 6:2

The book of Acts gives us a glimpse into the diversity within the Philippian church, which served people who came from all over the civilized world. No wonder Paul was concerned about unity amid such a variety of backgrounds. In the church at Philippi, there were:

Different People in the Church at Philippi

Person	Passage	Background
Lydia	Acts 16:14	A Gentile from Asia who was a convert first to Judaism and then to Christ through Paul's ministry. She was a wealthy businesswoman.
Slave girl	Acts 16:16–18	She first harassed Paul because she was possessed by a demon and used by her masters for fortune-telling. Paul cast the demon out of her and she believed in Christ. Commentators believe she was originally from Greece.
Jailer	Acts 16:25–36	He was probably a Roman who was assigned to Philippi to guard it as one of the Roman colonies. His family was with him, and all of them came to know Christ after Paul was miraculously freed of his chains during an earthquake.

Being unified doesn't mean never having disagreements or having a separate opinion. It does mean to willingly be open to God's guidance about our own ideas and to willingly release what may seem absolutely the only way to think! When we are open to other people's ideas, we're really showing the Holy Spirit's presence in a powerful way. That brings such glory to God in the eyes of others.

Don't Have a "Party" Spirit

PHILIPPIANS 2:3–4 *Let nothing be done through selfish ambition or conceit, but in lowliness of mind let each esteem others better than himself. Let each of you look out not only for his own interests, but also for the interests of others. (NKJV)*

Paul doesn't just say, "Don't be <u>ambitious</u> or self-centered," but wisely tells the Philippians the positive of what they should do—be humble and seek the <u>good</u> of others. He constructively exhorts them about both what they should avoid and what they should do. If they follow his instructions, they will achieve unity, for unity is the result of giving up wanting your own way and humbly seeking the good of others. We can only be humble and loving when we esteem others and value their interests just as highly as our own.

lift
James 4:10

secret
Matthew 6:1–2

rewards
Matthew 16:27

what others say

C. S. Lewis

If anyone would like to acquire humility, I can, I think, tell him the first step. The first step is to realize that one is proud. And a biggish step, too. At least, nothing whatever can be done before it. If you think you are not conceited, it means you are very conceited indeed.[3]

Jill Briscoe

But the Lord delights to hear the prayers of inadequacy—those requests that speak of our desperate need of Him. The one who prays in humility is heard loud and clear in the heavenlies. God delights, not only to hear such prayers, but to answer them. He loves to lean out of heaven and assure us that He has not made us like King David, but He has made us like us.[4]

When you instruct or teach people, don't just tell them what *not* to do—but also tell them what they should do. Being practical and positive gives people hope. If we tell them only, "Don't do this," they won't know what they really should be doing. This is especially true in family life, and particularly with our children.

Humility is not thinking of myself as a worm—lacking in value to God and others. Humility wisely acknowledges my abilities and talents and credits them as gifts from God. Therefore He deserves the credit, not myself. Paul gave an explanation of true humility in his letter to the Romans: "For I say, through the grace given to me, to everyone who is among you, not to think of himself more highly than he ought to think, but to think soberly, as God has dealt to each one a measure of faith" (Romans 12:3 NKJV).

Humility is a by-product of completely trusting God. When we believe He can <u>lift</u> us up if that is appropriate, we don't need to try to parade ourselves before others as worthy of credit. Instead, we can be content behind the scenes, knowing our God sees everything done in <u>secret</u> and <u>rewards</u> those who serve Him with a humble heart.

In addition, humility is not something that we actively develop by concentrating on it. Saying, "I'm going to be humble today" only makes me focus on myself. But by saying, "I'm going to meet the needs of others today," we inadvertently fertilize and loosen the soil where the seeds of humility will grow deep.

go to

privileges
John 17:5

sin
Hebrews 4:15

servant
Mark 10:45

will
John 5:30

despicable
Galatians 3:13

God-nature
John 1:1

nature
Hebrews 2:17–18

rights
Matthew 24:36

limitations
2 Corinthians 8:9

willingly
John 10:18

incarnation
God becoming
human

Beam Me Down

PHILIPPIANS 2:5–8 *Let this mind be in you which was also in Christ Jesus, who, being in the form of God, did not consider it robbery to be equal with God, but made Himself of no reputation, taking the form of a bondservant, and coming in the likeness of men.*

And being found in appearance as a man, He humbled Himself and became obedient to the point of death, even the death of the cross. (NKJV)

It must not have taken long for Paul to come up with the best example of humility—Jesus, of course! Talk about humility. In beautiful, descriptive language, Paul describes Jesus's willingness to give up the advantages and <u>privileges</u> of being a part of the Trinity and take the temporary form of a man—yet without <u>sin</u>. Such a transformation is called the **incarnation** of Jesus. Jesus became a <u>servant</u> to God's <u>will</u>, even to the point of dying the most <u>despicable</u> death ever invented, death on a cross. That's humility to the nth degree.

Jesus's <u>God-nature</u> never left him, even as He took on the "<u>nature</u>" of a human. The human form changed because He was born a baby and His body grew into a man. In the Resurrection, He changed his form again, and went to heaven with the form of both His divine nature and a human one.

But through all His time on earth as a human, He didn't leave His divine nature behind, only His <u>rights</u> as the Son of God. He was willing to obey the Father and subject Himself to the <u>limitations</u> that every human faces. And the greatest limitation He faced was death—a death He <u>willingly</u> chose.

When someone is willing to not use the abilities and rights that they are entitled to, that's ultimate humility. It would be like the president of the United States choosing to ride in a commuter airline rather than on Air Force One. Jesus with premeditation gave up His ability to be protected as God and willingly allowed Himself to suffer as a human, even to the point of sacrificing His life. Paul could not have given a more descriptive and powerful example of humility.

Jesus truly was selfless in making such a huge sacrifice. It's only an inadequate comparison, but from a human standpoint, it would be like someone losing their sight, or hearing, or ability to feel, or ability to move. Until we've lost something that we take for granted, we can't imagine the loss. Jesus willingly sacrificed His ability to have

His needs met in supernatural ways. He was hungry and <u>tempted</u> in the wilderness, He grew <u>tired</u>, He felt the sting of <u>rejection</u>, and He <u>cried</u> at the death of a friend. He humbled Himself by taking on our human nature for one grand purpose: to reveal the Father's love through sacrificing His own life on a cross.

go to

tempted
Matthew 4:1–11

tired
John 4:6

rejection
John 18:25–27

cried
John 11:35

---

what others say

Kenneth S. Wuest

The expression could be translated in a number of ways, each of which while holding to the main idea, yet brings out a slightly different shade of meaning. For instance: "Be constantly thinking this in yourselves"; "Be having this mind in you"; "Reflect in your own minds, the mind of Christ Jesus" (Lightfoot); "Let the same purpose inspire you as was in Christ Jesus" (Way). The sum total of the thought in the exhortation seems to be that of urging the Philippians to emulate in their own lives, the distinctive virtues of the Lord Jesus spoken of in 2:2–4.[5]

Lloyd John Ogilvie

By disposition [attitude] I mean more than countenance or facial expression; it is the inner quality of life which expresses itself in attitudes, actions, and awareness. It is the outer expression of the integration of thought, feelings, and will around a unifying motive.[6]

C. S. Lewis

The Eternal Being, who knows everything and who created the whole universe, became not only a man but (before that) a baby, and before that a fetus inside a woman's body. If you want to get the hang of it, think how you would like to become a slug or a crab.[7]

The Incarnation

Scripture	Details About Jesus's Transformation from God into Human Form
John 1:1–14	Jesus became a man with the purpose of showing God to people and saving them from their sins.
Romans 1:2–5	Jesus's resurrection confirms that He was God and man.
2 Corinthians 8:9	Jesus left the riches of heaven to encounter the poverty of earth.
1 Timothy 3:16	Jesus was affirmed as God and man in many different ways.
Hebrews 2:14	As a man, Jesus defeated death's control through His own death and resurrection.
1 John 1:1–3	Many testify to Jesus's form as a human with divine characteristics.

go to

exaltation
Hebrews 2:9; 12:2

bow
Romans 14:11;
Revelation 15:3–4

adoration
Isaiah 45:23–24

Old Testament
Deuteronomy 16:11

Bow the Knee

PHILIPPIANS 2:9–11 *Therefore God also has highly exalted Him and given Him the name which is above every name, that at the name of Jesus every knee should bow, of those in heaven, and of those on earth, and of those under the earth, and that every tongue should confess that Jesus Christ is Lord, to the glory of God the Father. (NKJV)*

Jesus's sacrifice as a man on the cross prepared Him for <u>exaltation</u>. He didn't obey God with the motive of being exalted, but God lifted Him up nonetheless. When Paul says God bestowed on Jesus "the name," this is not some ordinary naming, for the definite article "the" appears in the Greek text and refers to a particular name.

Because this name of Jesus is so great and above every name, every knee will <u>bow</u> before Him. What a glorious thought! When you and I are in heaven, every single being will acknowledge that Jesus is God, and they will worship Him! That includes every human along with angels—even the fallen angels. Not only will they say, "Jesus is Lord," they will worship Him, praising Him as almighty God. What glory that will be! Our beloved Savior will finally receive all the <u>adoration</u> He deserves—which He didn't receive when He was on earth.

The title "The Name" is a very common Hebrew title, denoting office, rank, and dignity. If we can think of how that term is used in describing God in the <u>Old Testament</u>, we can begin to have a feel for its significance. It denotes the divine presence, the divine majesty, as the object of adoration and praise. It includes all that the majesty of God represents.

what others say

Evelyn Christenson

Jesus was completely victorious over Satan on the cross of Calvary. There are no future rematches. No best two out of three tries. It was a final, complete victory for Jesus.[8]

Anne Graham Lotz

Whoever, or whatever, sets themselves against Christ will find themselves sooner or later on their faces before Him.[9]

The fact that everyone will acknowledge Jesus as God can give us some sense of satisfaction, since people in our day often turn up their noses at the thought of God or Jesus. They disdainfully profess that they don't need God, believing that Jesus wasn't God while on earth and certainly isn't relevant now.

But someday, regardless of how self-righteous their efforts and independence, they will confess that Jesus is indeed God . . . and bow before Him. And since the word *confess* means to "declare or confess openly or plainly" and "to offer praise or thanksgiving," their confession and acknowledgment will not be concealed in some hidden place. No, we all will be there to witness it and join in!

Prophecy

I Thought I Was Saved by Grace

PHILIPPIANS 2:12–13 *Therefore, my beloved, as you have always obeyed, not as in my presence only, but now much more in my absence, work out your own salvation with fear and trembling; for it is God who works in you both to will and to do for His good pleasure.* (NKJV)

Even though Paul is going to strongly exhort them, he does it lovingly, calling them his "beloved" friends. Then he reminds them that they have always obeyed, both when he is there and when he is absent. Paul graciously shone the best light on their behavior, since no one could obey completely. Obviously, he's hoping to inspire them to continue obeying—especially in the area most uppermost in his mind right now: church unity. He wants them to work together in harmony and living the way they should—to represent that they have indeed been saved.

Knowing that God will judge them in the end, Paul says they should live like Christians who have already been set free from the sin that had previously held them bondage. But that kind of obedient living can't be done in their own power; it must be done through God's power and their cooperation. Therefore, he says, "Obey because God motivates you from the inside out." That doesn't mean Paul is telling them to earn their salvation through their fear and trembling.

Something to ponder

This is one of those verses in the New Testament that have created controversy. On the one hand, people say that Paul's words to "work out your own salvation" prove that we must earn our salvation. They say, "Earn salvation through your works. It's all up to you."

And it would continue to be confusing if we didn't compare these verses with others to clarify Paul's meaning. That's what Paul's writings in the Epistle to the Ephesians do for us. In Ephesians 2:8–9,

go to

conformed
Romans 12:1–2

image
Romans 8:29

Paul assures us, "For by grace you have been saved through faith, and that not of yourselves; it is the gift of God, not of works, lest anyone should boast" (NKJV). And Paul writes to Titus, "Not by works of righteousness which we have done, but according to His mercy He saved us, through the washing of regeneration and renewing of the Holy Spirit" (Titus 3:5–6 NKJV). Paul would not contradict himself; therefore, we can look at the whole message to be sure that Paul is saying:

- Salvation is through faith in Christ's substitutionary death on the cross alone and not by earning it with good works.

- Once we're saved through faith, we continue allowing the Holy Spirit to empower us to change.

Paul wants them to demonstrate their salvation through living the way God wants them to live—thus being <u>conformed</u> to the <u>image</u> of Jesus.

what others say

Warren Wiersbe

The Christian life is not a series of ups and downs. It is rather a process of "ins and outs." God works *in,* and we work *out.* We cultivate the submissive mind by responding to the divine provisions God makes available to us.[10]

William Barclay

This is not the fear and trembling of the slave cringing before his master; nor fear and trembling at the prospect of punishment. It comes from two things. It comes, first, from a sense of our own creatureliness and our own powerlessness to deal with life triumphantly. . . . It comes, second, from a horror of grieving God. When we really love a person, we are not afraid of what he may do to us; we are afraid of what we may do to him.[11]

Pat Boone

I was brought up lovingly . . . with a deep reverence for God's Word, and I tried to live out Philippians 2:12: *"Continue to work out your salvation with fear and trembling."* That's a very tough job, and I gave it a good shot. But inevitably I would fail and "goof up" and feel guilty as a result.

Twenty years later I got around to reading the next verse, Philippians 2:13: *"For it is God who works in you to will and to act according to his good purpose."* When I finally invited Him to breathe His Holy Spirit into me, I realized He would

> create in me the desire to obey Him and give me the ability to do it! He knew how impossible it was for me to obey Him on my own initiative, but had already provided the fuel if I would just receive it.[12]

determined
Isaiah 25:1

wilderness
Exodus 16:7;
1 Corinthians 10:10

The Greek word for "work," *energein*, which Paul uses in the phrase "It is God who works in you," means "to energize, to work effectively." The English words *energy* and *energize* come from it. Therefore, it is God who is energizing us within our inner beings to complete the great things He has planned for us to do. Of course, we still have to choose to obey, but for whatever He wants us to do, He provides sufficient power.

The meaning of this Greek word makes it very clear that it is not our efforts that make God's power work on a daily basis. We don't have to grit our teeth and tell ourselves we must make things happen to bring glory to God or to obey Him. He has already <u>determined</u> the things He wants us to do. We just have to cooperate, live close enough to hear His directions, and then do what He says. That brings freedom!

Don't Whine, Wail, or Whimper

> PHILIPPIANS 2:14–16 *Do all things without complaining and disputing, that you may become blameless and harmless, children of God without fault in the midst of a crooked and perverse generation, among whom you shine as lights in the world, holding fast the word of life, so that I may rejoice in the day of Christ that I have not run in vain or labored in vain.* (NKJV)

When we are successful in seeing God's work in our lives, we would expect that we would have good attitudes about everything and everyone. So why does Paul next need to write, "Don't complain or argue"? Because Paul knows that it's often our successes that make us want to grumble and complain about others. After all, if we've overcome problems in God's power, why can't others? If we've seen God work through us, why can't other Christians have the same effectiveness?

The word *complaining* is the same Greek word, *goggusmos*, that is used to describe the Israelites' grumbling in their <u>wilderness</u> wanderings. It carries the idea of "inward questionings," like the dissatisfied mutterings of a group who distrust their leaders and could

rewarded
1 Thessalonians
2:19–20

light-bringers
Matthew 5:14

distinguish
John 13:35

light
John 8:12

erupt into a violent mob at any moment. The other word Paul uses, *disputing*, is the Greek word *dialogismos*, which describes more vocal arguing. Behind these words is the idea of questioning another person's integrity with suspicion or doubt.

The word *blameless* means "above reproach," so that unbelievers cannot point a criticizing finger at the Philippian believers. We could assume it refers to living perfect lives, but it does not mean being without sin or performing perfectly. Paul wanted these believers to grow in their faith and in their ability to live godly lives more faithfully. Along those same lines, Paul uses the word *harmless*, which in the Greek applies to wine that isn't diluted and metal that isn't weakened. Paul wanted the Philippians to live powerfully in God's strength with no disunity diluting their message of love and joy in Christ.

Whining only brings bad representation for God. No wonder Paul wants the Philippians to "become blameless and harmless," "without fault," "holding fast the word of life," so that Paul's efforts will be <u>rewarded</u>. He wants them not to do anything that would make people point to them and say, "Look at those Christians! They call themselves holy, but see what they do?" It's only as we respond to unbelievers with righteous and loving behavior that we represent God as <u>light-bringers</u> on earth.

Since Paul's continuing theme is unity, he wants them to shine as people who have harmonious relationships. If they would, people would stare and say, "Wow! Those Christians sure know how to love each other." And that's exactly what Jesus said would <u>distinguish</u> His followers.

When Paul writes "holding fast the word of life," the word for "hold fast" is *epechontes*, which means to "hold forth" or "hold firmly." Therefore, he could be saying, "Hold the word of life close to you and don't let go," or "Offer the word to others." Some commentators think *epechontes* refers to how guests were offered wine at a secular Greek banquet. The fact that Paul then refers to Christians "[shining] as lights" would support this view, because they are offering or "holding forth" Jesus as the <u>light</u> to a darkened world.

what others say

John F. Walvoord

One of the most common failures of Christians who have lost sight of the wonder of God's grace is the tendency to complain, often about simple things such as food and drink, as illustrated in the children of Israel in the wilderness. Such complaining, however, is a symptom of a deep-seated spiritual problem—failure to really trust God and failure to be submissive to His providential provision.[13]

go to

unbelievers
1 Timothy 4:15

Gigi Graham Tchividjian

Not long ago I had a burr in my life that caused me much irritation, and I howled loud and long. Finally I gave up. "Lord," I prayed, "I'm tired of this burr. But I'm even more tired of howling about it." So I began to thank Him and praise Him for what He was doing in my life through this burr. To my amazement I found that, although the burr was still there, it had lost its power to irritate. Give Him your burrs, and He will give you the grace to overcome the habit of howling.[14]

As imperfect Christians, we could easily become discouraged thinking we aren't "blameless" and "harmless." But God knows we'll never become perfect on this earth and intends to use us regardless. Although we should be seeking His power to grow stronger in faith and in righteous living, there will always be something we'll need to work on.

something to ponder

Also consider these reasons that God doesn't allow us to become perfect on this earth:

- If we became perfect, we'd be proud of it and that would be a barrier to our witness.

- If we became perfect, we would be even more intimidating to others because they would think, *Well, I'll never be perfect, so why trust in their God? I can't do that.*

- Our testimony is still powerful, though based on imperfection, because of what God really is doing in our lives—and that's a lot!

- As we continue to struggle and then overcome each challenge, we are gaining more valuable insights to share with others in their struggles.

We usually feel justified when we are tempted to grumble and complain. But we need to stop and consider what kind of testimony we are presenting to others—especially <u>unbelievers</u> who are watching and ready to point an accusing finger. This is especially true in our marriage and family relationships. We often don't allow God's

strengthen your family

drink offering
Numbers 15:7

Spirit to help us guard against complaining with family members because at home we can "let our hair down." We think no one is aware inside our own home, but the truth will always be revealed. Besides, our motives should be to lovingly want the best for the most important people in our lives. That means being patient and thinking positively.

When we grumble and complain about anyone, particularly family members, we forget how much God has forgiven us. Instead of passing that wonderful grace along to others, we find ways to criticize, gossip, and backbite. Instead of arguing to change their opinions, we can believe that God will do according to His will and as we pray. We can calmly share our perspective and opinion and not try to force them to change. We'll have a sweeter attitude when we can trust Him enough to remember that He wants what's best for His bride, the body of Christ.

Don't Be Sad or Mad; Be Glad

PHILIPPIANS 2:17–18 *Yes, and if I am being poured out as a drink offering on the sacrifice and service of your faith, I am glad and rejoice with you all. For the same reason you also be glad and rejoice with me. (NKJV)*

In case the Philippians began to feel responsible for Paul's imprisonment and possibly his future death, Paul urges them not to feel guilt-ridden, but glad. Of course, the Philippians weren't the direct cause of Paul's potentially being tried and executed for his faith and service, but they were one of many groups Paul ministered to, and he wouldn't have been in prison if he weren't serving them. They could easily have thought, *If only Paul weren't going around to all of us preaching the gospel, his life wouldn't be in danger.* But Paul didn't want them brooding over what-ifs. He served them gladly, and he would give up his life if it were God's plan, especially if it advanced the gospel message. Paul didn't just want them not to be sad; he wanted them to actively rejoice in his sacrificial service.

When Paul referred to a drink offering he could have been thinking of two things—either the drink offering that the Israelites gave because of God's commands, or the cup of wine, called *libations*, that idol worshippers poured out to their gods. This second kind of "grace," which acknowledged their particular god, was given at the beginning and the end of the meal. Because the readers of his letter were primarily Gentiles and not Jews, and because Paul uses references to all elements of life, such as athletic games, some commentators believe he was most likely referring to the idol worship.

Although few of us will actually sacrifice our life in service for God, it would be a challenge to think through what our attitude might be if we were ever brought to that point. Would we be sad, glad, or mad? In a sense we can employ Paul's selfless attitude as we make a daily choice of rejoicing while facing small sacrifices—even if it's not death. When things go different than we thought or people don't meet up to our expectations, we can choose to emulate his attitude: Be glad and rejoice!

something to ponder

Now, Here's Timothy!

PHILIPPIANS 2:19–24 *But I trust in the Lord Jesus to send Timothy to you shortly, that I also may be encouraged when I know your state. For I have no one like-minded, who will sincerely care for your state. For all seek their own, not the things which are of Christ Jesus. But you know his proven character, that as a son with his father he served with me in the gospel. Therefore I hope to send him at once, as soon as I see how it goes with me. But I trust in the Lord that I myself shall also come shortly. (NKJV)*

traveled
Acts 16:12

Derbe, Lystra
Acts 16:1

Eunice and Lois
2 Timothy 1:5

circumcised
Acts 16:3

taught him
2 Timothy 3:15

spiritual son
1 Timothy 1:2

set free
Hebrews 13:23

valuable
1 Corinthians 4:17

Paul has already cited Jesus as an example of humility and selflessness—the reservoir for unity. As if his readers might feel intimidated by such an extreme example of selflessness, he lowers his sights to "real" people like himself, Timothy, and Epaphroditus. First, he points his finger at his traveling buddy, Timothy. Timothy would have been well known to the believers in Philippi because Timothy traveled with Paul when he visited there.

Although we don't know a lot about Timothy, we do know that he was born in Derbe or Lystra, located in present-day Turkey. His mother, Eunice, was a Jewess and his grandmother's name was Lois. We don't know his father's name, but he was a Greek. Since Timothy had not been circumcised, that would indicate he was raised and educated in Greek ways. Eunice or Lois taught him about the Scriptures.

We don't know exactly how or when Timothy believed in Jesus as his Messiah, but evidently he was already a believer when Paul first met him on Paul's second missionary journey because Acts 16:1 refers to him as "a certain disciple [who] was there, named Timothy" (NKJV). But Paul refers to Timothy as his spiritual son, which would indicate the great affection Paul had for him. And they did spend much time together, because Timothy joined Paul's small but loyal band of companions traveling with him on his missionary journeys. At some point Timothy must have been imprisoned for his faith, because Paul refers to Timothy's being set free.

Paul had no trouble giving credit to another. And the credit he gave about Timothy was luxurious. "Timothy is my soul mate. He has the same purposes I do," Paul writes. "Many others aren't seeking the interests of Jesus Christ, but my son Timothy is. He has proven himself valuable." Because of Paul's own sincere humility, he has no hesitation in building up others.

As an example of humility and selflessness that brings unity, Timothy doesn't mind playing "second fiddle" to Paul. He doesn't have his own agenda to establish his own international ministry because Paul is sidetracked in prison. He's not hanging out his shingle, "Timothy Ministries," with the logo "Secondhand man to the apostle Paul: I try harder." There seems to be no jealousy or envy in him. He doesn't have a competitive spirit. Truly, those are the characteristics of a genuinely humble person who wants to foster unity among believers.

Paul was willing to sacrifice Timothy's helpful presence for the good of the Philippians and in order to hear how his friends in Philippi were doing. Paul was constantly thinking of the good of others. If Timothy could visit the believers in Philippi and be of assistance to them—plus carry back a report from them—then Paul would graciously arrange for him to visit them. He wanted the best for others.

Timothy's Strengths and Weaknesses

Scripture	Strengths	Weaknesses
1 Corinthians 16:10	Did the work of the Lord	Had a tendency to be fearful
1 Corinthians 16:11		Felt insecure, fearful of being despised
2 Corinthians 1:19	Preached faithfully in Macedonia	
Philippians 1:1	Paul identified Timothy as a bondservant like himself	
Philippians 1:20	Sincerely cared for others	
Philippians 1:22	Had a proven character	
1 Thessalonians 3:2	Established others in their faith	
1 Timothy 1:3–5	Stood strong as the pastor in Ephesus against false teachers	
1 Timothy 4:12		Insecure about his youthfulness
1 Timothy 4:14		Paul needed to remind him about his spiritual gifts
2 Timothy 1:7–8		Paul urged him not to be fearful or ashamed
2 Timothy 3:10	Faithfully followed and emulated Paul's life	

apply it

When we're truly humble, we don't have trouble building up others. We can brag on others because we don't need the stroking ourselves. In contrast, when we're insecure and feeling inferior, we need to have the focus on ourselves. Or sometimes we respond with <u>gossip</u>, thinking that tearing down someone else will put us a notch higher. But it does just the opposite. It makes people disrespectful of us as they see how unloving and mean we are. We can resist those mean-spirited responses by remembering that building up others makes us look good and that we can trust God to <u>elevate</u> us at the right time.

something to ponder

Paul was Timothy's mentor. Paul was grooming Timothy to take over his ministry when he died—either soon or in the future—as the Lord directed. In much the same way, each of us can "reproduce" ourselves by mentoring others. That might take the form of an <u>older woman</u> teaching a young woman how to be a good mom and wife. It can be a seasoned Bible teacher advising someone on how to walk the Christian life. Or a couple who have been married many years counseling a young couple who are having struggles. Jesus modeled a mentor who poured His life into twelve disciples. We should do the same—with the goal of their becoming Jesus's strong followers.

And Here's Epaphroditus Too!

go to

gossip
Proverbs 18:8

elevate
James 4:10

older woman
Titus 2:3–5

epistle
letter

PHILIPPIANS 2:25–30 *Yet I considered it necessary to send to you Epaphroditus, my brother, fellow worker, and fellow soldier, but your messenger and the one who ministered to my need; since he was longing for you all, and was distressed because you had heard that he was sick. For indeed he was sick almost unto death; but God had mercy on him, and not only on him but on me also, lest I should have sorrow upon sorrow. Therefore I sent him the more eagerly, that when you see him again you may rejoice, and I may be less sorrowful. Receive him therefore in the Lord with all gladness, and hold such men in esteem; because for the work of Christ he came close to death, not regarding his life, to supply what was lacking in your service toward me. (NKJV)*

Epaphroditus is only mentioned in this **epistle** of Scripture. Although variations of his name appear in other passages, it is generally agreed that they are not the person Paul refers to here. Paul speaks highly of this servant of Christ Jesus. Although he is the pastor or an elder at the Philippian church, he brought their greetings and a financial love <u>gift</u> to Paul and has been staying with him. Now Paul is ready to send him back home with this letter Paul is writing.

Although we don't know the disease that almost cost Epaphroditus his life, most commentators agree that Epaphroditus is homesick to the point that he actually is returning to his home church earlier than originally planned. He is "distressed" and "longing" for the Philippians. The word *longing* can be more clearly identified as "intense longing, accompanied by distress." Some scholars writing about this section believe that a fever overtook him, but some wonder whether his homesickness created his disease.

Although we don't know what truly happened, Paul describes how Epaphroditus served to the point of risking his life. In those days, anyone who associated with a prisoner, like Paul, could easily be regarded as criminal material himself. Epaphroditus knew he could be viewed as dangerous. No wonder Paul says to "hold such men in esteem" and uses a word for "esteem" that could be interpreted as "hold precious." Paul reminds the Philippians that Epaphroditus was representing them as he served Paul—something they weren't able to do. That was another reason they should welcome back their church elder with eager arms.

Paul had given Epaphroditus an incredible recommendation. But there is a behind-the-scenes reason for these mighty descriptions. Paul is going to bat for Epaphroditus. Originally, Epaphroditus was supposed to stay longer with Paul; therefore, Paul fears that when Epaphroditus returns to Philippi, he'll be labeled a "quitter" or a "wimp." Paul points out all the good things about this servant of Christ in defense and prepares the way for Epaphroditus to return as a hero, not a failure.

Whether Epaphroditus expressed his own fear that he wouldn't be accepted and approved, we don't know. Paul may have wisely seen the possibility without Epaphroditus's even expressing his dread of the Philippians' response. Regardless, Epaphroditus, although an example of humility for his sacrificial service, is weak in an area. To Epaphroditus's credit, he was willing to risk returning, knowing what others might think of him. If he hadn't truly been humble, he would have stayed in Rome with Paul, fighting his homesick urgings because he didn't want anyone to see him struggling. But instead, he serves Paul by returning with word of Paul's condition. Again he risked his life—and his reputation—in service to the Lord.

gift
Philippians 4:18

Epaphroditus almost died, yet Paul doesn't give any indication that he tried to pray for his healing. Also, Paul doesn't indicate that Epaphroditus was out of the will of God and that's why he was very sick. Although we don't want to make conclusions based on what's not said, it is interesting that Paul doesn't say he prayed for Epaphroditus's healing—something that we would assume he would say. He does acknowledge thankfully—and rightfully so—God's mercy in sparing his friend's life.

> **what others say**
>
> **William Barclay**
>
> Paul is saying that for the sake of Jesus Christ Epaphroditus gambled his life. In the days of the Early Church there was an association of men and women called the *parabolani*, the gamblers. It was their aim to visit the prisoners and the sick, especially those who were ill with dangerous and infectious diseases. In AD 252 plague broke out in Carthage; the heathen threw out the bodies of their dead and fled in terror. Cyprian, the Christian bishop, gathered his congregation together and set them to burying the dead and nursing the sick in that plague-stricken city; and by so doing they saved the city, at the risk of their lives, from destruction and desolation.[18]

True love defends and thinks the best of the beloved. Paul wrote to the Corinthians that it "bears all things, believes all things, hopes all things, endures all things" (1 Corinthians 13:7 NKJV). We can take a lesson from Paul. Just as he defended Epaphroditus, we need to defend and unconditionally love and support other people.

Chapter Wrap-Up

- Selfishness is a sure way for people to feel disgruntled and upset with each other—and certainly not be unified. Paul says being selfless and humble will bring unity and it will make him glad. (Philippians 2:1–4)

- Jesus is the perfect example for Paul to point out as humble. He willingly left the beauty of heaven to sacrifice His life as a human. Although Jesus didn't sacrifice His God-nature, He did choose to set it aside so that He would have to experience all the disadvantages of being a human being. (Philippians 2:5–11)

- Paul knows his readers are already saved, but he wants them to live out their salvation with good works—something for which they will be judged. Therefore he encourages them to be in awe of God and do His will—which includes not grumbling or disputing with other Christians. (Philippians 2:12–18)

- Timothy is an example of humility because he wanted to serve Paul and advance the cause of the gospel. Paul really appreciated how Timothy was selfless and focused on the needs of others, not his own. (Philippians 2:19–24)

- Epaphroditus was sick to the point of death, but God spared his life—for which Paul is very grateful. Epaphroditus is an example because he was willing to go anywhere to be a servant for Paul and his congregation. (Philippians 2:25–30)

Study Questions

1. What is the main thing Paul says will develop unity and why?

2. Who is the best possible example Paul could choose for humility and why?

3. What does it mean when Paul says for the believers to work out their salvation with fear and trembling?

4. Who is the human example of humility that Paul uses and why?

5. How was Epaphroditus an example of humility and what happened to him?

Philippians 3
Pursuing Christ Above All Else

Let's Get Started

When we don't succeed or fulfill our goals, we can easily feel like failures. We tend to have to be accomplishing something (rather than just sitting), and we think the highest compliment someone can give us is "My, but you're busy these days." We puff out our chests and respond, "Yes, I am, aren't I?" We equate busyness and accomplishment with value and importance. Because so many of us are wrapped up in this kind of thinking, we need a mental transformation from being a "human doing" to a "human being."

This is where the apostle Paul would put up his hand and yell, "What you do isn't as important as what you are and who you know." The "who" he would be referring to is Jesus Christ. We need to value a relationship with Him above all the human efforts and signs of success, which often are only a self-protective cocoon of false self-importance. We'll find out how to do that in this next chapter, the third in Paul's letter to the Philippians.

rejoice
Philippians 1:18;
2:17–18

times
Philippians 4:4, 10

Rejoice!

> PHILIPPIANS 3:1 *Finally, my brethren, rejoice in the Lord. For me to write the same things to you is not tedious, but for you it is safe.* (NKJV)

Paul never seems to be at a loss for words, and he doesn't mind repeating himself. He has already told the Philippians four times to rejoice. By the time he's finished, he will say it three more times. That's a total of eight times, including this verse! He didn't seem to have any fear that the Philippians were putting their hands over their ears, scrunching up their foreheads, and screaming, "Enough already!" He also says he doesn't have any trouble repeating himself because he knows the reminder will serve the purpose of making them aware again of the essentials and foundation of the Christian faith: being joyful regardless of their circumstances. At that point, if his readers had been in the room with him, he most likely would

go to

attacks
Ephesians 6:11

assurance
1 John 5:13

source
2 Timothy 3:16–17

have rattled the chains that encased his hands and legs as a reminder of how anyone can choose to rejoice even when they are stuck in bad circumstances.

It never hurts for any of us to review the basics of our Christian beliefs because it guards our hearts. The Bible is our safeguard against wrong thinking. Reexamining the foundational principles keeps us strong and able to respond with trust in God to the <u>attacks</u> of Satan when he tries to make us distrust God's faithfulness. One of Satan's key plans is to make Christians doubt that they ever became Christians. In order to counter that, many Christians write the date when they received Christ as their personal Lord and Savior on the front page of their Bible. That way they can have it readily available to remind them that they did indeed make that commitment and thus have the <u>assurance</u> that it was real.

Because Paul wrote, "For me to write the same things to you . . . ," some commentators believe that Paul is referring to things he wrote in other letters to the Philippians. In other words, there could have been more than one letter from him to them. This might very well be true, since he wrote many letters to many different groups and individuals for sixteen years (AD 48 to 64), but there are only thirteen letters left. Although it's possible he went for long periods of time without writing, knowing his pattern that seems unlikely.

---

what others say

J. Vernon McGee

"Finally, my brethren" gives us the impression that Paul is coming to the conclusion of this epistle. He must have intended this to be a very brief thank-you note to the Philippian believers. But we are just midway in the epistle; so obviously the Spirit of God prompted him to go on.[1]

apply it

Don't depend exclusively upon your feelings or the ideas of others for knowledge about the Christian life and faith. The Bible is the only sure way to know what God has to say and what He wants. Although other godly Christians can be a valuable resource for advice, the Bible is the only indisputable <u>source</u>.

Facts About Christian Joy

Scripture	Fact
John 16:33	Joy is possible because Jesus has overcome the world, including the hard things that happen.
Romans 8:35–39	Nothing can separate us from God; therefore we can rejoice.
2 Corinthians 5:1–8	Heaven is waiting for us; therefore we have the assurance of eternal life.
Philippians 4:11–13, 19	Joy comes from contentment, e.g., believing God provides all of our true needs.
Romans 8:28	God promises to use everything bad for our good as we trust in Him.

go to

deal
Acts 15:1

false teachers
2 Corinthians 11:13

circumcised
Genesis 17:10

dogs
Isaiah 56:10

circumcised
removal of foreskin
of a male's penis

Be a Human Being—Not a Human Doing

PHILIPPIANS 3:2–3 *Beware of dogs, beware of evil workers, beware of the mutilation! For we are the circumcision, who worship God in the Spirit, rejoice in Christ Jesus, and have no confidence in the flesh, (NKJV)*

One of the basics of the Christian faith that Paul wants these believers to review is the fact that a relationship with God comes through grace—not earning it. This is the foundation of being a "human being" and not a "human doing." A "human doing" is intent on earning his own salvation through his efforts in keeping the Law or in becoming perfect. Paul has always had to <u>deal</u> with such people. He often came into contact with those who claimed they were Christians and yet wanted to add something more to God's free gift of Jesus's sacrifice. But Paul says only Jesus's death and resurrection are needed.

Paul knew that the Philippians were being bombarded with a message from <u>false teachers</u> that they must be **circumcised** in order to be saved. They taught that only Jews could be "saved," not Gentiles. And of course, a Gentile was anyone who wasn't a Jew. Therefore, if a Gentile wanted to know God, he must not only follow an unlimited number of Jewish laws; he must also identify himself as a Jew by being circumcised. Salvation had nothing to do with Jesus's death on the cross.

Paul doesn't mince his words as he calls these people "<u>dogs</u>" and evil people. They taught that cutting the flesh through circumcision made a person acceptable to God, but Paul said such actions only

heart circumcision
Colossians 2:11

death
Romans 5:10

mutilated the body and did nothing to purify the heart. True worship, or "heart circumcision," comes through rejoicing in what Jesus did when He died in the sinner's place. That's giving Jesus the glory He deserves, rather than taking credit for making yourself acceptable to God through circumcision.

Paul uses very strong language to identify a group of teachers who were trying to persuade the Philippians of a theology different from Paul's. He called them "dogs" and "evil workers." No wonder Paul didn't want the Philippians to believe those false teachers; if they did, they could never be certain that their works were "enough" to earn salvation. They would always be wondering and feeling stressed.

When Paul called these false teachers "dogs," he wasn't writing about the favored and lovable pets in our culture. In Paul's time, dogs were scavengers who roamed the streets eating whatever they could find. As a result, they were "unclean animals" because they ate the foods that Jews were forbidden to eat. They often traveled in packs and were dangerous. These evil teachers may have thought they were teaching the truth, but Paul clearly believes they were dangerous because they turned people away from believing in Jesus's death as the only way to gain a right standing with God.

God had a different idea than what the "evil workers" were teaching. God's plan is for anyone to accept His free gift of eternal life and then be assured that they are indeed in God's family and going to heaven. The apostle John wrote, "These things I have written to you who believe in the name of the Son of God, that you may know that you have eternal life, and that you may continue to believe in the name of the Son of God" (1 John 5:13 NKJV). John didn't write "that you may *wish*" or "that you may *hope*"; he wrote "that you may *know*"—without a doubt. It's God's promise, not a possibility.

what others say

Charles R. Swindoll

These legalists taught that people were saved by works—by keeping the Law (an impossibility). Such folks live on to this day, spreading their heresy. Their message is full of exhortations to do more, to work harder, to witness longer, to pray with greater intensity, because enough is never enough. Such folks are "evil workers" who will take away what little bit of joy you may be able to muster.[2]

Paul was constantly defending the truth of the free gift of salvation, the kernel of the good news. In other letters he wrote, he protected the gospel against those who wanted to add something else to it. In his letter to the Colossian believers, he addressed those who said <u>angels</u> were needed. In his letter to the Romans, he argued against those who said <u>circumcision</u> was needed for true salvation. And there were always <u>those</u> who wanted to include circumcision along with Jesus's substitutionary death for true salvation. That was in the letter he wrote to the believers in Galatia. The Jewish Christians who believed that other works were necessary for salvation had great effort invested in their self-made salvation. They didn't want to give that up. No wonder Paul had to address them so frequently.

When the good news about Jesus was originally preached in the early church, believing Jews were primarily telling other Jews. There wasn't much difficulty in knowing how to encourage new believers to grow. But then believing Jews began to reach out to the Gentiles, and that's where the difficulties started. Because then there were questions like:

1. Is it necessary for a Gentile believer to observe the Law of Moses in order to become a Christian?

2. Should a male Gentile be circumcised after he believes in Jesus?

There was a meeting reported in Galatians 2 that covered these very issues. Paul was at that meeting and answered "NO!" to those questions by urging everyone, "A man is not justified by the works of the law but by faith in Jesus Christ, even we have believed in Christ Jesus, that we might be justified by faith in Christ and not by the works of the law; for by the works of the law no flesh shall be justified" (Galatians 2:16 NKJV).

Not everyone left that meeting convinced Paul was right, and unfortunately, the wrong ideas about how to be saved continued spreading. Thus, Paul was still dealing with these difficulties in the Philippian church approximately ten years later.

God originally gave <u>circumcision</u> to Abraham as a covenant between Him and his future descendants, who would become the Jewish people. It was a physical act intended as a sign of their uniqueness as the people of God; a symbol of what God wanted to

angels
Colossians 2:18

circumcision
Romans 2:28–29

those
Acts 15:12–21

circumcision
Genesis 17:9–14

based
Ephesians 2:8–9

occur in their hearts; a commitment to Him that would set them apart as His special people. The "evil workers" that Paul warns the Philippians about believed there was no need for a heart commitment, only a physical cutting of the flesh. Paul tells them they are "mutilating" their bodies, not "circumcising" them. Their motives are wrong—they are focused on "doing" rather than "being."

God wants all of us to have a circumcised heart, which represents the cutting away of rebellion and disobedience. Deuteronomy 10:16 says, "Therefore circumcise the foreskin of your heart, and be stiff-necked no longer" (NKJV). Paul names three evidences that a person is circumcised in their heart:

- *Worshipping God in the Spirit.* This shows a heart of worship toward God that isn't just a ritual, but a heartfelt love and commitment to acknowledge God as Lord in that person's life.

- *Rejoicing in Christ Jesus.* Such a person recognizes his salvation is <u>based</u> in Jesus alone, and nothing else.

- *Having no confidence in the flesh.* This is when we're dependent upon belief in Christ, not anything physical like circumcision or obeying the Law.

References to Circumcision of the Heart and Ears

Scripture	Point
Leviticus 26:41	Comes from humility before God.
Deuteronomy 10:16	Results from giving up stubbornness.
Deuteronomy 30:6	God circumcises the heart to make people love Him.
Jeremiah 6:10	An uncircumcised "ear" cannot hear the Word of God.

<u>Hey, Look at Me! I Was Perfect!</u>

PHILIPPIANS 3:4–6 *though I also might have confidence in the flesh. If anyone else thinks he may have confidence in the flesh, I more so: circumcised the eighth day, of the stock of Israel, of the tribe of Benjamin, a Hebrew of the Hebrews; concerning the law, a Pharisee; concerning zeal, persecuting the church; concerning the righteousness which is in the law, blameless. (NKJV)*

<u>Paul says that if anyone had the claim to salvation earned through works, it was him! He did it *all* right.</u> His parents gave him the perfect pedigree, and his own deeds were impeccable.

Paul says he had reached the ultimate and if anyone could have taken pride in being a "human doing," it was him.

- He was a Jew. He could trace his lineage all the way back to Abraham.

- He was born a Hebrew son of Hebrew parents. He followed his Hebrew language and customs, along with speaking Greek.

- He was born into the prestigious tribe of Benjamin, which in the Old Testament had proven its commitment to God time after time.

- He was circumcised on the eighth day in obedience to the law of Israel.

go to

commitment
Ezra 4:1

involved
Acts 9:1–2

Those were the result of his ancestry and gave him special distinction. But the next three elements were by his own choice and therefore even more valuable in setting himself up as good as the "dogs" whose theology he was disputing.

- *He was a Pharisee.* This was the strictest sect of the Jews and it was considered the most inflexible about the Law. Pharisees were actually laypeople, yet kept the Law as faithfully as the priests. There were never more than six thousand at a time. The name Pharisee means "the Separated Ones," and they were the most self-disciplined of all the Jewish groups.

- *He was zealous in persecuting those who were Christians.* Before he came to know Jesus as his Savior, he was involved in making sure Christians were put to death for their faith. Acts 9:1–2 tells us, "Then Saul, still breathing threats and murder against the disciples of the Lord, went to the high priest and asked letters from him to the synagogues of Damascus, so that if he found any who were of the Way, whether men or women, he might bring them bound to Jerusalem" (NKJV). The words *breathing threats* suggest in the Greek language the idea of a wild boar snorting in rage.

- *He believed he kept every point of the Law and considered himself perfect.*

Joyce Meyer

You and I are going to lean either on the arm of the flesh or on the arm of the Lord. Either we will spend our lives trying to take care of ourselves or we will let go and let God take care of us as we put our faith and trust in Him.[3]

apply it

Although Paul was proud about his lineage and accomplishments before knowing Jesus, he was eventually humbled. We need to make sure that our own accomplishments don't give us a big head. Otherwise, we'll need to be humbled.

It Wasn't Enough!

PHILIPPIANS 3:7–8 *But what things were gain to me, these I have counted loss for Christ.*

Yet indeed I also count all things loss for the excellence of the knowledge of Christ Jesus my Lord, for whom I have suffered the loss of all things, and count them as rubbish, that I may gain Christ (NKJV)

We've all made the mistake of thinking something like, *Once I get my new car, I'll be happy.* Or *As soon as I am promoted, life will be perfect.* Yet, when we gain that possession or accomplishment, we find it hollow. Paul didn't know his life was hollow from all those things he mentioned previously until he met Jesus face-to-face. Before his encounter with God, Paul's ego was bigger than his list of accomplishments or his ancestry. But after coming to know Christ, he was willing to die to his own self in order to participate in a righteousness found only in Jesus. He wants the Philippians to know that being a "human doing" doesn't bring satisfaction and doesn't make a person acceptable to God. He is thrilled that he is no longer held in the prison of his good works. Once he met Jesus on that road to Damascus, his eyes were opened to a heavenly perspective.

Before Paul met Jesus on that road, Paul's earthly accomplishments and heritage seemed to satisfy. But once faced with Jesus's claim of being the Messiah, he faced true righteousness and perfection. Suddenly, the old things lost their luster. He found out that no amount of "human doing" or earthly success can ever fully pacify the heart's search for God.

go to

humbled
Luke 14:7–10

die
Galatians 2:20

Damascus
Acts 9:3–5

And Paul is adamant in saying that absolutely nothing is more important to him than being a Christian. Everything he valued before, he considers one big loss. He doesn't put anything at the same level of value as knowing Christ. In fact, he considers it "rubbish." That strong word, *skubala* in the Greek, is the same as excrement or food thrown away because it is useless and even contaminating and harmful.

The word *count* carries the meaning "to evaluate, assess." Paul evaluated everything he had before Christ and everything he gained through knowing Christ, and he could say without a doubt that the present knowledge of Christ was far superior.

It's significant that Paul's words to the Philippians were penned thirty years after his conversion experience. We're not talking about new convert excitement. Thirty years later, Paul remembers what he gained in his earthly perspective, and after thirty years of "evaluating" what is really important, he can conclude that Christ still offers the best!

what others say

Warren Wiersbe

Yes, Paul gained far more than he lost. In fact, the gains were so thrilling that Paul considered all other "things" nothing but garbage in comparison! No wonder he had joy—his life did not depend on the cheap "things" of the world but on the eternal values found in Christ.[4]

Kenneth S. Wuest

The word *gain* is plural in the Greek, namely, "gains." . . . After mature consideration, Paul came to a settled conviction with regard to the matter. "Loss" is singular. The various gains are all counted as one loss.[5]

James I. Packer

What makes life worthwhile is having a big enough objective, something which catches our imagination and lays hold of our allegiance; and this the Christian has, in a way that no other man has. For what higher, more exalted, and more compelling goal can there be than to know God?[6]

go to

change
Romans 12:2

William Hendriksen

When he expresses his yearning to *know* Christ, he has in mind not only or even mainly the learning of certain facts about Christ but also and especially the sharing of certain experiences with him, as is clearly indicated by the rest of verse 10 and by verse 11. He wishes to become entirely "wrapped up" in Christ, so that Jesus will be "all the world" to him.[7]

Paul used part of a Greek verb that meant "to know experientially." The same word is used in the Old Testament to refer to sexual intercourse, such as in Genesis 4:11: "Now Adam knew Eve his wife, and she conceived and bore Cain" (NKJV). That's personal knowledge! Can you imagine the loss of intimacy in a marriage without sex? That kind of knowledge allows you to know your mate in the closest way. There's little hiding of ourselves as we reveal our bodies and then surrender both our bodies and spirits in intercourse. Paul wants that kind of knowledge of God: intimate and strong.

Coming to the place of considering all our earthly "doings" and accomplishments as "rubbish" is a lifelong process. Because it's easy to be trapped by the world's thinking that reaching our goals or climbing the ladder of success will bring satisfaction, we need to constantly and continually be alert to the world's influence and <u>change</u> our thinking to the truth. Nothing satisfies like knowing Jesus!

Got No Satisfaction in Things!

> PHILIPPIANS 3:9 *and be found in Him, not having my own righteousness, which is from the law, but that which is through faith in Christ, the righteousness which is from God by faith;* (NKJV)

Think of the most important thing that you value. Maybe it's being acknowledged as a good worker, or having a big house. Maybe it's being considered "all together" or driving a new car. Whatever it is, now imagine losing it. Feel tense? That might be an indication that your "thing" or "accomplishment" is too important. Paul learned the right priorities and is willing to give up the earthly values of respect from others, the privileges of righteous standing, the comfort of wealth, the self-satisfaction of pride, and the efforts of self in exchange for true, deep-down satisfaction, peace, contentment, and lasting joy.

Paul is stressing that all the works he previously did could not gain him the righteousness he now has because of his faith in Jesus. Paul believes that Jesus's robe of righteousness is wrapped around him and God no longer sees his sins—He sees only a cleansed and set-free believer. Paul wants his readers to think the same thing about themselves.

Paul uses the Greek word *dikaiosune* for the word *righteousness*. In the Greek, it has a multifaceted meaning, but basically Paul means a right relationship with God—one that wasn't earned by good works but given through grace.

go to

cleansed
1 John 1:9

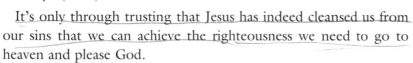

what others say

J. Vernon McGee

The Spirit of God chose just one little word, the preposition *in*, to explain what salvation is. What does it mean to be saved? It means to be *in* Christ. How do you get in Christ? Well, you get in Christ when you trust Him as your Savior, when you accept Him as your Savior.[8]

Nothing we accomplish can possibly be valuable enough to impress God. And being as good as possible cannot compare to the sinless perfection that God sustains. Isaiah 64:6 tells us, "But we are all like an unclean thing, and all our righteousnesses are like filthy rags; we all fade as a leaf, and our iniquities, like the wind, have taken us away" (NKJV).

It's only through trusting that Jesus has indeed cleansed us from our sins that we can achieve the righteousness we need to go to heaven and please God.

something to ponder

Share with God

PHILIPPIANS 3:10–11 *that I may know Him and the power of His resurrection, and the fellowship of His sufferings, being conformed to His death, if, by any means, I may attain to the resurrection from the dead. (NKJV)*

known
Ephesians 1:17

resurrection
Revelation 22:1–7

We can want to know someone more deeply as a friend, but if they don't want to "be <u>known</u>," there's not too much we can do about it. Paul wants to know Christ, and, thankfully, God wants to "be known" intimately. But since God is not like a human friend whom we can have a cup of coffee with and share our lives, Paul describes what this knowledge of God should focus on and what the result will be.

Paul suggests that we know:

- *The power of His <u>resurrection</u>.* When we see His power in our lives, we will know God better because we identify His powerful nature. It also refers to the resurrection to eternal life that every believer will experience at death or when Jesus returns.

- *The fellowship of His sufferings.* We can know God through standing up for righteousness' sake because we'll experience what Jesus did—persecution.

- *Conformity to His death.* By dying to our own selfish desires, we come to know God in truth. We see life through eyes of selflessness and <u>we aren't blinded to the real reason for life: to glorify God.</u>

To be in the same form as someone else means knowing them at their inner core. That's what Paul wanted and it's what God wants for us in our relationship with Him.

When Paul used the words *if, by any means,* he wasn't expressing doubt or uncertainty. He was musing about the way in which he would meet death: Would it be through immediate martyrdom, or would he die a natural death much later? He didn't know, but he trusted in God's control over his life and future.

> ## what others say
>
> ### Kenneth S. Wuest
>
> When these four things are true of Paul, namely, to be discovered by men to be in Christ by the very life he lives, by coming to know Him better all the time, by experiencing the same power that raised Christ from the dead surging through his own being, and by becoming a joint-participant in His sufferings for righteousness' sake, then Paul will constantly be made conformable to Christ's death. The words *made conformable* mean literally "to bring to the same form with some other person."[9]

go to

commitment
Psalm 89:30–33

provider
Psalm 68:10

seek
Jeremiah 29:13

satiate
completely satisfy

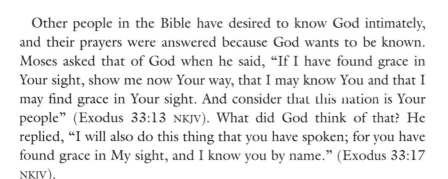

what others say

Joni Eareckson Tada

To hunger is to be human, but to **satiate** yourself on God is to send your heart ahead to heaven. Feed on Him in your heart, and you will be yanking that foot out of the mud of earth and stepping closer to eternity.[10]

Jan Frank

I have discovered that the greatest joy is to be found in His presence, not in the resolution to a problem, the answer to a long-awaited prayer, or the end of a waiting season.[11]

something to ponder

Other people in the Bible have desired to know God intimately, and their prayers were answered because God wants to be known. Moses asked that of God when he said, "If I have found grace in Your sight, show me now Your way, that I may know You and that I may find grace in Your sight. And consider that this nation is Your people" (Exodus 33:13 NKJV). What did God think of that? He replied, "I will also do this thing that you have spoken; for you have found grace in My sight, and I know you by name." (Exodus 33:17 NKJV).

But we shouldn't just seek God in order to find the solutions for our problems or struggles. We need to seek Him for the pure joy of getting to know Him more. Let's evaluate our motives in seeking God to make sure we really want to know God.

Why should we want to know the almighty God of the universe? Because:

- He's the One who loves us unconditionally with an everlasting <u>commitment</u>.

- He's the sovereign Lord, who not only knows the right thing for each one of us but can carry it out.

- He's the patient <u>provider</u> who generously blesses far beyond what we deserve.

- He's the kind gentleman who calmly waits for us to <u>seek</u> Him.

- He calls us to Himself through an eternal perspective that acknowledges that nothing we do on this earth has as much value—isn't even close—to the surpassing value of knowing Jesus in truth.

Knowing Jesus more and more involves the wise commitment of

judge
2 Corinthians 5:10

spending time in Bible study and prayer. That can be a difficult choice because our lives are so busy. But if we will make that decision, even if it means starting out with a few minutes a day, we will reap the benefits of seeing the value of fellowship with God.

Strain and Train Those Spiritual Muscles

PHILIPPIANS 3:12–14 *Not that I have already attained, or am already perfected; but I press on, that I may lay hold of that for which Christ Jesus has also laid hold of me. Brethren, I do not count myself to have apprehended; but one thing I do, forgetting those things which are behind and reaching forward to those things which are ahead, I press toward the goal for the prize of the upward call of God in Christ Jesus.* (NKJV)

Of all people in the Bible, most would vote for the apostle Paul as the most accomplished Christian, maybe even having reached perfection. He represented God faithfully, he brought multitudes to Christ through his personal interaction and letters, and he didn't seem to have any faults. Yet, Paul himself says he hasn't achieved perfection and because he hasn't, he's still pressing on toward faithful Christian living for Jesus.

But to counter that idea, Paul used a literary word picture to let his readers know that he also was still in the process of learning and growing. The Greek word for "reaching forward" is *epekteinomenos*, and Paul uses it to refer to the runners in the Greek games who strained forward to reach the finish line before other opponents.

key point

In Paul's metaphor, of course, he isn't competing against other people—only himself—in seeking to be the best Christian he can be in God's power. He may have had in mind a picture of godly character that he hoped he would attain before he died. He most likely pictured the list of the fruit of the Spirit he wrote about in his letter to the believers in Galatia: "But the fruit of the Spirit is love, joy, peace, patience, kindness, goodness, faithfulness, gentleness, self-control. Against such there is no law" (Galatians 5:22–23 NKJV).

The prize in the Greek games was awarded by a judge, and Paul knew that God would judge him in heaven and award him his "prize" of salvation because Jesus's robe of righteousness was wrapped around him.

In Paul's example of a runner, we envision the athlete concentrating so hard on the goal ahead of him that he doesn't look around to see where the other runners are. To do so would slow him down. In the end, Paul could say that he had reached the goal and prize. He wrote to Timothy in his last letter before his death, "I have fought the good fight, I have finished the course, I have kept the faith. Finally there is laid up for me the crown of righteousness, which the Lord, the righteous Judge, will give to me on that Day, and not to me only but also to all who have loved His appearing" (2 Timothy 4:7–8 NKJV).

letter
Philippians 1:6

When Paul said he hadn't been "perfect," he used the Greek word *teleios*, which he used twice in this chapter, verses 12 and 15. In verse 15, it's translated "mature." The two different uses are because *teleios* has many diverse yet interconnected meanings. In verse 12, Paul uses it to mean "perfection," but in verse 15, it's the idea of being "full-grown." Paul says it's impossible for anyone to become perfect, but some have attained the state of being full-grown in their faith, like a full grown person is contrasted to an immature youth.

Paul was taking a risk when he said he hadn't attained perfection because the teaching of "evil workers" said they had reached perfection—through keeping the Law. For those in the church at Philippi who might think it was bad news not to reach perfection, Paul's message could be unattractive. Paul still told the truth and trusted God to convince Philippian believers that being "in process" was God's will—not reaching perfection on earth.

Yet, for those who were frustrated because they realized they couldn't reach perfection, Paul's admission would be fabulous news! The pressure was off them to become perfect. They could relax in God's power, knowing He was working in them and would until they died just as Paul had stated earlier in this letter.

Paul is not saying that his readers shouldn't remember the past, or else he wouldn't have rehearsed the past as he did earlier in this chapter. But he is saying that they shouldn't be held captive by the past, which could include past accomplishments, past heritage, past sins that have been forgiven, or past hurts that others had done to them.

Actually, there is value in remembering the past. But we want to remember it, and not let it control us. Although God can forgive and forget sin, we humans haven't been given that ability for the most part.

go to

press on
Galatians 6:9

Heb 10:30-33

We can make a choice to forgive people who have hurt us and then stop rehearsing those hurts. Remembering our own sin even after we've received God's forgiveness and forgiven ourselves has value because God can use it to keep us humble and dependent on Him.

> **what others say**
>
> **Beth Moore**
>
> Many well-meaning Christians take out of context the exhortation in Philippians 3:13, "forgetting what is behind," and apply it as a command to never look at the past. Paul was talking about all the trophies of life he had to leave behind to follow Christ. God's Word clearly expresses what a good and effective teacher the past can be.[12]

As Christians we can become easily distracted by possessions, comparing ourselves to others, feeling inadequate, wanting the approval of others and many more things. Let's <u>press on</u> and keep our eyes centered on Jesus continually.

We can always reach greater heights as a Christian. We need not grow weak on the plateau of Christian living, saying, "Well, this is just about as far as I can go." But just off in the distance is another mountain to climb that will make us even closer to the image of Jesus. Therefore we must never say things like, "Well, you'll just have to accept me as I am, warts and all. I can't get any better."

apply it

Paul's Metaphors

Paul was fond of using metaphors in his writings as he was inspired by the Holy Spirit. He used several of them to describe the Christian life in his letters. Here are four of them:

Scripture	Metaphor	Aspect of Christian Living
1 Corinthians 9:24–27	Race	Just as a runner trains his body, a Christian needs to train his spirit and soul to be strong in Christ.
Hebrews 12:1–2	Race	Just as a runner focuses all his or her energy on reaching the finish line, a Christian needs to stay focused on living in God's power and not be distracted by unimportant things.
1 Timothy 4:7–8	Exercise	Just as an athlete disciplines his body, a Christian needs to discipline himself to choose godly behavior.
2 Timothy 4:7–8	Race and fight	Just as an athlete and a boxer must persevere in training, Christians should persevere until the day they see Jesus face-to-face.

We Aren't Made—We're in the Making

PHILIPPIANS 3:15–16 *Therefore let us, as many as are mature, have this mind; and if in anything you think otherwise, God will reveal even this to you. Nevertheless, to the degree that we have already attained, let us walk by the same rule, let us be of the same mind. (NKJV)*

in Christ
Colossians 2:10

If you want to know whether you are mature, just see what Paul points to for his definition of maturity: it's the things he has been talking about. Things like pressing on, not being proud of accomplishments, desiring to know God and growing in trust in God. Paul doesn't define maturity as perfection but growth. And it's also not falling back into old habits, but continuing to live at the level a person has already reached. Another perspective about Paul's comment could be that these believers should live up to the position <u>in Christ</u> that God has already given them.

These verses were most likely carefully written by Paul to refute the teaching of another group of teachers, called the antinomians. They taught that there was no effort required in the Christian life, believing a Christian could do anything they wanted and then any sins would be forgiven by God. That was their warped definition of grace. But Paul counteracts that by saying that discipline and continued growth are part of normal Christian life. This does require thought and seeking God, even as we recognize we'll never become perfect.

The word *antinomism* was first coined by Martin Luther, and it comes from *anti*, meaning "against," and *nomos*, meaning "law." Therefore, it's the idea of believing the Christian doesn't need to obey any law of God, not even living a moral life. Although Christians are not expected to keep the Jewish law, there are other "laws" to obey, like the law of love. Paul wrote to the Galatians, "For all the law is fulfilled in one word, even in this: 'You shall love your neighbor as yourself'" (Galatians 5:14 NKJV). And Paul's words, "But if you are led by the Spirit, you are not under the law" (Galatians 5:18 NKJV), indicate there are standards to follow and grow in.

In verse 15, Paul is gently but firmly urging believers to consider whether they are mature and to fight the ideas of antinomism. If they would only honestly come to God and ask Him what to believe, Paul was confident that God would reveal the truth to them. Such openness to God's changing a person's mind shows their maturity.

go to

presented
John 4:7–29

worry
Philippians 4:6–7

ostracized
separated

something to ponder

apply it

Jesus had such an incredible trust in God's ability to change the perspective of people that He wasn't tense about trying to make them believe in Himself as Savior. He simply <u>presented</u> the truth that He was God and the Messiah and allowed people to form their own opinions. We can learn from His example and stop trying to control people and make them think the way we think. We should present the truth and trust that God will work in their hearts and minds to reveal a confirmation of the truth. And sometimes, releasing them to form their own opinions actually helps them do it faster than if they think we're controlling them. God can change anyone's mind.

Sometimes we can feel discouraged as we evaluate our thinking and wonder if we're falling short of God's desires for us. But we needn't <u>worry</u>. God doesn't want us to worry even about that. He promises that He will make clear to us anything that isn't right. We don't need to fret; we just need to be open to whatever God might reveal to us.

What Pattern Are You Sewing From?

PHILIPPIANS 3:17–19 *Brethren, join in following my example, and note those who so walk, as you have us for a pattern. For many walk, of whom I have told you often, and now tell you even weeping, that they are the enemies of the cross of Christ: whose end is destruction, whose god is their belly, and whose glory is in their shame—who set their mind on earthly things. (NKJV)*

Paul knows he's not perfect, but by golly, he *is* a wonderful "pattern" of Christian persistence for others to learn from and copy. He doesn't flinch from seeing himself as a good example for his friends. That's confidence! But that confidence isn't in being perfect; it's in what he has been describing about himself: that he unceasingly wants to seek to know Christ more and live in His power. As far as he's concerned, that kind of pattern is something every person should seek for himself.

But Paul is not the only person they could copy. Some are good examples and some are bad—like the false teachers who believe in circumcision for salvation, whom he doesn't want the Philippians to imitate. They are actually enemies of Jesus because they steer people in the wrong direction: as having gained salvation through pulling themselves up by their own bootstraps. Some also think that being a Christian gives them no responsibility or accountability for living a godly life. Since <u>sin</u> can be forgiven, they think they can act any way they like. It was a twisted view of Christian liberty. Paul is so concerned about such a destructive path that it brings tears to his eyes. He is burdened to think that they won't see the difference.

sin
Romans 6:15

Paul lists four very big differences between himself and those who claim to be Christians yet teach the wrong things:

- *Their destiny is destruction:* They won't go to heaven but to hell.

- *Their god is their stomach:* They want to satisfy only their own needs, not the needs of others.

- *Their glory is in their shame:* They pride themselves on gaining salvation through self-effort rather than depending on God's provision through Jesus's death.

- *Their mind is on earthly things:* They aren't concerned about spiritual growth that brings benefit while on earth.

Paul said for these believers to follow him. That may sound heretical. Why didn't he say, "See what Jesus is like and emulate Him"? But these believers had never seen Jesus and because the Gospels (biblical books written by Matthew, Mark, Luke, and John) were not yet circulated, they couldn't even read about Him. So Paul gave them his own example and felt confident that he was acting like Jesus and they could act like him.

Some commentators believe that at the time Paul wrote this letter, there was an additional group of people who believed what later became labeled as "Gnosticism." Those who believed this worldview were called Gnostics, which loosely means "the intellectual ones." That's because they highly stressed having knowledge but without applying it to living a moral life.

key point

Paul is subtly trying to neutralize their influence because they lived immoral lives and defended it through their philosophy. They

sinned
Romans 6:1–2

stimulate
Hebrews 10:24–25

libertine
immoral

believed that the body is essentially evil, and since it can't be improved, a person might as well just go ahead and do whatever they want. Living immorally didn't affect them. Paul's letter to the believers in Colosse particularly addressed this incorrect viewpoint.

Additionally, there was a group within this philosophy that said everyone should participate in as many sins and virtues as possible in order to be truly "complete." No wonder Paul stressed that being "complete" in Christ meant attaining maturity and a moral life—which was the example he gave them.

In Paul's letter to the Romans, he makes it very clear that we shouldn't sin by choice. "What shall we say then? Shall we continue in sin that grace may abound? Certainly not! How shall we who died to sin live any longer in it?" (Romans 6:1–2 NKJV).

what others say

Malcolm O. Tolbert

Paul said: "They glory in their shame." This probably reflects **libertine** theology. There were people who said that the more they <u>sinned</u>, the greater was their witness to the grace of God. Instead of being ashamed of their sin, they were proud of it.[14]

Tony Evans

Many Christians going down the wrong road are traveling alone. When you know a brother or sister who doesn't come to church anymore and there's no good reason, you can predict something is wrong. You need to say something to them, go after them, <u>stimulate</u> them to join the assembly.[15]

Every single one of us is an example whether we want to be or not. There are always people watching us and being inspired to live for God or being turned away from Him because of our model. We must always be careful to do the best we can in God's power—knowing our actions have eternal consequences in the lives of others.

On this earth, there are many secular things that could become our mentors if we let them: the media, television, radio, magazines, movies, service groups, even billboards. All of those "enemies" of Christ purport to share truth, but it's not heavenly truth.

Who are your mentors and examples? Do you desire to emulate those who are like Christ or those who want success in earthly things? We may say we're only following someone's example because they are good in business, but are we really ignoring their immoral way of life? What a person does is not as important as the character behind his actions. Be careful whom you are imitating, and also who is imitating you.

go to

transported
1 Thessalonians
4:13–18

apekdechometha
Romans 8:19, 23,
25;
1 Corinthians 1:7

Three Rocks from the Sun

PHILIPPIANS 3:20 *For our citizenship is in heaven, from which we also eagerly wait for the Savior, the Lord Jesus Christ,* (NKJV)

If you were in a foreign country and longed for the good ol' USA, you might try to go to the local American embassy to get a little shot in the arm of the United States. In any country, the land that the embassy is situated on is land that is owned by that country. When a citizen visits his embassy, he again is on his own country's land, even while being a foreigner.

That is the picture Paul paints of a Christian's heavenly citizenship. The Philippian believers would have completely understood this metaphor. Philippi was a Roman colony and they were "citizens" of Rome even though they lived outside of Rome's borders. Everyone there enjoyed the benefits of being a Roman citizen, and in effect, they were stepping on Roman ground—though far from Italy. And as Roman citizens, they dressed, acted, talked, and were governed by Roman rule even though they weren't in Rome.

Paul uses this word picture of "citizenship" to help the Philippians understand their role as Christians while still on earth. They actually belong to another country—heaven—yet they must live on earth. In other words, they can still enjoy their heavenly rights but must keep their heavenly responsibilities until they are <u>transported</u> from earth to heaven through Jesus's appearance or after they die. Just as the transplanted Romans must live as Romans, Paul says Christians must live on earth exhibiting the same behavior they will in heaven: being obedient to God and living holy lives.

something to ponder

The Greek word "*apekdechometha*" is translated "eagerly wait" and suggests a tiptoeing kind of anticipation. It's actually a combination of three words in the Greek: *to receive*, *off*, and *out*.

- "receive": like welcoming a friend
- "off": taking the focus off something and turning it to something else
- "out": called away from something

Abraham
Hebrews 11:8–10

tears
Revelation 21:4

expendable
able to be used up

Therefore, Paul is saying we should concentrate our attention on the coming of Jesus with great longing.

what others say

Max Lucado

As we get older, our vision should improve. Not our vision of earth but our vision of heaven. Those who have spent their life looking for heaven gain a skip in their step as the city comes into view.[16]

Joni Eareckson Tada

Let's not get too settled in, too satisfied with the good things down here on earth. They are only the tinkling sounds of the orchestra warming up. The real song is about to break into a heavenly symphony, and its prelude is only a few moments away.[17]

Joseph Stowell

The pilgrim mindset, best exemplified by <u>Abraham</u>, recognizes that as aliens we don't belong here and that we live seeking the country to which we do belong.

To claim a pilgrim's identity means that we always know we're not home yet. For us the best is yet to come. Therefore, everything is **expendable** here, free to be used for the glory and gain of the King.[18]

The thought of eternally living with Christ should make whatever we experience on this earth of minute perspective. Second Corinthians 4:16–18 tells us the attitude we should have: "Therefore we do not lose heart. Even though our outward man is perishing, yet the inward man is being renewed day by day. For our light affliction, which is but for a moment, is working for us a far more exceeding and eternal weight of glory, while we do not look at the things which are seen, but at the things which are not seen. For the things which are seen are temporary, but the things which are not seen are eternal" (NKJV).

It may not seem like our problems are momentary and light, but with an eternal perspective we can view them that way. This doesn't mean we won't feel sad and even grieve in the face of loss, but in our hearts we can have faith, knowing God is in control. We're only passing through; there's a far better joy waiting for us—no pain, no confusion, no struggle, no <u>tears</u>, no grief!

Beam Me Up, Jesus

PHILIPPIANS 3:21 *who will transform our lowly body that it may be conformed to His glorious body, according to the working by which He is able even to subdue all things to Himself. (NKJV)*

go to

transformation
1 Corinthians
15:51–54

die
Romans 6:9–11

rise
1 Thessalonians
4:15–17

We are excitedly looking with great anticipation toward Jesus's return because our <u>transformation</u> will bring great benefits. We're going to be transformed into the perfection we've been wanting all along. In God's powerful ability, He will take the powdered dust of the saints long dead and fashion them again into their original likenesses, but this time with spiritual bodies that will never <u>die</u> again. In His amazing greatness, He will call those of us who are alive and instantaneously change our flesh-and-blood bodies into bloodless, spiritual beings that will <u>rise</u> through the air and greet Him in the sky, leaving behind the pull of gravity that formerly held it in bondage to the earth. We'll fly without wings and shout or sing our praise of such an awesome God.

The concept of Jesus's returning in what is called the Rapture is a doctrine that not everyone agrees with. Each person's take depends on how that person interprets the events in the biblical book of Revelation. Some believe the Tribulation will come first before Jesus returns to take His people home to heaven. Those who believe in the Rapture base it upon 1 Thessalonians 4:16–17: "For the Lord Himself will descend from heaven with a shout, with the voice of an archangel, and with the trumpet of God. And the dead in Christ will rise first. Then we who are alive and remain shall be caught up together with them in the clouds to meet the Lord in the air. And thus we shall always be with the Lord" (NKJV).

The Greek word for "the working by which He is able" is the same English word we use for "dynamite." That's power! Dynamite can blow things apart, and God's dynamite power can rearrange our molecules to become something supernatural and indestructible.

When Paul refers to our physical bodies as "lowly," he's not saying there's anything morally wrong with them, just that they are inferior in comparison to the eternal bodies we will receive in heaven.

go to

house
John 14:2

what others say

Billy Graham

The resurrected body of Jesus is the design for our bodies when we are raised from the dead also. No matter what afflictions, pain, or distortions we have in our earthly bodies, we will be given new bodies![19]

Max Lucado

We aren't home yet. We are orphans at the gate of the orphanage, awaiting our new parents. They aren't here yet, but we know they are coming. They wrote us a letter. We haven't seen them yet, but we know what they look like. They sent us a picture. And we're not acquainted with our new <u>house</u> yet, but we have a hunch about it. It's grand. They sent a description.[20]

Resurrected Body

Scripture	Description of Resurrected, Glorious Body
Romans 8:29	"conformed to the image of His Son" (NKJV)
1 Corinthians 15:49	"bear the image of the heavenly" (NKJV)
1 John 3:2	"We know that when He is revealed, we shall be like Him, for we shall see Him as He is." (NKJV)
1 Corinthians 15:42–44	Our bodies will be imperishable, glorious, powerful, and spiritual.
1 Corinthians 15:53	Our bodies will be immortal, therefore indestructible and without pain.

Chapter Wrap-Up

- If Paul could encourage the Philippians to believe anything, it would be that they should rejoice regardless of anything that happens to them. (Philippians 3:1)

- There were false teachers who were always trying to incorrectly influence believers, and Paul was concerned that those who proposed circumcision for salvation would make the Philippians earn their salvation that way. Paul said that such an act only mutilated the body and didn't save the soul. (Philippians 3:2–3)

- If anyone deserved to go to heaven based on his own activities and family qualifications, it was Paul. He had done it all right and had come from the right family background. Yet after meeting Jesus personally and putting his faith in Him, Paul realized that only the free gift of salvation could get him into right standing with God. (Philippians 3:4–11)

- Paul recognizes that he hasn't become perfect, but the imperfect past is no longer of value to him. He can remember how his efforts didn't gain him salvation, but after that, he wants to concentrate on being the best he can be for God's use in the future. (Philippians 3:12–19)

- Paul is more concerned that his readers press on to maturity and know their citizenship in heaven. They can have joy because they know this earth isn't the final whistle stop. It's heaven—where each believer will receive his or her heavenly bodysuit. (Philippians 3:20–21)

Study Questions

1. What is Paul's continuing message throughout his letter to the Philippians?

2. What group of people was Paul concerned would influence the Philippian believers, and why was he concerned?

3. What qualifications did Paul have as a Jew that he now realizes don't give him favor with God?

4. What is Paul's viewpoint of the past and its value?

5. What future thing does Paul want his readers to focus on?

Philippians 4 Peace with People and Circumstances

Let's Get Started

If you were to ask someone about the two most difficult things they face, you probably wouldn't be surprised to hear "conflict" and "worry." Relationships are often the most challenging aspect of life, and closely related—because we worry about people—is anxiety. Put them together, and what do you have? People worrying about other people who don't cooperate with their ideas of what's right.

No wonder Paul addresses these two joy stealers in his letter about joy! People and worry create lots of tension and pose a threat to fully trusting God. And when someone isn't happy, then nobody's happy in that household—or church. Paul focuses his aim on these two aspects of life, along with contentment, in this final part of his letter. He has some practical ideas as he shares more about his deep feelings for his friends. No wonder they loved him so.

key point

Like a Glorious Hat

PHILIPPIANS 4:1 *Therefore, my beloved and longed-for brethren, my joy and crown, so stand fast in the Lord, beloved.* (NKJV)

We readily call the special people in our lives a "spiritual brother" or "spiritual sister" and tell them we love them. But if you told your friends, "You are 'my joy and crown,'" they might think you were a little crazy. We don't generally think in those terms. However, that is how Paul describes his feelings about his friends in Philippi. He uses those very words because his friends give him reason to rejoice and be proud. For Paul, they are like the victory wreath a runner wears after crossing the finish line in a race. He's confident they will follow the principles he's been sharing with them; therefore he, as their spiritual father, can boast of God's work in them and wear them like a proud papa (or victory crown). Traditionally, a new papa hands out cigars when his baby is born, but Paul wants to boast about his spiritual children by putting them on display like a winning runner wears the victor's wreath. Like that runner who knows his training was not in vain, Paul is proud of his "children" because they have stood firm in the Lord. He knows his efforts have not been in vain.

There are two Greek words for the word *crown: diadema* and *stephanos*. Paul didn't choose to use *diadema* because that refers to a kingly crown. He uses *stephanos* because it conveys two meanings:

1. crown of the victorious athlete at Greek games

2. reward at a banquet for public service, military accomplishments, or a time of great joy, like a wedding

Either of these two definitions would communicate the feeling Paul has for the Philippians. Symbolically, he pictured wearing them as his crowning glory when he sat at the final banquet of God in heaven. To Paul, one of the most important things he can do on earth is lead people to knowledge of Christ. He knows they'll enjoy heaven with him, and never once does he think he'll "wear" the material possessions or accomplishments from this earth.

Then Paul goes on to urge his friends to "stand fast in the Lord." *Stand fast* in the Greek is *stekete*, which was used to denote a soldier standing fast during battle, even though the enemy is attacking. *In the Lord* should be thought of as submission to God, which is the only way anyone will stand fast in their convictions and not succumb to the spiritual enemies' strategies of temptation and distrust of God. More specifically, since "in" means being within something, such as "he went in the water" and is therefore surrounded by the water, we want to be "in the Lord" by remembering that He is surrounding us in His omnipresence. We can always call upon Him at any time for strength to stand firm in our commitment to Him.

apply it

Just as Paul so often in his letter tells the Philippians how much they mean to him, we should also tell people how much they mean to us. Even if they don't always perform the way we think they should, we can still tell them we love them. Saying, "I love you," doesn't mean we're also saying, "I approve of what you're doing." By saying simply "I love you," we express unconditional love, which could motivate them to godly living.

All Isn't Hugs and Kisses

PHILIPPIANS 4:2–3 *I implore Euodia and I implore Syntyche to be of the same mind in the Lord. And I urge you also, true companion, help these women who labored with me in the gospel, with Clement also, and the rest of my fellow workers, whose names are in the Book of Life. (NKJV)*

Paul said in verse 1 to "stand fast." Although he certainly meant that for everyone in the Philippian church, he had some particular people in mind—in fact, two women: Euodia and Syntyche. He wants them to stand fast in unity.

It's a little surprising for us to hear of this conflict; as positive as Paul has been in this letter, we might think everything was coming up roses among the believers in Philippi. Evidently that's not true, because Paul refers to conflict between these two women. Paul knew both of these women—and loved them equally. Although they had "contended" alongside Paul trying to win people to Christ, they were now contending with each other—but that wasn't the kind of "contending" Paul desired. Nevertheless, he didn't try to play favorites or even sort through the mess—he urged them to agree with each other. He also urged others in the church there to get involved in helping these women get their act together. No wonder Paul had a theme of unity throughout his letter to this congregation. He knew there was conflict.

Euodia and Syntyche weren't living up to the meanings of their names. Euodia means "a prosperous journey," and Syntyche means "pleasant acquaintance." They were not journeying together pleasantly, and Paul must have ached, thinking and wondering how this was affecting the witness of the church. It must have especially bothered him since they were prominent workers in the church, which also shows us that women were actively involved in its success.

Paul urges these two women, along with the help of others in the church, to deal with their conflict. But conflict certainly hadn't

settled
2 Timothy 4:11

eluded Paul in his own ministry. Acts 15:36–39 tells of a disagreement with Barnabas about whether they should take John Mark on a second missionary trip after John Mark had abandoned them on a previous trip. There was such "bad blood" between them that they each took a different man and went their separate ways. But in time, that conflict was peacefully <u>settled</u>, and God used it to spread the gospel to more places than if Paul and Barnabas had traveled together.

> **what others say**
>
> ### Charles R. Swindoll
>
> Why did this mean so much to Paul that he included it in his letter? Because these women were important. They had "shared in the struggle" with Paul, and they belonged to the same spiritual family. Their clash was hurting the fellowship among the Christians at Philippi, so it needed resolution . . . soon.[2]

Paul refers to the Book of Life, within which every true believer in Jesus is listed—only those on that list will enter heaven. Other than Paul's mention of the Book of Life in this letter, the phrase is not used elsewhere in Scripture except in the apostle John's book, Revelation. There are, however, other ways it is described, such as "Your names are written in heaven" (Luke 10:20 NKJV).

Facts About the Book of Life

Verse(s) in Book of Revelation	Information
3:5	He who overcomes shall be clothed in white garments, and I will not blot out his name from the Book of Life; but I will confess his name before My Father and before His angels. (NKJV)
13:8	All who dwell on the earth will worship him, whose names have not been written in the Book of Life of the Lamb slain from the foundation of the world. (NKJV)
17:8	The beast that you saw was, and is not, and will ascend out of the bottomless pit and go to perdition. And those who dwell on the earth will marvel, whose names are not written in the Book of Life from the foundation of the world, when they see the beast that was, and is not, and yet is. (NKJV)
20:12	And I saw the dead, small and great, standing before God, and books were opened. And another book was opened, which is the Book of Life. And the dead were judged according to their works, by the things which were written in the books. (NKJV)

Facts About the Book of Life (cont'd)

Verse(s) in Book of Revelation	Information
20:14–15	Then Death and Hades were cast into the lake of fire. This is the second death. And anyone not found written in the Book of Life was cast into the lake of fire. (NKJV)
21:27	But there shall by no means enter it anything that defiles, or causes an abomination or a lie, but only those who are written in the Lamb's Book of Life. (NKJV)
22:19	And if anyone takes away from the words of the book of this prophecy, God shall take away his part from the Book of Life, from the holy city, and from the things which are written in this book. (NKJV)

judges
Revelation 20:11–15

said
John 13:35

Is your name written in the Book of Life? One day when God <u>judges</u> every single person, He will bring out a book where it is recorded whether a person received Jesus as his Lord and Savior. Only those who made that decision will be permitted to live in heaven. Is your name written there?

The solutions that Paul gives for this conflict are threefold:

1. Be of the same mind in the Lord.

2. Have fellow church members intervene to bring unity.

3. Rejoice in whatever circumstances or conflict they are experiencing (verse 4). We'll deal with this conflict-manager in our next verse.

Paul's phrase *in the Lord* has great significance because we can never "be of the same mind" unless we are committed to God and His glory. If our focus is on pleasing Him, we'll be looking around us at other people with eyes of unity.

Jesus <u>said</u> that it was through our love for fellow Christians that other people would know we are His disciples. When we are in conflict, we're not just making our own lives miserable but we're also giving Christ's name bad representation. For that reason alone, we should be willing to give up our own rights and even suffer injustice—if it will represent Jesus positively.

The fact that these two women whom Paul addressed were obviously actively involved in ministry is very revealing of the place women occupied in the city of Philippi, which was located in Macedonia. If these same women had been living in Greece, a nearby country, the situation would have been entirely different. In

Greece, the attitude toward women was like the attitude Americans had toward children years ago: that they should be seen and not heard. Actually, women didn't have it even that good—they weren't even supposed to be seen very much. Each woman within a household had her own living quarters and wasn't allowed to join the men for meals. She wasn't supposed to be on a street alone. The purpose of all these restrictions was to keep women sexually pure and make sure the children of the Greek husbands were truly their own children.

The contrast to these women in Philippi is striking, and it represents two very different cultures. It also indicates the extent to which the Christian church allowed and encouraged women to serve the Lord.

Be Joyful

PHILIPPIANS 4:4 *Rejoice in the Lord always. Again I will say, rejoice! (NKJV)*

Paul can sure sound like a broken record at times. He's already requested repeatedly that his readers be joyful, and now he says it again. But how appropriate for him to say it after mentioning two women who weren't rejoicing. When we are rejoicing, there's not as much of a possibility that we'll be finding things to disagree about with others. Rejoicing and unity are like the thumb and index finger—they work together and accomplish great things.

Yet Paul didn't have in mind that everyone should go around being happy only when good things are happening. His definition of joy is different from happiness. Happiness is something that happens to you; joy is something you choose by believing God will <u>bring good</u> out of everything, including bad things. Paul maintained his rejoicing attitude even though he was under house arrest and chained to guards, without his freedom and seemingly powerless to share the gospel as he'd prefer. Yet, he said everything should be a reason for rejoicing in God. He didn't want people to just rejoice, but to rejoice in God. Keeping our eyes on Jesus will help us have the right attitude of <u>rejoicing</u>.

bring good
Romans 8:28

rejoicing
James 1:2–5

go to

joy
Nehemiah 8:10

what others say

J. Vernon McGee

In other words, "Your power is in your joy—don't weep!" A great many people seem to think that God commanded fasting and wearing sackcloth and ashes. God never did that. You won't find that in the Word of God. Of the seven feasts that God appointed for His people, every one of them was to be a time of rejoicing.[3]

Rick Warren

God doesn't expect you to be thankful for evil, for sin, for suffering, or for their painful consequences in the world. Instead, God wants you to thank Him that he will use your problems to fulfill His purposes.[4]

Jesus is the ultimate example of rejoicing, even in difficult circumstances. From His very first human awareness of His role in His Father's plan of redemption, He knew He was traveling toward Calvary and His painful death. Yet He kept His cheerful perspective. He is an example to us of believing that if God is in control, then we can rejoice in anything God allows.

apply it

Rejoicing concentrates on the good things of life and on the good efforts that people make—even if it's not always exactly the way we would have liked or preferred. Few people will complete things totally to our expectations, and not many will perform in order to entirely satisfy us. When a spouse makes an effort, even if it's not all that we would like, we must give the credit he deserves. That will actually motivate him to try to please us the next time. But if we never credit his efforts, he may begin to give up, thinking, *I shouldn't even try, I can't please her anyway.* Acknowledging someone's desire to help is far better than focusing on how they were lacking—and it will bring about better overall results.

Catch Me Being Gentle

PHILIPPIANS 4:5 *Let your gentleness be known to all men. The Lord is at hand.* (NKJV)

If we truly believed Jesus could appear at any moment and see what we're doing, we might react to life and other people more carefully with godliness and gentleness. Joy is an inner response, yet gen-

go to

forgave
John 8:11

Samaritan
John 4:1–30

Peter
John 21:15–19

tleness is how joy and trust in God are demonstrated in outward behavior. When we really believe God is in control, we don't need to be harsh in our words or actions. When we're really thinking Jesus could return at any moment, we want Him to catch us being kind to others. And kindness means I don't have to force anyone to do anything—because God can work within them to do the right thing. If we believe Jesus is coming back soon, we're reminded that life is short and choosing joy and gentleness is the best way to live. Bitterness and animosity really don't get us what we want.

The concept of "gentleness" includes not taking revenge or destructive action toward someone who has hurt you. It's the idea of being gracious and understanding of someone's weaknesses and inadequacies, even when you have every right to take justice against that person. Interestingly, this word is translated in a variety of ways in other Bible versions: patience, softness, patient mind, forbearance, forbearing spirit, even "meet a man halfway." The Greeks used this word to deal with situations that called for extra compassion or mercy rather than strict enforcement of a law. This is certainly what God does for every sinner by offering salvation instead of spiritual death, which we all deserve.

Jesus exemplified gentleness to those who were treated with contempt by others. He surprised His followers by paying attention to the needs of people whom others didn't care about. Gentleness is often the hardest way to respond when we encounter a person who isn't respected. Yet Jesus saw the person's inner need of Him and didn't respond to their outward appearance or circumstances.

- He <u>forgave</u> the woman caught in adultery.
- He interacted with the <u>Samaritan</u> woman at the well who wasn't respected in her village.
- He forgave and comforted <u>Peter</u> after Peter denied Him.

what others say

Kay Arthur

We *should* act with sweet reasonableness or forbearance because "The Lord is near"—watching, observing our behavior and our faithful obedience, or lack of it. Then if we look at the phrase from a different perspective, we see that we *are able* to maintain a sweet reasonableness because "The Lord is near"—available to infuse His strength into us![5]

Often, the very opposite of the way we naturally respond is the way God's kingdom works. Because we are naturally sinful, our first reactions aren't often the best—or what will glorify God. If we are in doubt about how to behave toward someone, maybe we should consider doing the opposite of our natural response—it just might be the godly one.

Prayer Plus Thanksgiving Equals Peace

PHILIPPIANS 4:6–7 *Be anxious for nothing, but in everything by prayer and supplication, with thanksgiving, let your requests be made known to God; and the peace of God, which surpasses all understanding, will guard your hearts and minds through Christ Jesus. (NKJV)*

Paul is on a roll in delineating the characteristics of a Christian walking with God: he or she has joy, gentleness, and, Paul adds now, peace. The Philippians certainly worried about many things, just like any of us, but they could also add possible persecution or death to their list. For believers in the first century, life was dangerous.

In the midst of that fearful possibility, Paul focuses on how to find peace because there are so many things that try to steal it: worrying and being anxious, for example. Paul commands his readers not to be anxious about *anything*. The fact that Paul commands the Philippians not to be anxious indicates that it is something they can control. Some people think of worry as something they can't control—something that they can't fight against. But Paul says they can stop being anxious by taking the positive steps of praying and being grateful. His formula goes like this:

- *Recognize:* Nothing is worth being anxious about, nor even a little worried. And God is interested in everything in our lives.
- *Pray:* Approach God.
- *Petition:* Request God's help in a specific need.
- *Thanksgiving:* Along with requesting, thank God for what He will faithfully do.
- *Present requests:* Call God's attention to the things that are of concern.
- *Peace:* Expect by faith that God will relieve your soul of the painful expectation that bad things will happen.

The word *guard* is a translation of the Greek word *phrouresei*, which was a military term meaning "to protect or **garrison** by guarding." Soldiers in Paul's day would stand at attention with ready weapons to make any attackers know they would defend their position. Through the Holy Spirit's power in the heavenly realm, when we pray, God establishes a guard around our hearts that protects further fear and worry from entering our heart's door.

Being anxious is different from being concerned. Paul was concerned about many things: the conflict between two women at the church, that the Philippians would criticize Epaphroditus, and that he wanted his friends to experience unity. But he wasn't anxious about those things. He did what he could about them and left the results to God. He didn't think that worrying would make things better but took the action that he could within his limited abilities.

> **what others say**
>
> ### Elisabeth Elliot
>
> Today's care, not tomorrow's, is the responsibility given to us, **apportioned** in the wisdom of God. Often we neglect the thing assigned for the moment because we are preoccupied with something that is not our business just now.[6]
>
> ### Max Lucado
>
> The German word for worry means "to strangle." The Greek word means "to divide the mind." Both are accurate. Worry is a noose on the neck and a distraction of the mind, neither of which is befitting for joy.[7]

apply it

Whenever we're worried or anxious, we are trying to be "god" in that situation. We believe that we can control the situation and that we know best. The next time you're tempted to be worried because you can't control what's happening, stop trying to take God's place in your life.

We really can't make or force inner peace to occur; it comes as a result of trusting God with our concerns. It also occurs within the heart when it seems impossible that such peace could be found under difficult and trying circumstances. When it does, that person knows it was God's work, not something he could make happen.

The peace that God offers is different from the peace of the world. There is a certain level of peace that can be obtained from society if someone concentrates enough on positive thoughts. But invariably, life will get out of control, and only then can a peace "higher" than the world—which <u>Jesus</u> referred to—bring the comfort that is needed.

Some Things to Think On

here

go to

Jesus
John 14:27

lies
John 8:44

truths
John 14:6

following
Proverbs 8:6

respected
1 Timothy 3:8;
Titus 2:2

PHILIPPIANS 4:8 *Finally, brethren, whatever things are true, whatever things are noble, whatever things are just, whatever things are pure, whatever things are lovely, whatever things are of good report, if there is any virtue and if there is anything praiseworthy—meditate on these things. (NKJV)*

Paul doesn't just say "Don't worry"; he tells his readers what to think about instead. The wonderful objects of thought he wants us to concentrate on will not only dispel worry and anxiety, but will also keep us focused on God. He encourages the Philippians to meditate on what is:

- *True:* Satan is the author of <u>lies</u> and wants us to go against the <u>truths</u> God has established in the world. Society may not believe that there are absolutes, but God has established certain unchangeable ideas that represent His perspective of the world He made. Wisdom is found in <u>following</u> those truths, not society's false claims.

- *Noble:* Being noble is no longer valued in the world. But God says think on those good things worthy to be <u>respected</u>, like values and the importance of people over things.

- *Just:* Just as there are truths, there is right and wrong and those things that are fair to all involved. In God's economy and from His viewpoint, there are certain correct ways to do things. Those are explained in the Bible. Not everything in our world has a right and wrong way, but when God says, "This is right, and this is wrong," you can be sure that He knows what He's talking about.

- *Pure:* <u>Purity is when there isn't a mixture. Pure gold is all gold</u>, not mostly gold and some metal. When we think on those things that are pure, we avoid putting in just a little of the opposite and calling it right or true. <u>The word *pure* is the word for wholesome</u>.

- *Lovely:* This word in the Greek refers to what promotes peace rather than conflict. When we think on lovely things, we will see the best in other people and not pick fights with them.

- *Of good report:* Worthy to be followed after and copied. It's when someone acts with a positive, constructive attitude rather than a negative, destructive viewpoint. When we see such a godly response in someone, we want to be like them, acting in the same ways. The things we admire are those things that are beyond our own ability and that challenge us to rise above our own inadequacies.

Paul then summarizes all these wonderful things in two distinct ways:

- *Virtue:* When people think about the qualities that Paul just related, they will think the best things.

- *Praiseworthy:* When someone deserves to be credited, we need to do so. We'll be able to if we've been focused on the first six things Paul talks about. Praising could mean giving a coworker credit even if it diminishes your own favor. Or it could be crediting a child's efforts at putting away toys, even though she didn't do it as neatly as you would have.

These are the things Paul wants every believer to dwell upon; to think upon. Not just to casually focus on every once in a while, but to meditate on continually. When someone focuses on the first six things, they have meditated on that which is virtuous and praiseworthy.

Paul's wording of "meditate on these things" isn't quite as passive as it initially sounds. It actually means "fill all your thoughts with these things." Paul doesn't want any corner of our minds to think on anything other than the wonderful things he mentions. If we don't sweep away negative and mean thinking from even one shelf in our mind's cabinets, it could gather more dust bunnies of negative thinking and then grow stronger.

what others say

Charles R. Swindoll

I say things like, "Okay, Chuck, it's time to let your mind dwell on better things." And then I go over the list and deliberately replace a worry with something far more honorable or pure or lovely, something worthy of praise. It never fails; the pressure I was feeling begins to fade and the peace I was missing begins to emerge.[8]

Just think of the difference it would make in a person's life if they chose to dwell on Paul's formula for positive thinking. The person who is depressed most likely wouldn't be depressed as much because they could see the good things that were shrouded by negative thinking. There is always something good to think about—even when life seems overwhelming and bad things happen. Every single experience has some good in it. And when we get to heaven, there won't be any memory of the bad.

The kind of positive thinking Paul is suggesting doesn't mean we don't acknowledge sin and confess it. There is a valid place for focusing on the wrong things we do and making them right with God. On the other hand, Satan wants us to continually hit ourselves mentally and emotionally over the head with negative and condemning thoughts. He knows that focusing on the past, even if our actions are forgiven, will discourage us from seeking God's power for right living. God, on the other hand, wants us to ask for His forgiveness, consider ourselves cleansed, and then focus continually on the things Paul writes about—because God's children are not condemned.

The spiritual things Paul is talking about are the opposite of what the world offers through television, movies, and the media. Which are you focusing on more? Whatever you concentrate on will determine how you respond to life and other people.

Monkey See, Monkey Do

> PHILIPPIANS 4:9 *The things which you learned and received and heard and saw in me, these do, and the God of peace will be with you.* (NKJV)

Paul is very confident that if people do what he does, they will be living the way God wants them to live. We already know he doesn't claim to be perfect—he said as much in chapter 3. But Paul knows that he has learned enough in his walk with God that he offers a worthy example to follow.

Paul may be referring to different ways that we acquire knowledge:

- *Learned:* Paul's personal instruction.
- *Received:* We must accept fully what we learn.
- *Heard:* We must have open ears to receive.
- *Seeing:* We observe others and learn what not to do from their

good
Romans 8:28

confess
1 John 1:9

condemned
Romans 8:1

~~wrong choices and we learn what to do from their correct choices.~~

Then Paul indicates that doing these things will bring about a relationship with God, who not only is peace Himself, but brings peace into a life dedicated to Him.

strengthen your family

Be careful, little eyes, what you see. If little eyes are watching you, what will they see? Is there anything worthy in you to mimic? Be aware that someone is always observing your life and that if you proclaim to follow Jesus, they are crediting your behavior to Jesus.

Many people say—especially to their children—"Do what I say, not what I do." But that is a philosophy that dishonors God. God wants us to be consistent in our responses—in both words and actions. He desires to give us the power we need to live by actions and words that reflect the way Jesus would act. Don't just listen to God's instructions; put His principles into action.

A Shift That Brought a Gift

PHILIPPIANS 4:10 *But I rejoiced in the Lord greatly that now at last your care for me has flourished again; though you surely did care, but you lacked opportunity.* (NKJV)

Epaphroditus brought Paul word about the Philippian church and, along with it, a financial gift. Since Paul was under house arrest and could not work for a living, he was totally dependent upon the gifts of others. It wasn't as if he were looking for enough money to live high on the hog—in fact, most likely he was barely making ends meet.

But the church's financial gift meant more to him than just money: It also expressed their concern for him. Paul feels the Philippians' love just like a father would rejoice in a child caring for an elderly parent. Paul may not have been elderly, but he was confined and dependent upon other caring people just like an elderly person in a nursing home.

Notice Paul's attitude of trust. He didn't beg anyone to help him. He just trusted that God would provide all his <u>needs</u>. The Philippians were unable to send a gift for about two years at one point, because they didn't know where Paul was located. But once they heard he was in prison, they sent their gift.

Paul didn't always accept financial gifts. He actually refused to accept a gift that the believers in <u>Corinth</u> offered him. At that time, he didn't want anyone to think he was preaching with the motive of getting money. Yet, Paul believed that a missionary should be <u>supported</u> by other believers, even though he sometimes had to help support himself by making tents.

needs
Philippians 4:19

Corinth
1 Corinthians
9:11–18

supported
1 Corinthians 9:14

what others say

Charles R. Swindoll

When he says, "You were concerned before, but you lacked opportunity," he means they had wanted to send an offering to him earlier, but they either didn't know where he was or they had no way to get it to him. Normally it is the other way around! We have an opportunity to send our support, but we lack concern.[10]

Of course, missionaries need financial support, but often they need more than that: They need <u>emotional support</u>. A financial gift demonstrates that support—even on an emotional level. When missionaries are out on the field and separated from their old friends, they need letters from home, phone calls, and other forms of contact.

Contentment Has Nothing to Do with Happiness

PHILIPPIANS 4:11–13 *Not that I speak in regard to need, for I have learned in whatever state I am, to be content: I know how to be abased, and I know how to abound. Everywhere and in all things I have learned both to be full and to be hungry, both to abound and to suffer need. I can do all things through Christ who strengthens me. (NKJV)*

limited perspective
Isaiah 55:8–9

experienced
2 Corinthians 6:4–10

Paul says he has learned to be content even when life isn't the way he would like it. Contentment can be described as seeing God's hand and surrendering to His plan no matter whether it seems good or bad, happy or unfortunate. The key word here is *seems*, because from our <u>limited perspective</u>, something may seem bad, but in the end, God creates good out of it.

That was Paul's perspective. Paul made the choice to surrender to God's plan for him even though he <u>experienced</u> the extremes of life: At times he lived well and had every need met. But more often, he was physically abused, persecuted almost to the point of death, deprived of food and water, and even experienced the deep grief of being misunderstood and called a heretic. Yet in the midst of all that, he depended upon God's strength to rejoice and trust that God's way and plan for his life were better than what he would prefer.

Paul's statement of "I can do everything" could be construed as pride in himself, so he's careful to include that his strength is based on God's power within him. Paul knew he could do anything in God's strength—if God wanted him to do it!

We all can take comfort in the fact that even the great apostle Paul had to *learn* to be content. Of all people, we would expect that he wouldn't have had to learn it—that it came naturally. Yet, even Paul needed to go through a process that taught him to choose contentment.

In Paul's day, a group of religious people, the "Stoics," taught that the goal of contentment was to give up having emotions about everything. The Greek word for *content* is *autarkes*, which is translated "self-sufficient." Their warped idea of "self-sufficient" meant that even if your husband or wife died, you replied, "I don't care." The goal was to divorce themselves from having feelings. Paul used the same word for contentment in a revolutionary way: to trust in God, not yourself, and also have emotions.

> **what others say**
>
> **Rick Warren**
>
> Put Jesus Christ in the driver's seat of your life and take your hands off the steering wheel. Don't be afraid; nothing under His control can ever be out of control. Mastered by Christ, you can handle anything.[11]

Charles Stanley

It is God's responsibility to provide the things we need. It is our responsibility to trust Him and to keep our focus on who He is and what He supplies rather than on what is missing or lacking in our lives. Too often, we shift our focus so that it is exactly the opposite of God's plan. We start trusting in what we have and looking at what we don't have and blaming God for our lack! Rather, let's trust God to be the source of our total supply and keep our eyes on what He provides.[12]

Paul's great statement, "I can do all things through Christ who strengthens me," was specifically referring to being content—the subject of the previous verse. But because he says "all things," we can apply it to anything in our lives: whether it's strength to give a testimony when you're afraid to speak in public, or a need to believe God can heal your marriage. And at the core of all those "all things" is the need for contentment. When we are content, we show we're trusting God.

Contentment can only come from truly trusting God, believing that He knows what is best—even when life is unhappy or disappointing. A lack of contentment means that we are trying to force life to be the way we think it should be—rather than the way God has chosen for us.

Coming to My Aid

PHILIPPIANS 4:14–16 *Nevertheless you have done well that you shared in my distress. Now you Philippians know also that in the beginning of the gospel, when I departed from Macedonia, no church shared with me concerning giving and receiving but you only. For even in Thessalonica you sent aid once and again for my necessities. (NKJV)*

Even though Paul is content, he is grateful for the help of others. Paul again expresses that he isn't just interested in getting their money: He wants them to support him in his troubles. He needs their financial support, yes, but even more, he needs their emotional support: to know that he is cared about and valued. And Paul knows that he has indeed received that consistently and lovingly from these dear believers. He credits their involvement in his ministry and reminds them that he hasn't forgotten their faithful support.

Thessalonica
Acts 17:1

shared
Acts 16:1–40

something to ponder

what others say

Malcolm O. Tolbert

"Partnership with me in giving and receiving" expresses one of Paul's major ideas about the church. Believers bring what they have to the fellowship of the body and receive from it what they lack. The Philippians had received from Paul. Through him they had heard the gospel. They had given material gifts to Paul at least twice previously during his ministry in Thessalonica.[13]

The Philippians had supported Paul from the very beginning when he first shared the gospel message with them. When he left their town for another on his missionary journey, they sent money along with him to support him. Then, when Paul was ministering in Thessalonica, the Philippians sent him a monetary gift two times.

Paul's Piggy Bank Has a Big Balance

PHILIPPIANS 4:17–18 *Not that I seek the gift, but I seek the fruit that abounds to your account. Indeed I have all and abound. I am full, having received from Epaphroditus the things sent from you, a sweet-smelling aroma, an acceptable sacrifice, well pleasing to God.* (NKJV)

Paul suddenly seems to realize that maybe his comments could be misinterpreted, so he quickly explains that he's not just interested in getting money from them, but for the blessings they receive from being generous. He believes that their giving will not be forgotten by God and that they will receive a reward in heaven. He doesn't want them to miss out on that. They aren't just giving for an earthly project; they are investing toward an eternal one.

Paul doesn't want his letter to come across as a plea for money. He says he's quite taken care of because of their generosity. He also doesn't want to appear ungrateful for their wonderful care.

Paul's phrase "a sweet-smelling aroma, an acceptable sacrifice, well pleasing to God" refers back to the Old Testament sacrifices. When animal sacrifice was burned, the smell was something that pleased God because the sacrifice represented His people's dedication and obedience.

The first record in the Bible of a sacrifice's aroma being pleasing to God was when <u>Noah</u> offered a sacrifice. Then the Israelites in their wanderings were given rules for giving <u>sacrifices</u> to God. And now in the New Testament Paul uses it as a symbol for being pleasing to God. In Ephesians 5:1–2 he writes, "Therefore be imitators of God as dear children. And walk in love, as Christ also has loved us and given Himself for us, an offering and a sacrifice to God for a sweet-smelling aroma" (NKJV).

Noah
Genesis 8:20–22

sacrifices
Leviticus 1:9

generous
Matthew 20:15

owns
Psalm 50:10

> **what others say**
>
> **Malcolm O. Tolbert**
>
> Paul wanted the Philippians to know that he did not expect anything else from them. Whatever they owed to him, they could consider the bill paid in full. "Received full payment" is a technical financial expression often found on receipts of the period.[14]

It's not always a selfish desire to have people contribute to a worthy goal—even if it's your own mission outreach or organization. When people give with the desire to see God glorified and to help people, it pleases God and that brings a blessing from Him. Today's missionaries can ask freely for support because they can know it will actually bring a reward to those supporters from God.

When someone gives generously to you, you may not have the means to pay them back and you might never be able to reciprocate. But God can. He can bless them for their generosity to you. So commit their loving support to your great God and know that you don't have to feel guilty if they've helped you without your ability to give back.

There's More Where That Came From

> **PHILIPPIANS 4:19–20** *And my God shall supply all your need according to His riches in glory by Christ Jesus. Now to our God and Father be glory forever and ever. Amen. (NKJV)*

Paul assures his readers that God won't leave them high and dry because of their support of him. God is not only <u>generous</u> (after all, He created and <u>owns</u> everything); His love wants to provide for them.

Beth Moore

God is not only the answer to a thousand needs, He is the answer to a thousand wants. He is the fulfillment of our chief desire in all of life. For whether or not we've ever recognized it, what we desire is unfailing love. O God, awake our souls to see—You are what we want, not just what we need.[15]

Anne Graham Lotz

We may intellectually grasp the truth that God's power is adequate, but we can never know that by experience if we stay in our comfort zone. If all you ever attempt is what you know you can do yourself, if all your needs seem to be met through someone or something other than God, if you never have any difficulties that are greater than you can bear—how will you know the awesome greatness and personal availability of His infinite power?[16]

God promises to meet all our true needs. We might think that we can ask for anything we want, but His promise refers to "true" needs—not our wants. If we get our wants and our needs mixed up, we're going to think God should give us a new car every year or the fanciest wardrobe—but that isn't what this promise is about. Literally, our needs are actually only those things needed to stay alive. Anything else is a "want." But because God is generous, He often gives us our desires, our wants, too.

Don't Cry for Me

PHILIPPIANS 4:21–23 *Greet every saint in Christ Jesus. The brethren who are with me greet you. All the saints greet you, but especially those who are of Caesar's household. The grace of our Lord Jesus Christ be with you all. Amen. (NKJV)*

Remembering that a "saint" is any believer of Jesus, we can say a gentle good-bye to Paul's letter to the Philippians. He has concluded after exhorting them to adopt many wonderful qualities: love, humility, joy, unity, and faith. He wants the Philippians to know they are not alone in their belief and service for the Lord—Paul is surrounded by believers also—even in the secular world of Rome. What fruit from his ministry! No wonder Paul's conclusion isn't some sad last words, but a rich greeting accompanied by a declaration of God's grace—as was his <u>custom</u> in his letters.

custom
Ephesians 6:24, 3
Philemon 25

When Paul writes "those who are of Caesar's household," he doesn't mean exclusively the relatives of Caesar. Commentators have varying opinions about the extent of what "household" means, but it could be those who were relatives and worked within the palaces, including slaves and staff. Or it could mean everyone who served the Caesar all over the world. The important thing is that there were even believers surrounding Caesar—and those who were local to Paul most likely came to know the Lord through Paul as he was imprisoned.

The Roman believers send their greetings to their Philippian brothers and sisters in the Lord. These believers in different locations—those in Philippi and those in Rome—had never met, and yet they shared a common interest and commitment. There could be unity and concern among them all, even though they comprised every strata of society, because Jesus was the most important person in each of their lives.

> ## what others say
>
> ### John F. Walvoord
>
> The Christian life, which is an expression of grace, is by grace sustained, and the final verse to some extent summarizes all of Paul's yearnings for these Christians who had manifested their love and care for him.[17]

Paul has a lack of bitterness about his situation throughout his letter—from the first verse to the last. He is a refreshing model of faithfulness from start to finish. If you've become discouraged because living the Christian life is just too difficult, take a dose of inspiration from Paul—and take hold of that grace and "greeting" that he talks about. As a result, you'll experience the wonderful character qualities that Paul desired for his Philippian friends.

apply it

Chapter Wrap-Up

- Just like a runner proudly wears the wreath after winning a race, Paul says he's "wearing" a crown representing the believers in Philippi. That's because he's proud of their maturity in the Lord. (Philippians 4:1)

- Paul wisely doesn't try to control the conflict between Euodia and Syntyche but advises a fellow Christian in the congregation to help them resolve their disagreement. And Paul says that overall, everyone should be gentle toward everyone else. (Philippians 4:2–5)

- Everyone can be tempted to worry and think negatively, so Paul gives practical ideas for coping by telling God your concerns and thanking Him for the way He'll answer. He also says for people to focus on the things that are good, things like truth, honor, purity, loveliness, praise, and excellence. (Philippians 4:6–9)

- Paul was very grateful for the financial support from the Philippians that showed their love and confidence in him. But he didn't want them to think that he was discontented without it. He stresses that he knows God will provide all his needs and encourages them to follow his example of trusting God. (Philippians 4:10–23)

Study Questions

1. In what interesting way does Paul express how important his Philippian friends are to him?

2. Who is creating some conflicts in Philippi, and what does Paul say should be done?

3. How does Paul say believers should cope with anxiety and negative thinking?

4. How does Paul give an example of contentment?

Part Three
COLOSSIANS

Let's Get Started

While Paul was imprisoned, he heard that the Christians in the Asian city of Colosse were being influenced by some incorrect teaching. Of course, he didn't want that to continue, so he wrote them a letter, sometime between the years of AD 60 and AD 62, and today we call that letter Colossians—in other words, Paul's letter or epistle to the church members in the city of Colosse. He called upon the service of <u>Tychicus</u> to take his letter to Colosse, and Tychicus also delivered Paul's letter to the Ephesians about the same time. Paul reached out to his Colossian brothers and sisters, but there is no record that he actually ever visited there. Yet commentators believe he directed the church's beginnings there from a distance. The members there were primarily Gentiles. Based on Colossians 4:12, commentators believe <u>Epaphras</u> founded the churches in Colosse, Hierapolis, and Laodicea.

Tychicus
Colossians 4:7

Epaphras
Colossians 4:12

Colosse was located in the Lycus Valley, about one hundred miles east of Ephesus in Asia Minor. Other cities in the valley included Hierapolis and Laodicea. Colosse's name may have been after the city's large statue, *Colossus*. The large stone statue may have been carved from the stony deposits that were a part of the geography there. Colosse was rich in mineral deposits but also had frequent earthquakes.

There were two primary trades of the valley where Colosse stood: first, it was the greatest center of the woolen industry because of the rich pastureland that supported flocks of sheep. Associated with that was the second commerce, dyeing of the wool that those sheep produced. The River Lycus that flowed through the valley deposited chalk, which contributed to a high level of quality dyeing. In fact, a particular dye was named after Colosse. Over time, Hierapolis and Laodicea prospered but Colosse failed. Today there are standing ruins that show the greatness of the first two, but nothing to show where Colosse stood. Many scholars say that Colosse was the most insignificant town Paul ever wrote to.

The problem the Colossians faced was big enough, though, to warrant Paul writing his letter. He was concerned that they were begin-

asceticism
relentless (sometimes excessive) self-denial

ning to be pulled away from true faith in Christ. Regardless of the impact of Paul's letter, this competing philosophy would continue and eventually turn into what became known as Gnosticism. This heresy of Jewish, Greek, and pagan threads of thought that Paul contended with had these distinguishing points (although not all commentators believe that there was a definitive heresy being taught):

1. It stressed the need for observing Old Testament laws and ceremonies, therefore it was Jewish in nature.

2. It taught that believers had to know some special or deeper knowledge in order to be included.

3. Angels were worshipped as mediators between men and God.

4. It believed only its own converts were true believers and they were given the distinction of special privileges and a state of "perfection."

5. It denied the deity of Christ.

Paul, without specifically naming these qualities, addressed this heresy in his letter, particularly addressing the deity of Christ and the needed spiritual growth of Christians so that they wouldn't believe wrong ideas.

The Colossian Heresy[1]

Paul answered the various tenets of the Colossian heresy that threatened the church. This heresy was a mixed bag, containing elements from several different heresies, some of which contradicted each other (as shown below).

The Heresy	Reference in Colossians	Paul's Answer
Spirit is good; matter is evil.	1:15–20	God created heaven and earth for His glory.
One must follow ceremonies, rituals, and restrictions in order to be saved or perfected.	2:11, 16–23; 3:11	These were only shadows that ended when Christ came. He is all you need to be saved.
One must deny the body and live in strict **asceticism**.	2:20–23	Asceticism is no help in conquering evil thoughts and desires; instead, it leads to pride.
Angels must be worshipped.	2:18	Angels are not to be worshipped; Christ alone is worthy of worship.
Christ could not be both human and divine.	1:15–20; 2:2–3	Christ is God in the flesh; He is the eternal One, Head of the body, first in everything; supreme.

The Colossian Heresy (cont'd)

The Heresy	Reference in Colossians	Paul's Answer
One must obtain "secret knowledge" in order to be saved or perfected—and this was not available to everyone.	2:2, 18	God's secret is Christ, and He has been revealed to all.
One must adhere to human wisdom, tradition, and philosophies.	2:4, 8–10; 3:15–17	By themselves, these can be misleading and shallow because they have human origin; instead, we should remember what Christ taught and follow His words as our ultimate authority.
It is even better to combine aspects of several religions.	2:10	You have everything when you have Christ: He is all-sufficient.
There is nothing wrong with immorality.	3:1–11	Get rid of sin and evil because you have been chosen by God to live a new life as a representative of the Lord Jesus.

go to

authority
Ephesians 1:1;
2 Corinthians 1:1

what others say

Charles R. Swindoll

Gnostics taught that matter was evil, and that whatever was physically pleasing to humans was spiritually displeasing to God—which would include things like marriage and eating certain foods. So they taught, "You're not to marry, and you shouldn't eat certain foods."[2]

Paul's purpose in writing this letter is to say, "Jesus is enough. Nothing additional is needed." He wants his readers to grow strong in a mature faith and knowledge of Jesus and His role in their lives. Therefore he stresses Jesus's deity and His lordship over their lives.

Calling All Those Holy and Faithful

COLOSSIANS 1:1–2 *Paul, an apostle of Jesus Christ by the will of God, and Timothy our brother, to the saints and faithful brethren in Christ who are in Colosse: Grace to you and peace from God our Father and the Lord Jesus Christ.* (NKJV)

As an apostle, Paul needed to identify himself as a person in <u>authority</u> in order to have the power he needed to fight against the

go to

Philippians
Philippians 1:8

see
Acts 9:1–5;
1 Corinthians 9:1

miraculous
2 Corinthians 12:12

Gentile
Acts 16:1

mother
2 Timothy 1:5

Scripture
2 Timothy 3:15

creeping heresy that he would be addressing, especially since he didn't have a personal relationship with these believers like he had with the <u>Philippians</u>. He had never been to Colosse but only knew of them through Epaphras. Although he was not one of the original twelve followers of Jesus—the usual requirement for apostleship—Paul did <u>see</u> Jesus personally and he had <u>miraculous</u> powers. The Greek word for *apostle* is *apostolos* and means "one who is sent out." Paul clarifies that it was God who called him and sent him out ("*by the will of God*"), not his own choice.

Paul never starts his letters with "worldly" kind of accomplishments as his qualifications. He doesn't say, "I've now written eighty letters and led millions to the Lord. I've traveled bazillions of miles in my travels and have frequent-flier miles for every airline. I have every right to write to you—so that's why you should pay attention to me." No, he writes as a fellow Christian who is qualified by being called and sent by God.

Timothy must have been known to the Colossian believers because Paul refers to him. Timothy was the son of a <u>Gentile</u>, but his <u>mother</u> and grandmother were godly Jewesses who had taught him the <u>Scripture</u> from childhood.

Paul affirmed to these believers that in God's sight they were saints and faithful. He is encouraging in his words to them and reminds them of their position in Christ—saints and faithful—something that they would not benefit from if they chose to follow the heretical teachings that some were trying to have them believe.

Paul's use of the word *saints* doesn't mean Christians who had achieved some super-special attainment or award. In Greek, it's the word meaning "set apart, sanctified, consecrated, or holy." Every Christian is a saint because their sins have been cleansed by Jesus's death. That qualifies them to have a relationship with God and to go to heaven. Thankfully, it has nothing to do with earning that description because none of us could.

A characteristic greeting of grace and peace helps us identify this letter as one of Paul's. That was the opening for most of his letters, referring to the grace that meant in Greek "Rejoice!" (*Charis*) and shalom (*eirene*). These were both greetings to the Colossians and an expression of Paul's desires for them. If they had those two things through knowing Jesus, they would have joy, gratification, harmony, and everything intended for a person's good. Although these two words were the common greetings of people at that time, as Paul so often did, he took frequently used ideas and applied them to Christian living. And in this case, the results of salvation and living in tune with God.

go to

faithfulness
Galatians 5:22

holiness
1 Corinthians 1:30

what others say

Stuart Briscoe

The root from which we get the word *holy* is the word meaning "to cut," to separate something from the rest, to make it distinctive, other, something else. When God picks a word to describe Himself, He uses the word *holy*. That means He's distinct, separate, other.

People who are "in Christ" spiritually are required to be holy and moral—to live distinctively. There are some things holy people won't get into. They're too smart.[3]

Faithfulness is something that we each have a choice about including in our lives. It takes action and wise choices. We, as followers of Jesus, can see ourselves as "holy" in God's sight, but we must make a moment-by-moment decision to stay faithful to God's plan and desires for us. And when we do, we live out our holiness.

apply it

here Oct 6

You Mean I'm a Saint?

> **COLOSSIANS 1:3–4** *We give thanks to the God and Father of our Lord Jesus Christ, praying always for you, since we heard of your faith in Christ Jesus and of your love for all the saints;* (NKJV)

Paul didn't pounce upon the believers about the heresy they were considering. He could have started his letter, "You are stupid for beginning to believe something that isn't true! Wise up!" Instead, he trusted God enough to tell them he was praying for them and, in a sense, holding them accountable before God with his prayers. But Paul didn't just say, "I'm praying for you"; he told them exactly *what* he was praying for them. How powerful that must have been. When these believers received his letter, they knew they were hearing the words that were being prayed on their behalf before the very throne of God. That must have really gotten their attention! And since he wasn't just praying for them but expressing gratitude, they must have been encouraged.

love
Galatians 5:6

covenantal
Genesis 6:18

fidelity
allegiance

Paul was grateful for them because of their faith and love. They believed in Jesus as Lord and Savior, and they expressed God's <u>love</u> toward other believers—other saints—even when some saints didn't always act "saintly." Paul was good at rehearsing people's good points, and he was eager to point out the Colossian believers' worthy attributes.

---

what others say

Robert Wall

Paul's frequent use of *Father* alludes to an important Old Testament metaphor for God's <u>covenantal</u> relationship with Israel. Thanksgiving is given to God, then, within the framework of a covenant of mutual **fidelity**. Thus, to express thanks to God as our Father not only acknowledges God's faithfulness to us but also assumes our covenantal obligation to obey God in return, even as the child is responsible to bring honor to his or her father.[4]

key point

When we are concerned about someone, especially if we fear they are starting to turn away from God, our natural tendency is to tell them everything they are doing wrong and what they should change. But Paul didn't do that. He trusted God enough to work in the Colossians' lives by saying he believed in them and by gently pointing out the truth. If we believe God is a big enough God to work in the lives of others, we will also be content with praying for our loved one and gently pointing out the truth. We can't control anyone else, but we can influence them with our example and words.

People are most encouraged to do the right thing when we express gratitude for them and concentrate on the positives. <u>Giving thanks and even letting a person know how we are thanking God for them could do more to influence them toward good behavior than constantly telling them the right thing to do.</u>

Paul is grateful for their love for all the saints. Because love isn't a feeling but a choice for a person's highest good, you must choose to love *all* people, not just the ones you like.

The Three Legs of the Christian Chair

COLOSSIANS 1:5–6 *because of the hope which is laid up for you in heaven, of which you heard before in the word of the truth of the gospel, which has come to you, as it has also in all the world,* *and is bringing forth fruit, as it is also among you since the day you heard and knew the grace of God in truth; (NKJV)*

go to

faith
Hebrews 11:6

love
Romans 5:8

hope
Romans 5:5

three
1 Corinthians 13:13

fruit
Galatians 5:22–23

world
Romans 1:8

Paul mentions faith and love in verse 4, and now he brings in hope. These three elements are the foundations for the three-legged stool of Christianity:

- *Faith* refers to believing that Jesus died in someone's place for his or her salvation.

- *Love* is God reaching out to people unconditionally even though they don't deserve love.

- *Hope* is the expected end of living with God in heaven after a person's death. Paul's phrase "laid up for you in heaven" refers to the security the believer has because salvation can't be taken from any Christian.

Those three aspects of Christianity are the basics that the Colossians would forsake if they were pulled into the heresy that some were preaching in that church. Paul doesn't mention "knowledge" because one of the aspects of that heresy was the belief that people who were truly saved had a special accumulation of knowledge. The heresy also included the belief that knowledge wasn't gained through Jesus because they didn't believe Jesus was God or that they needed Him to be their Savior. Paul counters the heresy by saying that's not truth; needing Jesus as Savior is truth—because it's "gospel." Besides, Paul urges these believers, "look at how this truth makes such a difference in people's lives." That's the fruit of changed lives, which Paul could say was happening all over the known world.

The Greek word for *gospel* is *euangelion*, meaning "good news." It's good news because the death and resurrection of Jesus offer eternal life and abundant life. It's also good news because salvation is a free gift; we need only to receive it, not work for it. All other "religions" are designed to tell people how they can work toward or be good enough to deserve a right relationship with their god. But Christianity is different because God offers relationship with Him based on what He did to make it happen.

go to

alone
Romans 11:6;
Titus 3:5–7

Epaphras
Philemon 23

Bible Knowledge Commentary

Faith is the soul looking *upward* to God; love looks *outward* to others; hope looks *forward* to the future. Faith rests on the past work of Christ; love works in the present; and hope anticipates the future.[5]

Robert Wall

God's grace is a difficult notion for most people to grasp, partly because it contradicts so much of what we learn and experience from the non-Christian society that surrounds and conditions us. Everyday experience teaches us that receiving gifts from others is conditioned on first giving gifts.[6]

key point

It's not what you know that saves you, but who you know—Jesus. Don't add anything to the gospel. Nothing else is needed for salvation. Some people say that we can only be saved through Jesus and works. But that's not grace at all. Jesus—and Jesus alone—is sufficient for a person's salvation.

When we desire to grow stronger in Christ, we so often think we have to spiritually grit our teeth and try harder. But Paul says that the gospel bears fruit and causes us to grow. We don't make it happens—it happens as we get to know God better and obey Him more and more. You don't need to strive by performing; instead, just cooperate with God's Spirit within you and let Him do it.

Popping His Buttons with Pride

COLOSSIANS 1:7–8 *as you also learned from Epaphras, our dear fellow servant, who is a faithful minister of Christ on your behalf, who also declared to us your love in the Spirit. (NKJV)*

Almost two hundred years before Jesus walked the earth, Jews from Israel were forced to disperse to other countries. In doing so, some found their way to Colosse. Years later, Epaphras—a convert because of Paul's ministry—preached the truth about Jesus in that city and a church was born. Paul acknowledges their "spiritual father" Epaphras, and gives him the credit he deserves. Evidently, Paul heard about the Colossian church from Epaphras, who was popping his buttons in pride talking about what God had done there.

Epaphras is the shortened name for "Epaphroditus." Paul mentions an, "Epaphroditus" in his other writings. The one mentioned in Philippians was the pastor or elder of the church at Philippi. Commentators don't know if the man mentioned by Paul in connection with the Colosse church is the same man from Philippi.

Paul graciously talked about his fellow servant Epaphras. Jesus was like that too, and He was especially gracious and merciful toward those who were needy. With the <u>woman</u> taken in adultery, He didn't condemn but forgave. When <u>Nicodemus</u> wanted to argue theology, Jesus patiently revealed the truth.

go to

woman
John 8:3–11

Nicodemus
John 3:1–21

reprimand
Matthew 21:12

Philippians
Philippians 2:16

jealousy
Romans 13:13

schemes
Ephesians 6:11

what others say

J. Vernon McGee

Have you noticed how graciously Paul could talk about other servants of God? Paul had something good to say about those who were preaching the Word of God. But when he found a rascal, he was just like our Lord in that he would really <u>reprimand</u> evil when he saw it.[7]

Paul doesn't mind giving credit where credit is due. He wasn't the "spiritual father" of these believers like he was with so many of the other groups he wrote to, like the <u>Philippians</u>. He couldn't take credit for their growth. But instead of being jealous of someone else who was having an impact, he gladly credited Epaphras. If we really want God's glory, we won't mind giving credit to others who deserve it. <u>Jealousy</u> and envy are Satan's tools for dividing the body of Christ. We should do nothing to cooperate with his devious <u>schemes</u>.

apply it

You Don't Get an Edge with Knowledge

COLOSSIANS 1:9–12a *For this reason we also, since the day we heard it, do not cease to pray for you, and to ask that you may be filled with the knowledge of His will in all wisdom and spiritual understanding; that you may walk worthy of the Lord, fully pleasing Him, being fruitful in every good work and increasing in the knowledge of God; strengthened with all might, according to His glorious power, for all patience and longsuffering with joy; giving thanks to the Father* (NKJV)

knowledge
1 Corinthians 8:1

worthy
Ephesians 4:1

thank
Ephesians 5:26

The heresy being spread at the Colossian church said something like, "Just get knowledge, and the more the better. It doesn't need to make a difference in your life, but it does serve the purpose of pointing out who the special believers in God are. You want to be one of the special ones, don't you?"

Paul counters that by saying in effect, "That's bunk! <u>Knowledge</u> isn't only to be stored up in your mind; it's supposed to make a difference in the way you live." Then he goes on to point out the difference it should make, like:

- *Knowing God's will:* Having spiritual direction for problem solving and direction for making decisions.

- *Having spiritual wisdom and understanding:* Having insights that only God can give, and then applying them to daily living.

- *Living a <u>worthy</u> and godly life that pleases God:* Making choices that are moral and show Christlike character.

- *Being fruitful in every good work:* The things God would lead them to do would cause others to know Jesus personally.

- *Increasing in the knowledge of God:* They would change any lies about God to be the truth of who He really is.

- *Strengthened with all might:* They would be able to endure trials patiently in God's strength.

- *Patience and longsuffering with joy:* They would not just put up with difficult circumstances but victoriously give glory to God by the way they reacted. "Patience" refers to dealing with life, and "longsuffering" refers to dealing with people. Both can be done, Paul says, with joy, a deep trust in God.

- *Having a grateful heart:* Regardless of their circumstances, they would <u>thank</u> God.

The knowledge that Paul is talking about is an enlightened viewpoint of life that sees through God's eyes and responds the way Jesus did. And it is a practical outworking that is able to respond to problems or trials in a godly way—just like Jesus would have. Solomon wrote, "The fear of the LORD is the beginning of knowledge, but fools despise wisdom and instruction" (Proverbs 1:7 NKJV).

key point

It may sound like Paul was praying for these beloved people twenty-four hours a day, but that's not what he meant. He means

that he remembered to <u>pray</u> for them any time he regularly prayed, and that most likely meant daily.

pray
Acts 20:31

God
2 Corinthians 5:9

people pleaser
Galatians 1:10

inheritance
Ephesians 1:1–14

spiritual blessings
Ephesians 1:3

what others say

Bill Hybels

Nothing is too big for God to handle or too small for him to be interested in. Still, I sometimes wonder if my requests are legitimate. So I'm honest with God. I say, "Lord, I don't know if I have the right to ask for this. I don't know how I should pray about it. But I lift it to You, and if You'll tell me how to pray, I'll pray Your way."[8]

Have you ever wondered how to pray for someone when you don't know their needs? Paul gives us an example in these verses of the things that every believer needs. You could apply these verses by adding someone's name and making them into a prayer for that person. If you do, you will have covered their spiritual needs thoroughly—without even knowing what they are.

The only person we need to please is <u>God</u>. So often we are more concerned about what other people think of us than what God thinks. Being a <u>people pleaser</u> is an emotional disease that prevents us from responding to life and other people like Jesus wants us to do. Because if our eyes are on people, we won't stay focused on God's direction and will.

<u>What Benefits! What Blessings!</u>

COLOSSIANS 1:12b–14 *who has qualified us to be partakers of the inheritance of the saints in the light. He has delivered us from the power of darkness and conveyed us into the kingdom of the Son of His love, in whom we have redemption through His blood, the forgiveness of sins.* (NKJV)

If you want someone to be motivated to do what you say or to see your viewpoint, just point out the benefits of your comments. Paul did exactly that. He wants the Colossian believers to understand what wonderful blessings they enjoy from knowing God and following His ways. He lists several that should make every Christian rejoice:

- Qualified to partake in a saint's <u>inheritance</u> of living in the light. A Christian's inheritance includes all the <u>spiritual blessings</u> that

sealing
Ephesians 1:13

blood
Romans 5:9

set free
Galatians 5:1

redeemed
Hebrews 9:12

forgotten
Isaiah 43:25

delivered
2 Corinthians 1:10

come with knowing Jesus, like the <u>sealing</u> of the Holy Spirit, God's love, and knowing God's grace.

- Delivered from the power of darkness. Satan holds hostage every unbeliever, doomed for eternal destruction, until they are set free by Jesus's <u>blood</u>.

- Conveyed into Jesus's kingdom. A Christian is <u>set free</u> from sin and able to obey God.

- <u>Redeemed</u>. Means "to be rescued by ransom." Jesus paid the price that a person would normally pay themselves by dying spiritually. The word had the meaning "to purchase from the slave market," and of course every unbeliever is still held captive by Satan.

- Forgiven. Every Christian's sins are completely forgiven and <u>forgotten</u> by God.

The Greek word for *convey*, *methistemi*, is very interesting. When an army conquered a land, it was the custom to transfer the whole defeated population and all it owned back to the victorious country. Paul is saying that God has taken us to His kingdom—lock, stock, and barrel.

Paul uses the Greek word *ruomai* to describe the kind of "deliverance" every Christian has experienced. It's a word indicating that we were in serious danger, yet <u>delivered</u> from a hostile power in a very dangerous situation. Indeed! Without Jesus, we would all go to hell—the most dangerous place ever.

Deliverance Metaphors

Paul uses several different metaphors to describe deliverance in his numerous letters.

Scripture	Metaphor for deliverance
Romans 3:21–31	Paul describes deliverance from condemnation as the sinner stands (as in a courtroom) before God, accused and worthy of hell. But God "justifies" the believer as "righteous."
1 Corinthians 6:20	The believer is like a slave in the marketplace before God, worthy to be condemned and sold. But because of the payment of Jesus, the slave is set free.
2 Corinthians 5:18	The believer is like an enemy in war, fighting God with his wrong choices. But God declares him a friend, and he is delivered from sure defeat.
Ephesians 1:5	The believer is an alien child without a family. But because of Jesus's adoption, she becomes a member of God's family.
Ephesians 1:7	The believer is bankrupt, carrying an overwhelming debt. But Jesus pays the debt and the debtor is freed.

Philip Yancey

I grew up with the image of a mathematical God who weighed my good and bad deeds on a set of scales and always found me wanting. Somehow I missed the God of the Gospels, a God of mercy and generosity who keeps finding ways to shatter the relentless laws of ungrace. God tears up the mathematical tables and introduces the new math of *grace*, the most surprising, twisting, unexpected-ending word in the English language.[9]

If you are a Christian, then you are the most blessed person on earth. You enjoy many benefits and blessings, and it's easy to start taking them for granted if you don't focus on thanking God for them. Consider making a study of the different ingredients that make up your inheritance in Christ. You can begin by studying the first chapter of Ephesians, which lists many of them.

something to ponder

It's Not "The Force," It's Jesus

COLOSSIANS 1:15 *He is the image of the invisible God, the first-born over all creation.* (NKJV)

In case anyone doubts the power behind the promises of "living in God's light" that Paul had just made, he transitions into describing who Jesus is and the authority He holds. But his eloquent words describing Jesus's deity had a very important purpose: He was countering the false teachers' beliefs that "Jesus is pretty good, but He's not the only program in town. You can believe in any number of spiritual beings because they are all equal with Jesus."

Those preaching the heresy said Jesus was a prominent person, but Paul wants his readers to think of Him as not only prominent, but **preeminent**. He is the most important person ever to walk the earth, and that wasn't all: He was literally God in the flesh. He was and is God and <u>reflects</u> God the Father perfectly. If someone wants to know what God the Father is like, they just need to <u>look</u> at Jesus, His Son. In a sense, Jesus is the "mirror <u>image</u>" of God, just as if you or I looked into a mirror and saw the exact likeness of ourselves.

In addition to being preeminent, Paul stresses that Jesus is the firstborn over all creation. This is not saying that Jesus was born into

go to

reflects
Hebrews 1:3

look
John 14:8–9

image
2 Corinthians 4:4

preeminent
surpassing

the godhead or created, but that He preceded the whole creation and is sovereign over all creation because He was the force that created it. This statement refers to Jesus's place of authority because a firstborn human has a superior position in the family.

Many commentators believe that Colossians 1:15–20 is Paul's slightly changed version of a hymn that Christians were singing at that point in history. For his own purposes of stressing the lordship and sovereignty of Jesus, he made a few changes from the original hymn.

We all wonder what God is like. Well, wonder no more! We don't have to speculate or guess. We just have to read the Gospel accounts (Matthew, Mark, Luke, and John) in order to find out more about God's qualities and desires. If you want to know how God would respond to you, just find out how Jesus responded to someone in a similar circumstance. No more guessing or being uncertain. It's all recorded so that we can feel secure in God's love.

key point

"He's Got the Whole World in His Hands"

COLOSSIANS 1:16–17 *For by Him all things were created that are in heaven and that are on earth, visible and invisible, whether thrones or dominions or principalities or powers. All things were created through Him and for Him. And He is before all things, and in Him all things consist. (NKJV)*

What would you reply if someone said to you, "The physical world is evil, therefore God would never choose to dirty Himself by becoming human. Plus, since the world is evil, God couldn't have created it because a holy God can't create evil"? That is exactly the reasoning of the false teachers Paul was trying to fight against as he continued to persuasively argue a godly perspective. He is saying through these wonderful descriptions of Jesus: The world isn't evil, and God lovingly chose to come in human form to <u>demonstrate</u> His love. And yes, God did <u>create</u> our world through His Son, Jesus. In fact, everything was <u>created</u> by Jesus. Not only that, but He makes sure that the whole world doesn't disintegrate. He holds it all together like the Prudential Insurance "hands" on their TV ads.

Paul's reference to the spiritual world—thrones or dominions or principalities or powers—isn't just to include every created thing; it's to counter the false teachers' heretical instruction that angels were equal to Jesus and worthy to be <u>worshipped</u> just like Him. But Paul says, "They aren't equal at all, Jesus created *them*! Angels are created beings that Jesus made possible. See? Jesus is superior!"

go to

demonstrate
Romans 5:8

create
John 1:3

created
Hebrews 1:2

worshipped
Colossians 2:18

gradations
layers or levels

what others say

J. Vernon McGee

It is very interesting here to note that he mentions different **gradations** of rank in spiritual intelligences: thrones, dominions, principalities, powers. There are gradations in the angelic hosts.[12]

Dallas Willard

The biblical and continuing vision of Jesus was of one who made all of created reality and kept it working, literally "holding it together" (Col. 1:17). And today we think people are smart who make lightbulbs and computer chips and rockets out of "stuff" already provided! He made "the stuff"![13]

Anne Graham Lotz

Having brought everything into existence that exists, He has never become bored with or distracted from or unconcerned about His creation. The Living Logos personally hovers over all He has created, giving it His full attention.[14]

When life seems like it's on the edge of chaos and things feel out of control, just reflect on Jesus as the Master Sustainer. He holds everything together. He's not going to allow your life to disintegrate. If He has the power and authority to hold the whole world—

go to

church
Ephesians 1:22–23

body of Christ
1 Corinthians 12:12

part
1 Corinthians 12:13

rose
Matthew 28:6–9

Lazarus
John 11:43–44 ✓

rose
Acts 13:32–33

ascended
Acts 1:9

stone
Matthew 27:60

preeminence
domination

indeed, the whole universe—together, then He can hold your life together too. When life seems to be falling apart, just remember that Jesus has every piece in His loving hands.

Here Comes the Boss

> **COLOSSIANS 1:18** *And He is the head of the body, the church, who is the beginning, the firstborn from the dead, that in all things He may have the **preeminence**. (NKJV)*

Paul continues by naming another aspect of Jesus's supremacy: He's in charge of the <u>church</u>. Now, this doesn't mean that church on the corner you go to—only. It does refer to that too, but Paul is referring to the worldwide church that includes every believer. That's referred to as the "<u>body of Christ</u>," since it operates like a living organism. It grows, gives spiritual birth to new believers, and pulsates with life (the ability to respond to stimuli in a godly way). Every believer is automatically and immediately a <u>part</u> of that organism the second they ask Jesus to be their Savior and to cleanse them of their sins. What an awesome operation He oversees.

But that's not all! There's more that marks His superiority over anything else that false teachers might worship! Jesus is the only person who <u>rose</u> from the dead and never died again. Other people, like <u>Lazarus</u>, rose from the dead through Jesus's power—but each died a physical death again. Jesus, on the other hand, <u>rose</u> Himself from the dead and then <u>ascended</u> into heaven, never to die again. Nothing that the false teachers said could save a person—like angels or other spiritual beings—can claim that!

Jesus's resurrection established and emphasized His lordship over the material world. Death could not hold Him back from life. The physical grave, with its heavy <u>stone</u> that was rolled over the opening, could not keep Him inside. Jesus is the only person who controls the physical world. That's a supreme ruler!

what others say

N. T. Wright

The exaltation of Christ after His work on the cross gives Him, publicly, the status which He always in fact enjoyed as of right. The puzzle is caused by sin: though always Lord by right, He must become Lord in fact, by defeating sin and death.[15]

At times, conditions within the church and the mistakes that Christians make can cause us to scratch our head and wonder, "Is Jesus really in charge here?" But He has not withdrawn His hand nor relinquished His authority. He does allow His children to make mistakes, but He promises in everything to bring <u>good</u> and glory for His own name.

Since Jesus has that much power, we can trust Him with our lives. He is <u>interested</u> in every aspect of them and is powerful enough to do something about every single thing that concerns us or <u>worries</u> us. We need not fear life's problems or pitfalls. His hand is strong enough to pull us out and empower us to react the way He wants us to.

Oct 20

A Mended Heart; a Friend of God

> COLOSSIANS 1:19–20 *For it pleased the Father that in Him all the fullness should dwell, and by Him to reconcile all things to Himself, by Him, whether things on earth or things in heaven, having made peace through the blood of His cross.* (NKJV)

At this point, Paul must have thought, *If this isn't enough to convince you, I don't know what is!* But not wanting to leave anything out, and still needing to **refute** the teachings of the false prophets, Paul continues by describing Jesus as fully divine. The false teachers said that God wouldn't want to be restricted by earth's evil essence, nor would God clothe Himself with a human form that is evil. But Paul counters that by saying that Jesus was fully divine in a fully human body and because of that Jesus could <u>represent</u> all of humankind's sins on the cross while staying fully pure and sinless. That **atoning** death made it possible for people to become friends with God again. It was a part of God's plan that wasn't grudgingly offered, for God was pleased to make it available.

go to

resurrection
1 Corinthians
15:20–23

good
Romans 8:28

interested
1 Peter 5:7

worries
Philippians 4:6–7

represent
2 Corinthians 5:19

atoning
1 John 2:2

refute
disprove

atoning
pardoning

go to

reconciled
Romans 5:10–11

blood
Leviticus 17:11

lamb
John 1:29

reconciled
made friends again

hypostatic
humanity fused with
divinity

It was essential that Jesus's blood be shed on the cross in order for people to be **reconciled** to God because "according to the law almost all things are purified with blood, and without shedding of blood there is no remission" (Hebrews 9:22 NKJV). God determined from the very beginning that an animal's blood be shed in order for its sacrifice to be effective. Jesus was the final "sacrificial lamb," dying for the sins of the world. Since no person could be worthy—good enough—to earn their salvation, God devised a wonderful plan to make it possible through Jesus's sacrifice.

The Greeks of Paul's time claimed that no one could be fully divine and fully human at the same time. The Greeks and Romans believed that some humans had become gods, but that once a human became a god he ceased to be a human. Bear in mind that the Greeks thought of their gods in human form, so, for example, seeing the resurrected Jesus in human shape would mean to them that He couldn't still be divine.

The Greek and Roman gods whom the Colossians would be familiar with were considered gods, but without humanity, even if they did have human foibles. Therefore, the Greeks said Jesus couldn't be God and man at the same time, a theory that was affirmed by the false teachers at Colosse. But Paul says that Jesus was fully God and man. He lived in human flesh yet never sinned, and therefore could die for the sins of the world. The church's notion of the **"hypostatic** union"—that Jesus's human nature was fused to His divine nature, eternally joined but distinct—is extraordinary, and doesn't make sense from a purely human perspective. It even took the church a couple of centuries to figure out how to define it.

Paul's use of the neuter Greek word *panta* for "all things" means that he's referring to not only people but also the creation. Furthermore, he says that everything in the creation, both on heaven and earth, will be redeemed and made new.

what others say

Dallas Willard

Now, Jesus Himself was and is a joyous, creative person. He does not allow us to continue thinking of our Father who fills and overflows space as a morose and miserable monarch, a frustrated and petty parent, or a policeman on the prowl.[17]

Although Jesus made the way for people to be reconciled to God, not everyone is saved. Only those who trust in Jesus's redemptive act are actually saved and made friends again with God.

key point

Everything You Wanted to Know About Reconciliation

COLOSSIANS 1:21–23 *And you, who once were alienated and enemies in your mind by wicked works, yet now He has reconciled in the body of His flesh through death, to present you holy, and blameless, and above reproach in His sight—if indeed you continue in the faith, grounded and steadfast, and are not moved away from the hope of the gospel which you heard, which was preached to every creature under heaven, of which I, Paul, became a minister. (NKJV)*

Paul brought up the topic of reconciliation earlier, and now he starts developing it even more. He explains that everyone starts out as an enemy of God because they do wrong things. God, who is holy, cannot have a friendship with someone who is not holy like Him because sinlessness cannot have fellowship with sinfulness. Knowing that a relationship was impossible, He devised a plan to make a person free from sin in His eyes: through Jesus's substitutionary death. Each of us deserved to die on the cross because of our sin, but God sent Jesus as the perfect substitute to die instead. When a person says, "Hey! That was for me! I take His action to be counted on my behalf!" that person's sin is removed from their account.

When believers are in heaven, Jesus will present each one to God, and because of their position in Christ (not their performance on

go to

reconciled
2 Corinthians
5:18–20

enemy
Ephesians 2:16

fellowship
Ephesians 4:18

substitute
Romans 5:6

go to

righteousness
Romans 3:22–24

Satan
Revelation 12:10

advocate
1 John 2:1

heavenlies
Ephesians 1:4

inducement
motivation

earth), God will consider each one "holy, and blameless, and above reproach in His sight." We could never earn that. The best thing we can do is accept such a standing as a gift of God's grace.

Paul stresses Jesus's physical body when he writes, "in the body of His flesh." That's because the false teachers taught that since the body is evil Jesus couldn't have a real body. Some commentators point out that Gnostics wrote that when Jesus walked, He didn't leave any footprints on the ground. He was a spiritual entity without a real physical body. Paul emphasizes that this claim isn't true. Jesus's body died on the cross, and His body was fully human.

Paul is also trying to convince his readers to "continue in the faith, grounded and steadfast." You can hear the pleading in his voice as he dictates these words: "Please, please, *please* stay with the original ideas that were taught you, not the false teachings of these new people."

what others say

H. A. Ironside

The "if" with which the 23rd verse begins has been the occasion of much perplexity to timid souls who hardly dare to accept the truth of the believer's eternal security, so conscious are they of their own weakness and insufficiency. But, rightly understood, there is nothing here to disturb any sincere believer in the Lord Jesus Christ.[19]

God sees us "without sin" because of Jesus's robe of righteousness wrapped around us. It has nothing to do with our own efforts. We will stand before God's judgment seat when Satan points his finger at us and says, "Guilty and sinful!" But Jesus, our lawyer or "advocate," will say, "This is My child, and he is innocent of any wrong." Satan won't be able to say a single thing to accuse or condemn us.

Knowing we have been forgiven in the heavenlies so much, we should be motivated to live here on earth as obediently as possible. Our position of being blameless and holy in God's sight is not a reason to take advantage of God's grace—but an **inducement** to live lives that are pleasing to Him.

Paul wrote that the Colossian believers—before knowing Christ—were enemies in their thinking. That explains clearly how sin begins in the mind. When we don't look at life from God's viewpoint, we think other ways of behaving will meet our needs. We grow selfish and have no confidence that God will meet those needs. Once we are believers, we can begin to look at life with God's perspective and we'll sin less, believing right choices will meet our needs.

No Mystery Here

sufficient
Hebrews 10:10–12

Gentiles and Jews
1 Corinthians 1:21

> COLOSSIANS 1:24–27 *I now rejoice in my sufferings for you, and fill up in my flesh what is lacking in the afflictions of Christ, for the sake of His body, which is the church, of which I became a minister according to the stewardship from God which was given to me for you, to fulfill the Word of God, the mystery which has been hidden from ages and from generations, but now has been revealed to His saints. To them God willed to make known what are the riches of the glory of this mystery among the Gentiles: which is Christ in you, the hope of glory. (NKJV)*

Paul now addresses a different aspect of reconciliation, and we might think he's saying that Jesus's death on the cross was not enough. But we know that's incorrect, for Paul has been saying all along that Jesus's act was <u>sufficient</u> to establish a person's relationship with Him. Commentators explain that Paul is not referring to salvation, but service. Jesus was no longer on the earth, so He needed people like Paul to serve the needs of the church. And Paul is that servant, chosen by God to explain the full message of the church. He calls the concept of the universal church a "mystery," not because it was like a whodunit, but because it was hidden until Jesus's appearance. Until Jesus's life, death, and resurrection, people—even students of the Old Testament—couldn't comprehend how <u>Gentiles and Jews</u> could become one entity. But suddenly, once Jesus completed His work, the "mystery" was clear. And of course, it not only made sense, but all the puzzle pieces fell into place to reveal God's plan.

Even in all of this, Paul is contending for the truth of the gospel against the Colossian false teachers. They taught that salvation comes from gaining enough information and knowledge—*if* you are one of the chosen ones. But Paul says that anyone can understand if they will choose to, and that it's open to all—both Gentiles and Jews. For Jews, that was a surprising, even shocking, twist; for Gentiles, an unexpected gift.

formed
Philippians 2:13

Jan Johnson

To follow through with our purposes, we need to face the voices of our brokenness and choose to live an examined life. Then we not only find redemption in Christ, but we also behave redemptively in this world. We can fulfill God's will, which is that Christ be <u>formed</u> in us and our character be transformed. God is more interested in who we are than in what we can do for Him, whether we're starting a counseling center or scrubbing floors for a chronically ill person.[20]

Oswald Chambers

This call has nothing to do with personal sanctification, but with being made broken bread and poured-out wine. Yet God can never make us into wine if we object to the fingers He chooses to use to crush us. We say, "If God would only use His own fingers, and make me broken bread and poured-out wine in a special way, then I wouldn't object!" But when He uses someone we dislike, or some set of circumstances to which we said we would never submit, to crush us, then we object. Yet we must never try to choose the place of our own martyrdom.[21]

Paul had never met the people that he was writing to, so he needed to give more information about himself and his ministry. He doesn't want his readers to misunderstand him, since they couldn't know personally his good motives and loving desires for them. As a result, he explains himself more fully than to a church group like the Philippians.

Burn Hot in God's Love

COLOSSIANS 1:28–29 *Him we preach, warning every man and teaching every man in all wisdom, that we may present every man perfect in Christ Jesus. To this end I also labor, striving according to His working which works in me mightily. (NKJV)*

Paul is so dedicated to this wonderful message of salvation and the church that he tells everyone he can about it. Plus, for those who come to receive Christ, he admonishes them by warning them of the things they shouldn't do, and by teaching them the truths about the gospel. His goal is to help each believer become mature in their relationship with Christ. The word *perfect* means being <u>complete</u> or mature, not sinless. Paul knows no one on this earth is <u>sinless</u> (except for Jesus), but each person can grow stronger in their faith until they respond to life's challenges with a godly perspective. That's maturity!

Paul credits and stresses that he doesn't put out all of this energy by himself. He is empowered by Jesus. He has an inner fire fueled by the Holy Spirit, and he wants everyone else to burn hot with God's love too.

It may seem a little extreme that Paul uses the phrase *every man* three times. But he has a purpose in it as he again refutes one of the teachings of the Gnostics. The Gnostics believed that only a few people who had the special knowledge they taught could get into heaven; only the intellectuals could be saved. But Paul says that every person has the ability to choose to be saved. There are no special qualifications needed—other than asking Jesus to be a person's Lord and Savior.

go to

complete
Colossians 2:10

sinless
Philippians 1:6

what others say

Joyce Meyer

When God is dealing with you, don't look at the training, correction, and discipline you are going through for the moment. Look at the fruit you are going to bear "afterwards." When you don't see the manifestation of your prayers, realize that God is building faith in you, and "afterwards" that faith will be used to bring you into a greater realm of blessing.[22]

Max Lucado

Look at Paul's aim, *to present everyone perfect in Christ*. Paul dreamed of the day each person would be safe in Christ. What was his method? *Counseling and teaching*. Paul's tools? Verbs. Nouns. Sentences. Lessons. The same equipment you and I have. Not much has changed, has it?[23]

It's hard for some people to comprehend that God wouldn't want them to become perfect on this earth. The truth is that God knows we won't become sinless, but we can become mature. If we could somehow become sinless, we would no longer need to depend upon God. We would think we can do it ourselves. Therefore, there's an advantage to continuing to struggle: We must seek God and grow ever closer to Him.

key point

Nothing we do should be in our own power or energy. In all circumstances, ask God to help you do the right thing. If you don't, you won't grow mature as a Christian and you'll continue to make lots of mistakes.

When we try to make an impact in other Christians' lives, we need to both warn and teach them. We should warn them about the pitfalls of living selfishly and teach them the right way to respond to life's problems.

Chapter Wrap-Up

- Paul was very concerned that the believers in Colosse might be deceived by the lies that some were teaching. They taught that Jesus wasn't sufficient for salvation but that people had to do other things as well, like worship angels and have special knowledge. (Colossians 1:1–8)

- To counteract the false teachers' beliefs that someone must have special knowledge in order to be godlike, Paul says he is praying that the believers will have knowledge about God and His will. (Colossians 1:9–14)

- Paul was concerned that the believers would believe the wrong things about Jesus, so he wrote some of the most eloquent descriptions about Jesus as both human and divine—in the same human body. He also stressed that Jesus created everything and was Head of the body of Christ. (Colossians 1:15–20)

- Everyone is alienated from God because of their sin, and so Jesus died in our place. But each person must decide whether they will receive that gift for himself. Paul wants the believers to know they've done that and don't need to do anything else. (Colossians 1:21–23)

- Paul knew his special assignment from God was to preach the news that even the Gentiles could be reconciled to the God of the Jews. He loved the challenge and felt that he was fulfilling the work that Jesus had begun on earth. (Colossians 1:24–29)

Study Questions

1. Why did Paul want to teach the Colossian believers that they were holy and redeemed through Jesus?

2. Paul prayed that the believers would have what kind of knowledge?

3. What did the false teachers believe about Jesus and what did Paul preach?

4. How does Paul explain that these believers have become friends of God?

5. Paul had a special job to do for God; what was it?

Colossians 2
Our Freedoms in Christ

Let's Get Started

Paul still isn't satisfied that the Colossian believers really understand his heart for them, nor how destructive are the offerings of the false teachers. He continues his thoughts from the first chapter about his own struggles on their behalf and then writes on to counteract the false teaching that some are daring to "enlighten" unprotected minds. Paul is determined to bring them true enlightenment. Like a candle shining in the darkness, Paul faithfully exhorts these believers in Colosse to follow the truth.

Although you and I may not hear about any Gnostic teaching which would pollute our minds, we can still learn a lot about our own rich inheritance in Christ through the wisdom that Paul shares. Let's ask God to give us knowledge of His desires for freedom for us.

Spoon-Feeding

COLOSSIANS 2:1–3 *For I want you to know what a great conflict I have for you and those in Laodicea, and for as many as have not seen my face in the flesh, that their hearts may be encouraged, being knit together in love, and attaining to all riches of the full assurance of understanding, to the knowledge of the mystery of God, both of the Father and of Christ, in whom are hidden all the treasures of wisdom and knowledge. (NKJV)*

Paul believes that his readers will be encouraged if they understand the motives behind his struggles. They haven't met him personally, so they can't picture the love in his eyes or the gentle way he might wrap his arm around someone's shoulder. They have never personally witnessed him preaching with passion, warmth, and concern. Words on paper, and even the spoken affirmation by Epaphras about Paul's desire for their good, can't convey the care and love that a personal conversation would, so Paul tries hard to communicate his

Laodicea
Acts 19:10

inheritance
1 Corinthians 1:30

wisdom
Romans 11:33

lukewarm
Revelation 3:14–22

love for them. He uses the Greek word *agon* for "conflict," from which comes our word *agony*. That's strongly communicating his feelings for them. He agonizes over their struggle between believing him or the false teachers in their midst.

His desire is that:

- They be encouraged, to have the ability to meet the challenges they are facing with wisdom

- They be knit together in love by loving and appreciating every member of their church

- They receive full assurance of the mystery that is Jesus, who has all wisdom and knowledge. *Wisdom* is the Greek word *sophia*, and *knowledge* is the Greek word *gnosis*. Together, they mean having the ability to see truth and then defend the truth with intelligent discussion.

The fact that Paul also mentions the Christians in <u>Laodicea</u> (which was located only a few miles northwest of Colosse) indicates that the heresy the Colossians were being spoon-fed was also being dished out elsewhere, although commentators believe that the Colossians were struggling with it the most. Maybe Paul also wrote a letter to the Laodicean believers and it hasn't survived. Some commentators believe that Philemon—the subject of that letter from Paul—actually lived in Laodicea, so that might have been a letter written to that city. We'll never know, but chances are Paul would have penned something similar to what is written here if those believers struggled with the same false teachings.

Regardless, Paul wants these believers to see his heart of love and concern for them and to be encouraged by reviewing all the wonderful things that are wrapped up in their <u>inheritance</u> in Christ—among them, <u>wisdom</u> and knowledge.

Laodicea would later be rebuked by Jesus for their "<u>lukewarm</u> commitment." Could it be that they ended up succumbing to the heresies taught there that Paul warned them about indirectly, through the Colossian letter? What a great reminder for us to refuse any wrong teachings so that we will be commended in heaven—not reprimanded.

When Paul speaks of a "mystery," he's not talking about something that God wants to keep from people. It's a reference to something that previously was unknown—like in the Old Testament.

Now, with Jesus's appearance on earth, God's gospel message of hope and salvation is available to all—<u>Jews and Gentiles</u> alike—which is the <u>body</u> of Christ. Paul stresses this even more in using the word *hidden*. The Greek equivalent is *apokruphos*, and it is the same word that the false teachers used to refer to their "hidden knowledge." Paul is digging at them by saying, "You say your knowledge is secret and only good for a few, but we see it available through Christ for every single person." Paul is very clever in his word usage and communicates a lot within one word.

go to

Jews and Gentiles
Romans 3:29;
1 Corinthians 12:13

body
1 Corinthians 12:12

wisdom
1 Corinthians
1:21–25

knows
2 Timothy 3:7

adulation
praise

> **what others say**
>
> **Beth Moore**
>
> When we rub shoulders with Christ day-to-day, His wisdom and knowledge rub off on us little by little. Wisdom is the application of knowledge—knowing what to do with what you know. God wants to guide us daily in His own wisdom and knowledge. Remember, He's the one with the plan.[1]
>
> **Billy Graham**
>
> Who do you think Jesus Christ is? If He is not who He claimed to be, He is a deceiver or an egomaniac. We cannot settle for a middle-of-the-road answer that He was "a good man," or the modern form of **adulation** as a "superstar." He himself eliminates a neutral answer. Either we decide He is a liar or a lunatic or we must declare Him to be Lord.[2]

A lot of people seek knowledge, but it's not much use without <u>wisdom</u>. Wisdom is being able to apply in daily life what a person <u>knows</u>. Many people have knowledge, but only with wisdom will someone be able to live it out in a way that pleases God. Don't just seek knowledge; seek the wisdom to apply it.

Truth Plus Falsehood Does Not Equal Truth

COLOSSIANS 2:4–5 *Now this I say lest anyone should deceive you with persuasive words. For though I am absent in the flesh, yet I am with you in spirit, rejoicing to see your good order and the steadfastness of your faith in Christ. (NKJV)*

Have you ever heard something and initially thought, *Yeah, that's right*—but then, upon thinking about it more and working it

go to

works
Ephesians 2:8–9

dependability
1 Corinthians 15:58

plausible
2 Timothy 2:23

abiding
John 15:4

plausible
deceitful

through in your mind or with someone else, recognized the holes in your logic? The theories that the Colossians were being dealt were like that—at least that's what Paul wished for them to see. The false teachers were passing out information that may have sounded right, but Paul wanted them to see the holes in their logic. It may have sounded right that people should add something like good <u>works</u> in order to be saved, but that wasn't the way God had set up salvation. It's all His doing through Jesus and our cooperation through belief and faith. We may like the idea of contributing through good works—it makes us feel important and necessary—but God says, "It's My entire gift. Just accept it, and let your good works speak of your salvation—not create it."

Paul compliments his readers, even though he must have known some of them were entertaining heresy. But by faith, he acknowledges their <u>dependability</u> and faith. Paul wisely complimented while speaking the truth of warning. Paul always seems to say and believe the best about other people, before getting to the point of judging them or declaring something is wrong. He knows that compliments and affirmations have a more attractive pull toward the truth than telling everyone they are wrong. We can learn much in the people management department if we follow his good example of encouragement.

Paul uses a Greek word, *pithanologia*, to describe the phrase *persuasive words*. This is the only time that word is used in the New Testament. It carries the meaning of persuasive speech that uses **plausible** but false arguments.

When Paul said "*good* order and the steadfastness of your faith," he most likely was referring to military analogies. Just like a military force is ordered and strong, so should these believers be. And it can only happen as they remain "in" Christ—in other words, rooted and <u>abiding</u> in Him, as Paul will clarify in the next verse.

what others say

H. A. Ironside

It is important to remember that no amount of intellectual culture or human learning can take the place of divine revelation. If God has not spoken, we may speculate and reason as we please. But if He has given the truth in His Word, there is an end to all our theorizing.[3]

Just because something may sound good or right doesn't mean it is. Everything we hear, even from our most trusted pastor or Bible teacher, should be <u>examined</u> through the magnifying lens of the <u>Bible</u>.

No Instant Route to Roots

COLOSSIANS 2:6–7 *As you therefore have received Christ Jesus the Lord, so walk in Him, rooted and built up in Him and established in the faith, as you have been taught, abounding in it with thanksgiving.* (NKJV)

You may have heard the story about the huge tree in a town plaza in Colorado. Everyone thought it was the most fabulous tree. It provided welcome shade and beauty for many years . . . until the day a storm came through town that was stronger than anyone could remember. That beautiful tree fell right over. Everyone was shocked. But when they gathered around, they found out how it happened. The roots of the tree were shallow—they didn't extend more than a few feet below the surface. It was surprising that the tree lasted as long as it did. In the end, its shallow roots couldn't support it.

Although Paul wrote long before that incident, he would say that's exactly what he didn't want to happen to his readers. If they started to believe the persuasive but <u>false</u> beliefs of the mistaken teachers, they would come crashing down in their faith; their spiritual roots wouldn't offer the foundation to determine that the teachings were wrong. Paul wants their spiritual roots—their belief system—to go deep into the truth of God's perceptions. If they would learn what God called truth, they wouldn't be <u>swayed</u> by someone purporting to know an alternate truth.

Paul could have easily said, "When you received Christ, your roots went into the truth that He <u>saved</u> you based only on your faith in Him—not that you deserved it or could earn it. So keep growing your roots deeply into that theology, not the false thinking that says you need special knowledge or that you must pray to angels. That wasn't the original soil of your faith. Throw out that putrid-smelling false <u>manure</u>, and go back to the original plan you heard from Epaphras."

go to

examined
1 John 4:1

Bible
2 Timothy 2:15;
Hebrews 4:12

false
Galatians 1:6

swayed
James 1:6

saved
Titus 3:5

manure
2 Corinthians 11:4

key point

Charles R. Swindoll

But before you get excited about whipping up a strong set of roots, better remember this: It takes time. There's no instant route to roots. And it isn't fun 'n' games, either. It's hard work. Nor is it a high-profile process. Nobody spends much time digging around a tree trunk, admiring: *"What neat roots you have!"* No, the stronger and deeper the roots, the less visible they are. The less noticed.[4]

Tony Evans

The only way to get deep roots is the knowledge and application of the Word. I can tell you right now whether you are on your way to deep roots. Is the only time you are in the Bible the hour or two you show up on Sunday?

Well, you are not going far. Imagine a person eating only a Sunday afternoon meal, even a big one, and not eating the rest of the week. By about Tuesday he's going to be in trouble. One meal can't last all week long.

It's the same with our spiritual nourishment.[5]

Growing Your Roots Strong in the Soil of God's Salvation

How to Grow	Scripture
Read the Bible. If you don't, any new thoughts you hear could sound correct.	Hebrews 4:12
Pray every day. Seeking God and being sure of His love and unearned grace will strengthen you not to be swayed to believe other things—like that you need to earn His love.	Romans 12:12
Memorize Scripture. Unless God's words are hidden in your heart, you won't have as much artillery to fight the flaming false messages of Satan.	Psalm 119:9–11; Ephesians 6:11
Fellowship with other Christians. It doesn't help to be a spiritual Lone Ranger. We all need support. Being able to talk through possible wrong ideas with others is essential.	Acts 1:14
Witness to others. Telling others about the difference Jesus makes in your life causes your roots to grow even deeper into the soil of your faith.	Mark 16:15

When we know we believe the right thing, we will be filled with gratitude. There is such security in following what we know is the truth that we can't help but be consumed with thanking God. If you're not flowing with thanks to God, make sure your theology is correct.

Coming to know Christ as our personal Lord and Savior is just the beginning of a lifelong journey. Some people never grow stronger in their faith after making that initial commitment. But we must continue learning about God, Jesus, and our faith for as long as we live. Growing strong in Jesus takes time. Be patient!

Keep Away from That Quicksand!

COLOSSIANS 2:8 *Beware lest anyone cheat you through philosophy and empty deceit, according to the tradition of men, according to the basic principles of the world, and not according to Christ. (NKJV)*

What modern captivating philosophy have you encountered lately? Maybe you've read about the actress who believes she can communicate with spirits from beyond. Or maybe someone has shared with you about a cult that says you must work to gain entrance into heaven and be given a special name. Some people believe they will meet a spaceship in the sky to take them to heaven if they commit suicide. Oh, there are any number of religions that are abnormal variations on Christianity, and there are many that wouldn't want to be associated with Jesus—and yet they offer eternal life later and special knowledge now. Since many of those human ideas often incorporate elements of Christianity—like meditation, prayer, and reading Scripture (their own)—it can seem fairly good, maybe even truthful. But that's exactly what Paul commanded his readers to avoid. He said, "Stay away from anything that doesn't depend totally on God's plan of salvation through Jesus's death on the cross." If we start to consider another way, our minds are being held captive—and Paul didn't want the Colossians to even tiptoe around such a quicksand of thought.

When Paul said "cheat" he meant "to strip and rob," and also "to carry off as prey." Paul wanted the Colossian believers to see how believing the false teachers' principles would cheat them and rob them of living in their inheritance in Christ. He feared that just as victorious armies carried off the conquered people as slaves, these false teachers would carry the Colossians away from their true commitment to Christ and enslave them to false ideas.

Some commentators believe the words *basic principles* (the Greek word *stoicheia*) refer to astrological inferences, especially the spirits of the stars and planets, which some thought controlled their fate. People believed they had to free themselves from those spirits, and

stars
Jeremiah 10:2

offered
Matthew 4:1–5

the false teachers at Colosse may have been teaching that submission to Jesus Christ wasn't enough to get rid of that control—additional secret knowledge was needed. Paul definitely believes in those spirits because he writes, "For we do not wrestle against flesh and blood, but against principalities, against powers, against the rulers of the darkness of this age, against spiritual hosts of wickedness in the heavenly places" (Ephesians 6:12 NKJV)—but he doesn't believe they control life. He counters those lies as he does throughout this letter: by saying that Jesus is enough for anything and everything.

what others say

H. A. Ironside

Scripture nowhere condemns the acquisition of knowledge. It is the wisdom of this world, not its knowledge, that is foolishness with God. Philosophy is but world wisdom.[6]

Paul wrote elsewhere, "casting down arguments and every high thing that exalts itself against the knowledge of God, bringing every thought into captivity to the obedience of Christ" (2 Corinthians 10:5 NKJV). We can do that by evaluating any thought that comes our way. When we think, *I'm having tough times; God must not love me*, we can take that thought captive and throw it out because John 14:21 tells us God loves us. If we begin to think, *I'm unhappy in my marriage; I'm going to find someone else who will make me happy*, then we can take that captive and correct it to be obedient to God's perspective by choosing to respect and love our spouse as Scripture says (Ephesians 5:33). And today, with the following of astrology, people might think they should consult their horoscope to see if it's going to be a good day. But God does not lead through the stars.

When Jesus was offered a variety of quicksand thoughts from Satan, He quoted Scripture and rehearsed the truth. Time after time, Jesus was tempted by Satan to do the wrong thing, and Jesus always answered, "It is written . . . ," and then gave a passage or principle from the Old Testament. We can do the same thing each time we hear the hollow and empty philosophies of the world.

Is Your Soul Growling?

COLOSSIANS 2:9–10 *For in Him dwells all the fullness of the Godhead bodily; and you are complete in Him, who is the head of all principality and power.* (NKJV)

There are many things offered in this world that would seem to bring complete happiness. The single person thinks that getting married will meet all their needs—but any married person knows their spouse eventually disappoints them and even creates empty feelings of "I'm neither loved nor lovable." The couple without children is convinced that having children will bring unlimited joy—but the couple waking up in the middle of the night to care for a sick child is ready to hand him over for any offer. Even the New Age offering, "You are God, so just live like it," becomes empty when each of us continues to do things that we know are wrong or unloving. And for those who believe that they must earn their way into heaven, a continual and pervasive gnawing fills their souls as they wonder, *Have I been good enough?*

Paul would say to those philosophies of our current world, "Enough! You don't have to experience those empty ideas. Jesus is enough. *Only* He is enough. Because He is completely God, He offers <u>abundant</u> life because He designed life to begin with. He knows what He had in mind and it's not accomplishments, worldly success, possessions, or even people. It's a relationship with Jesus, who qualifies as <u>fully</u> God and has control over every area of our lives. And He offers us fullness (or being complete) through knowing Him."

Paul uses the strongest possible word to claim that Jesus is actually God, and he is making a good point. He isn't saying that when we're given fullness in Christ we become a god. That's an age-old philosophy—one that started in the <u>Garden</u> of Eden—and is now being recycled in the New Age philosophy of our time. No, we are still completely human, but we do <u>share</u> in His nature in our ability to respond like He would—when we obey Him and allow ourselves to be empowered by Him.

abundant
John 10:10

fully
John 1:16

Garden
Genesis 3:5

share
2 Peter 1:4

Jesus Demonstrated His Deity

Demonstration	Scripture
Jesus forgave sins, which only God can do.	Mark 2:1–12
Jesus received the worship of others as God.	John 5:23
Jesus Himself claimed to be God.	Luke 1:76
Jesus contained the attributes only God can have, like omniscience and omnipotence.	Matthew 16:21; 28:18
Jesus was given titles of deity.	Matthew 26:63–64

[handwritten annotations: "all knowing, all powerful – always present" and "omnipresent"]

abundant
John 10:10

Abraham
Genesis 17:11

circumcised
Romans 2:29

apply it

Here Nov. 3

what others say

J. Vernon McGee

"Complete" is a nautical term, and it could be translated in this very vivid way: You are ready for the voyage of life in Him, and whatever you need you will find in Him.[7]

Warren Wiersbe

When a person is born again into the family of God, he is born complete in Christ. His spiritual growth is not by *addition*, but by *nutrition*. He grows from the inside out.[8]

If Jesus is the Head over every power and authority, then we need never fear or worry. *That* is fullness of life—<u>abundant</u> life. Worry, fear, anxiety, inability to love, bitterness, anger, frustration—all the things that steal our joy—are the reactions that take away abundant life. But Jesus has control over everything that could cause us to feel those emotions or to have ungodly reactions. Therefore, we can confidently respond with God's power and experience fullness.

<u>Buried, Raised, and Alive: That's Every Christian</u>

COLOSSIANS 2:11–12 *In Him you were also circumcised with the circumcision made without hands, by putting off the body of the sins of the flesh, by the circumcision of Christ, buried with Him in baptism, in which you also were raised with Him through faith in the working of God, who raised Him from the dead.* (NKJV)

The Colossian Christians were being taught incorrectly about freedom in Christ not only because of this beginning form of Gnosticism, but also because of legalism. Paul now addresses that issue. Some of those who were teaching and calling themselves Christians taught that the Gentiles had to be circumcised in order to truly become Christians. Jews, of course, customarily circumcised their children on the eighth day of life—just as Jesus was, and as <u>Abraham</u> had been instructed by God many years earlier. But Paul says that's no longer needed for identification with God. Salvation through God's grace is enough to make a person fully a Christian because he or she has been circumcised spiritually. Jesus had done that at each person's conversion when their "sinful nature" was circumcised from their heart. That doesn't mean a Christian loses the ability to sin, but it does mean he has the capacity to obey because he is a new creature in Christ.

When did that happen? Paul explains that it was at the moment of salvation, which is a spiritual burial—when a person dies to his own way of trying to get into heaven and instead believes the only way is through Jesus. They are then spiritually raised as a new creature, able to enjoy the full life God desires for them.

go to

creature
2 Corinthians 5:17;
Galatians 6:15

burial
Romans 6:4

dies
Galatians 2:20

way
John 14:6

covenant
Genesis 17:11

what others say

Malcolm O. Tolbert

The Colossians, of course, had been baptized. Christian baptism is equated by Paul with dying and being buried. Christ died and was buried in a tomb. We die and are buried with Him in a watery grave. This means that there is a radical dividing line between what the Christian now is and what he used to be.[9]

Stuart Briscoe

No matter which mode of baptism people use, it is never a substitute for heart discipleship. Paul makes this clear in the rest of verse 12, when he insists the key even to baptism is faith. Baptism unrelated to faith is an empty tradition. Baptism as an outward and visible sign of an inward and spiritual grace is profoundly significant.[10]

Baptism is the outward act of an inner commitment. It is "going down" into the waters of symbolic spiritual burial and then being raised up as a symbol of new life in Christ. Baptism itself as an act does not save anyone. If a person who hasn't truly trusted Jesus to forgive them of their sins is baptized, they still won't be saved. It takes first the heart-changed attitude—and then baptism, which is the outward act to let others know of the inward commitment.

something to ponder

Circumcision was originally the outward evidence of a man's obedience to God's covenant. People then didn't understand that there was also a hygienic reason that God gave them the practice. Today, Christians can still have their male babies circumcised, not because of the old covenant but because science recognizes there is a physical benefit from it.

go to

abundant
John 10:10

law
Romans 3:19

pay
Romans 8:2

Paid in Full!

COLOSSIANS 2:13–14 *And you, being dead in your trespasses and the uncircumcision of your flesh, He has made alive together with Him, having forgiven you all trespasses, having wiped out the handwriting of requirements that was against us, which was contrary to us. And He has taken it out of the way, having nailed it to the cross. (NKJV)*

It may seem a little strong for Paul to say that these people were dead in their sins before they came to know Christ. None of us like to think of our lives as being worthless and empty. After all, we are alive and living. But spiritually, Paul is saying, without Christ, a person is not living the <u>abundant</u> life Jesus promised, and is in fact headed for judgment and hell. But the good news is that Jesus prevents that for anyone who wants to be cleansed from their sins. Their sins separated them from a holy God, but Jesus pays off the balance on their sin account.

In the same way, Paul explains that Jesus already sent through the check of His death to pay the account of salvation for you. Some people try to resend the check—but it's not necessary. The account has already accepted the payment, and it's paid in full.

Yet, legalism is like trying to send the check back through. It's trying to convince God with our own efforts of doing certain things that we deserve to be forgiven. To the Christian, God's reply would be, "Hey, your account was already paid in full through Jesus. There's no debt. Your account of sins is debt-free."

But before that happens, every person's account with God is still open and filled with sins that separate us from God's fellowship. God still loves us, but He can't be our friend because sin separates us from a holy God. God knew that would happen and wanted to make a way for the account to be cleared out. People will try to clear it out themselves through doing good works or following the written code—the Jewish <u>law</u>—but no amount of good works is enough. So God made a plan for Jesus to <u>pay</u> the account in full—remove the sin—if a person takes that privilege for himself.

Paul uses some interesting Greek words to state his case. The first is *handwriting*, which could be called an "autograph" or "charge list." It's the Greek word *cheirographon*, and it is like our version of an I.O.U. Specifically, it's defined as "a note written by the hand which makes one obligated to fulfill what is written." Sin creates a list of debts to God saying, "I'm in debt to You because You have every right to punish me for my sins." Jesus's death prevents that from happening because He paid the price of sin. In every heart, there's a conscience that says, "I signed my name, my autograph, to a list of my sins and I know I'm guilty." Paul says that list is "wiped out" by Jesus's death.

The words *wiped out* give us the other interesting Greek word, *exaleiphein*. It's the idea of wiping a slate or a blackboard clean of chalk—with no residue at all.

what others say

Henry T. Blackaby and Claude V. King

You did not initiate a love relationship with God. He initiated a love relationship with you. In fact, God loved you before you came into the world. He began to demonstrate his love for you on the cross of Jesus.[11]

Max Lucado

Between His hand and the wood there was a list. A long list. A list of our mistakes: our lusts and lies and greedy moments and prodigal years. A list of our sins.

Dangling from the cross is an itemized catalogue of your sins. The bad decisions from last year. The bad attitudes from last week. There, in broad daylight for all of heaven to see, is a list of your mistakes.

The list God has made, however, cannot be read. The words can't be deciphered. The mistakes are covered. The sins are hidden. Those at the top are hidden by His hand; those down the list are covered by His blood. Your sins are "blotted out" by Jesus.[12]

Some people really have trouble truly believing that their sins have been forgiven. They keep asking Jesus to come into their life over and over again. They conclude that because they keep sinning, they must not have fully received Jesus or done enough or done the right thing to be a Christian. But none of that is true. When a person sincerely receives Christ, crediting Him with forgiving them, everything needed is done! No more checks need to go through heaven's bank. Their account is paid in full.

If you keep thinking you should ask Jesus into your life over and over again, STOP! You don't need to do it more than once. Now

something to ponder

predicted
Genesis 3:15

accept the truth by faith—even if you don't feel like it—and start acting as if it's true. Because it is! You only need to ask Jesus into your life once. First John 5:13 says, "These things I have written to you who believe in the name of the Son of God, that you may know that you have eternal life, and that you may continue to believe in the name of the Son of God" (NKJV).

Don't Let Anyone Boss You Around— Especially Legalistic Rulers

COLOSSIANS 2:15–17 *Having disarmed principalities and powers, He made a public spectacle of them, triumphing over them in it. So let no one judge you in food or in drink, or regarding a festival or a new moon or sabbaths, which are a shadow of things to come, but the substance is of Christ. (NKJV)*

Jesus's death defeated Satan's ability to keep Christians in bondage to their sin; Jesus "disarmed" or stripped the evil spirits of their power. Conquering Satan and his spirits gave Jesus the authority to lead them as in a parade. In those days, a victorious military leader paraded through the streets with the conquered king and his people following him. That was the truth, but Paul didn't want the Colossians to live as if it weren't true and they needed to do the conquering themselves—by the old rules of the Law.

When we believe the old lies of legalism or Gnosticism, like the Colossians were tempted to do, we are in effect still being held captive by spiritual elements that serve Satan—demons and evil powers. Paul already mentioned those beings in the previous chapter: "For by Him all things were created that are in heaven and that are on earth, visible and invisible, whether thrones or dominions or principalities or powers. All things were created through Him and for Him" (Colossians 1:16 NKJV). Satan and his allies concoct all sorts of distorting philosophies to distract unbelievers from following God's ideas. His schemes include diverting Christians from taking advantage of their benefits as new creations in Christ. Paul is saying that the Colossians (and we) don't have to obey those evil beings because they are defeated. They can't have a hold over us if we don't cooperate with them. And since they were defeated by Jesus's death on the cross—something that God predicted from the very beginning—we no longer need to fear them or bow to them.

Paul goes on to point out some of the diverting and distorting philosophies that these spiritual enemies use. The first is being legalistic about what a person can eat or drink. God originally did give specific laws for what the Jews could eat and drink. But when Jesus opened a new covenant of freedom, those laws were no longer needed.

Then Paul mentions restrictions by some who say a festival should only be celebrated in a certain way on a certain day. Or that the Sabbath should continue to be celebrated on Saturday when Christians had begun meeting together for worship on Sunday—because that was the day of Jesus's resurrection. Paul says all of these restrictions are not needed because they were all things that formerly pointed to the need for a Messiah's forgiveness. But now that Jesus, the Messiah, has forgiven sins and revealed the way of a full life, Christians are free to live as God directs each one individually or corporately.

go to

laws
Leviticus 11:1–47

opened
Matthew 5:17

needed
Hebrews 9:10

festival
Galatians 4:9–10

pointed
Hebrews 8:6

forgiven
Romans 8:3

judge
Romans 14:10

wrong
Philippians 3:15

what others say

Oswald Chambers

In the Cross we may see the dimensions of Divine love. The Cross is not the cross of a man, but an exhibition of the heart of God. At the back of the wall of the world stands God with His arms outstretched, and every man driven there is driven into the arms of God.[13]

Some Christians still follow certain laws—like not eating certain foods or worshipping on the Sabbath. That's fine as long as they don't do it in an attempt to earn God's love or salvation. God loves worship from a pure heart—a heart that is seeking Him, not trying to gain His approval through works—and for some, worship or obedience includes the things Paul is talking about. It's all a matter of the heart's motives.

God's original motive in ordaining laws about eating certain foods and celebrating certain festivals on certain days was to distinguish His people from the pagan people around them. If they worshipped God in unique ways, they would be noticed as belonging to Him; it would keep them separate from those who didn't worship the only true God.

The important thing is that none of us should criticize or judge anyone else. If they are seeking God, then God will let them know if they are doing something wrong in His sight.

Nov. 10

go to

worship
Exodus 20:3

being right
2 Timothy 3:5

angels
Revelation 22:8–9

growth
John 15:1–5

way
John 14:6 ✓

prize
1 Corinthians
3:10–15

rewards
1 Corinthians 3:14

body
1 Corinthians 12:14

Don't Be Puffed Up Like a Blowfish

COLOSSIANS 2:18–19 *Let no one cheat you of your reward, taking delight in false humility and worship of angels, intruding into those things which he has not seen, vainly puffed up by his fleshly mind, and not holding fast to the Head, from whom all the body, nourished and knit together by joints and ligaments, grows with the increase that is from God. (NKJV)*

Paul goes on to describe other distortions and distractions that those defeated evil spirits try to use to steal a Christian's full new life: pride and the <u>worship</u> of angels. The false teachers took great delight in <u>being right</u> and in making sure everyone else knew it! They claimed to know what God wanted from their followers, and they wore their spirituality right on their shoulder for everyone to notice and be impressed by. They also encouraged people to worship angels and even claimed that Jesus was a glorified angel. But these false objects of spirituality are wrong, Paul says. They distract and distort God's true message: that Jesus made salvation possible and He is the Head of the church—and therefore in charge. <u>Angels</u> aren't in charge. Being proud of one's own accomplishments doesn't put a person in charge. Those false teachers aren't in charge, either. Only Jesus is in charge, and He also dictates the actions of the body of Christ—along with creating its <u>growth</u>. If we don't grow, we have "lost connection" with Jesus and aren't following Him closely.

The false teachers of the Colossian church taught that God was too distant to be reached directly, and that therefore He needed to be reached through a series of angels at different levels. By worshipping the angels, a person could eventually gain the privilege of worshipping God. But Paul refutes their premise, saying, as always, that Jesus is fully God and the only <u>way</u> to God.

The growth that Jesus desires for His bride, the church, could be stolen from them if they followed wrong teachings. As a result, they would "lose the <u>prize</u>." This doesn't mean they would lose their salvation, but they could lose the <u>rewards</u> in heaven that they would be due if they continued faithfully serving the Lord.

what others say

Tony Evans

God saved you to be part of His <u>body</u>. Just as your finger can't work without your hand; your hand can't work without

> your wrist; your wrist can't work without your arm; your arm can't work without your shoulder; and your shoulder can't work without your body; so you can't be what God wants you to be by yourself.[14]

True humility isn't self-focused; it's God-focused. True humility considers oneself an important and valuable creation of God, crediting Him for the talents and gifts God gave him. And a humble person sees the importance of every person in the body of Christ. A truly humble person acknowledges God and doesn't take the credit.

apply it

Jesus, who is the Head of the church and is responsible for each believer's growth, has different purposes for each one. That means we shouldn't judge or be critical if someone isn't growing as fast as we think they should. We can be patient, knowing the Holy Spirit is working in them according to His will.

Let's Get Past It!

> COLOSSIANS 2:20–22 *Therefore, if you died with Christ from the basic principles of the world, why, as though living in the world, do you subject yourselves to regulations—"Do not touch, do not taste, do not handle," which all concern things which perish with the using—according to the commandments and doctrines of men?* (NKJV)

In some religions or even factions of Christianity, people will hurt their bodies to show their faith in God. In some parts of the world, people cut their skin, or crawl on their hands and knees long distances in order to gain God's favor or to show their love for God. That's called **asceticism**, and it's the last distraction Paul addresses.

Mankind's plan for reaching God is always based on "Look, God, what I'm not doing wrong. And look what I'm doing in order to please You. Aren't I wonderful and deserving?" Paul points out that such a self-absorbed, man-made salvation blueprint is a mere world system that can't succeed in God's eyes. A person can never not "handle, taste, or touch" enough to deserve God's friendship. Such an effort always <u>falls short</u> because even our human best is far from God's holiness. It just won't work, so Paul says those things are of the past in a Christian's life, and that we should get past them. He stresses, "Don't go back to those things. They don't work!"

go to

falls short
Psalm 143:2

asceticism
man-made system
of rules for salvation

go to

omniscient
Romans 11:33

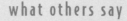

what others say

Henry T. Blackaby and Claude V. King

By nature God is <u>omniscient</u>—that is, He is all-knowing. He possesses all knowledge—past, present, and future. Nothing is outside the knowledge of God. Whenever God expresses Himself to you, therefore, His directions are always right. When God gives you a directive, you can count on the fact that God has already considered every factor that must be considered.[15]

something to ponder

Because God knew man's efforts would fall short, He devised a plan for reaching out to us. Since we couldn't reach Him, He bridged the gap with Jesus's death and offer of salvation through a free gift. If you're still trying to earn God's love through your efforts, take heart. Even if you could become perfect, God can't love you any more than He does right now.

Legalists are good at making it seem like they find favor with God through keeping rules. But God isn't so much interested in the sacrifices of "Don't touch!" as He is in a heart that says, "I love You, Lord; help me to obey." Which direction is your heart seeking today?

It May Look Like Gold, but It's Straw

COLOSSIANS 2:23 *These things indeed have an appearance of wisdom in self-imposed religion, false humility, and neglect of the body, but are of no value against the indulgence of the flesh. (NKJV)*

Asceticism may seem like a great idea. After all, depriving yourself should have *some* benefit. Some people might even call it self-discipline. But unless it's done in the power of the Holy Spirit and directed by Him, it's merely self-imposed pride calling attention to self. It doesn't really create a different heart of worship of God. It usually ends up elevating self, because we wind up thinking, *Look at what I did. Why can't everyone else do as well as me?* It doesn't change the real reason for sin: selfishness.

what others say

Warren Wiersbe

This is not to suggest that Christians are lawless. Paul was not counseling us to be rebels, but he was warning us not to think we are spiritual because we obey certain rules and regulations that pertain to the body.[16]

Modern cults—even those going back to Paul's day—stress things like:

- Being good enough to earn God's love and favor
- Not depending upon God's grace to be saved
- Being extremely judgmental about who is allowed to be a part of the group
- Believing they have secret information that is only available to a select group
- Adding to or deleting from the Word of God
- Positioning a human into near equality with Jesus in importance

Whenever we succeed in self-discipline in our own power, we give ourselves credit. We must depend upon God's help and then give Him the praise.

Chapter Wrap-Up

- Paul hasn't met the Colossian believers, but he wants them to know the great depth of his love and concern for them—especially that they will stay firm in their faith in Christ and grow deeper in their commitment to Him. (Colossians 2:1–7)

- The false teachers who are trying to lure away the Colossians are teaching something that can't bring the fulfillment Christ can. Paul stresses that only Jesus is fully God in human form. The false teachers who emphasize a worship of angels can't claim that angels can offer the same. (Colossians 2:8–10)

- The Colossians were being tempted to think they needed to be circumcised in order to have a relationship with God. Paul counters that by saying that circumcision only brings an outward change, but the circumcision of the heart through repentance and baptism shows a true relationship with God. (Colossians 2:11–14)

- Christians are set free from being judged by others and thinking they must hurt their bodies (asceticism) to gain acceptance by God. That occurred because of Jesus's victorious death and resurrection, which defeated any efforts that evil spirits might attempt toward Christians. (Colossians 2:15–19)

- Some people think that treating their bodies poorly will show God how much they want to love Him, but that doesn't mean much to God. He's more interested in the heart commitment of a person and wants us to treat our bodies well in service to Him. (Colossians 2:20–23)

Study Questions

1. Why is Paul concerned that the Colossians see his right motives in their growth in Christ? *He isn't trying to bind them as false teachers. He wants them freed*

2. Why is it so important that the Colossians resist being deceived by the false teachers? *The false teacher would impose thing on them that bind them*

3. How does Paul reason that physical circumcision is no longer necessary to be friends with God? *It take the circumcision of the heart.*

4. Whom did Jesus have victory over when He died on the cross, and what freedoms does that bestow upon a believer? *Satan His death was enough. Freedom in Christ*

5. Why does a Christian not need to be held hostage by treating his body badly as if it would gain him more acceptance with God? *It does no good. He loves us as we are, not what we do.*

Nov 17

Colossians 3:1-17
The Before and After of Believing

Chapter Highlights:
- It's Our Heavenly Life
- Just Say No!
- Clothe Yourselves with Love

Let's Get Started

Paul has been faithfully dealing with the issues that could distract the Colossian believers from following Christ, but now he focuses his attention on explaining what they should be doing. He will give them (and us) a remarkably beautiful challenge to the spiritual inner life with Christ: If we have died to our old way of living, then we should experience new life in Christ. When he tells us what that means, it will spur us all on to living victoriously and powerfully in God's power.

It's not an easy challenge that he'll be giving us. Putting off the old life and putting on the new isn't easy, but it's simple; it's just a matter of what we concentrate on. So let's take a look at what Paul values and then choose to value it ourselves.

go to

death
Romans 6:1

seated
Hebrews 1:3;
Psalm 110:1

It's Our Heavenly Life

> COLOSSIANS 3:1–2 *If then you were raised with Christ, seek those things which are above, where Christ is, sitting at the right hand of God. Set your mind on things above, not on things on the earth.* (NKJV)

Paul continues his thoughts by talking about what happens to those who "die" to self by believing in Jesus and symbolizing their belief through baptism. He says believers are supposed to live like heavenly citizens here on earth—but since they had never been to heaven, how can they know what it's like? How can they—and we, by extension—apply God's heavenly perspective over their earthly vision and see earth through His eyes? It just seems too difficult. But evidently Paul knew it was possible, for he told these believers it was what he desired for them. And that potential reality is based on <u>death</u> to themselves and being raised to new life in Christ. They can choose to "set" their hearts and minds on heaven's goals by remembering that Jesus is exalted as a victorious leader <u>seated</u> at the most

perfect
Colossians 2:10

important place in heaven: the right hand of God. Jesus is right beside God the Father because they are equal. No one else can claim that.

For the Christian that means his earthly sinful desires are in effect dead. Jesus was victorious over those desires, destroying them on the cross. Of course they still rear their ugly heads, but none of us who are in Christ need to be controlled by them. We have a choice, and that choice is strengthened when we view life from a heavenly perspective.

Although it's a weak comparison, the power available to us because Jesus conquered sin is like knowing the president of the United States personally because you grew up on the same block. Now that he's in the most powerful position in the country, he has the ability to do anything for you that you desire—so long as it's in your best interests. You can even sleep in Abraham Lincoln's bedroom if you want. Of course, the president's power is small in comparison to the incredible power that Jesus has.

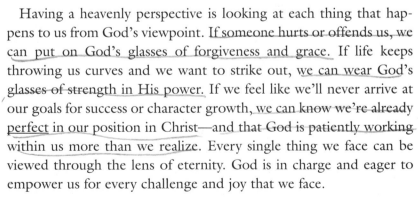

what others say

Elisabeth Elliot

Do not try to "think about nothing." "Set your mind," Paul says, not, "Empty your mind." Set it on Christ, not on earthly things. It is helpful for me to start with the Word, expecting God to direct and control my thoughts within that context, leading me to others as He chooses.[1]

Having a heavenly perspective is looking at each thing that happens to us from God's viewpoint. If someone hurts or offends us, we can put on God's glasses of forgiveness and grace. If life keeps throwing us curves and we want to strike out, we can wear God's glasses of strength in His power. If we feel like we'll never arrive at our goals for success or character growth, we can know we're already perfect in our position in Christ—and that God is patiently working within us more than we realize. Every single thing we face can be viewed through the lens of eternity. God is in charge and eager to empower us for every challenge and joy that we face.

We don't truly change our inner being by trying. That's what the false teachers were telling the Colossians. Just do this or do that . . . yet it didn't work. Only by allowing the Spirit of God to work within us will we actually be changed. And if we think change hasn't occurred in our lives because the <u>progress</u> is so slow, we can look back over a year or five years and see the changes God has made. We will have learned to depend upon Him more than if it had been fast or instantaneous. Through a process of growth, we're learning things that we'll then be able to pass along to others.

Hiding and Seeking the New Life in Christ

COLOSSIANS 3:3–4 *For you died, and your life is hidden with Christ in God. When Christ who is our life appears, then you also will appear with Him in glory.* (NKJV)

Dead people care about nothing because they don't have cares or desires. You may say, "If I'm supposed to be spiritually dead, does that mean I'm not supposed to care about anything? How about if my child or spouse isn't yet saved? God wants me to care about that, doesn't He?" Of course. Being dead <u>spiritually</u> means that you care less and less about the earthly, sinful things of this world (immorality, impurity, lust, selfishness) and care more about the spiritual, moral things of this world that affect eternity. The lures of this world: materialism, success, perfect relationships—all those things grow less desirable. All of them are <u>temporary</u> and won't bring the satisfaction that we need or desire. Only when our eyes are opened to the glory of giving selflessly will we find true happiness wrapped in the gift box of joy.

If your grandmother gave you a piece of antique jewelry worth thousands of dollars, you would probably keep it in a safe place and bring it out only for very special occasions. You would want it hidden in order to keep it in the family. It's the same way with our life in Christ: it is hidden within us and is safely <u>guarded</u> by the Spirit—since nothing can take it away from us. And it is concealed in the sense that it can't be seen when someone is just looking at us. We "bring it out" at every occasion—living as God would desire in each situation. But when Jesus is <u>revealed</u> for all to see, our "hidden" life with Him will also be revealed for all to see. And not just in our usual "earthly" clothes, but <u>glorified</u> with new heavenly and spiritual raiment.

go to

progress
1 Timothy 4:15

spiritually
Galatians 2:20

temporary
2 Corinthians 4:18

guarded
John 10:28–29

revealed
1 Thessalonians
4:16–18

glorified
1 John 3:2

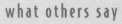

N. T. Wright

The Christian <u>hopes</u> not merely for the coming of the Lord, but for the full revelation of what he or she already is. Then will it be seen with what faithful diligence and perseverance many outwardly "unsuccessful" and forgotten Christian workers have served their Lord. Paul, the prisoner, an eccentric Jew to the Romans and a worse-than-Gentile traitor to the Jews, will be seen as Paul the apostle, the servant of the King. The Colossians, insignificant ex-pagans from a third-rate country town, will be seen in a glory which, if it were now to appear, one might be tempted to worship. This is how they are to regard their life, and on this foundation they are to build genuine holiness and Christian maturity.[2]

Since Paul just told us that asceticism—the denial of physical pleasures—is not the way preferred by God, we can know that being "dead" to this world doesn't mean forsaking the joys that God has declared as His gifts to us—like eating, sex, exercise, or other physical acts. He wants us to <u>enjoy</u> those things—but keep them in proper balance.

Just Say No!

COLOSSIANS 3:5–7 *Therefore put to death your members which are on the earth: fornication, uncleanness, passion, evil desire, and covetousness, which is idolatry. Because of these things the wrath of God is coming upon the sons of disobedience, in which you yourselves once walked when you lived in them.* (NKJV)

Paul makes people who love lists very happy. Some practical folks may have been reading Paul's comments so far and scratching their heads. "Now exactly what is he getting to?" they ponder. "I'm supposed to be dead, but what does that really look like?" Paul knows some of his readers need specifics, so he writes out a list. And it's a hefty <u>list</u> too. He tells them—commands them—to give up:

- *fornication:* sex outside of marriage or as a single person.
- *uncleanness:* the result of a tainted character because of immoral sin.
- *passion:* any uncontrolled lust. In this context it refers to a sexual nature, but could refer to any overwhelming passion, like overeating.

go to

hopes
Romans 8:18,
1 John 3:1

enjoy
1 Timothy 4:1–4

list
Romans 1:29–31;
1 Corinthians 5:11

- *evil desire:* thoughts that precede lust. They must be controlled but are not sinful until given free rein.

- *covetousness:* wanting anything that God doesn't want to give. Greed is basically idolatry because it makes something more important than God.

These are the evils that plague God's created beings and His world, which was created to worship only Him and to operate in godliness. Therefore, God must do something about it. He will someday destroy the earth and bring the deserved judgment. Paul uses the verb "comes" here, literally meaning that God's wrath is already <u>going</u> on. It will end in His <u>judgment</u>.

But Paul stresses that <u>judgment will not bother these Colossian believers because they are now protected "in Christ."</u> Besides, it's no longer the way they live. They are new <u>creatures</u>.

Our sin nature is already <u>dead</u> because of Jesus's death, but we must make a conscious choice to <u>not cooperate</u> with it . Paul's use of the Greek tense for "put to death" suggests a decisive action. It's a choice not to go along with the wrong things that our natural self wants to do. We just say "no" to those evil promptings, and the Spirit will come alongside us to strengthen us to keep our commitment.

go to

going
John 3:36

judgment
Romans 2:5;
2 Thessalonians
1:7–9;
2 Corinthians 5:10

creatures
2 Corinthians 5:17

dead
Romans 6:5–14

not cooperate
1 Corinthians 10:13

Jesus
Hebrews 4:15

tempted
Matthew 4:1–11

birth
James 1:15

what others say

Neil T. Anderson

The law of sin is still strong and appealing, but because of our position in Christ, we can rid ourselves of sinful behavior and habits. "Putting to death" is to render inoperative the power of sin—something we cannot do in the flesh, only through Christ.[3]

Sexual temptation—or any other temptation—is not sinful in itself. It is only as we give in to the temptation that it becomes sin. Every single one of us has desires that could be evil. <u>Jesus</u> was <u>tempted</u> but resisted sin and remained sinless. As Christians following Him, our thoughts need to be resisted and controlled before they give <u>birth</u> to sin.

Putting Myself to Death Daily

go to

outburst
2 Corinthians 12:20

new nature
Ephesians 4:24

COLOSSIANS 3:8–10 *But now you yourselves are to put off all these: anger, wrath, malice, blasphemy, filthy language out of your mouth. Do not lie to one another, since you have put off the old man with his deeds, and have put on the new man who is renewed in knowledge according to the image of Him who created him,* (NKJV)

When we change clothes, we put on one layer at a time. That's exactly what Paul advises in order to live as if we have this new self that controls the old nature. Like filthy clothes, we're supposed to take off each layer of disgusting behavior and motives. The previous verses gave the first layer: immorality. Then he gives two more layers: anger and wrong language. Paul uses several words to describe different aspects of anger and words:

- *Anger:* continuing attitude of smoldering hatred
- *Wrath:* sharp outburst of anger
- *Malice:* ill will toward others
- *Blasphemy:* injuring a person's reputation
- *Filthy language:* shameful or abusive speech, including obscenities
- *Lying:* telling something that isn't true

All of these negative results of the old nature bring dishonor to God, but they also limit a Christian's ability to represent the Lord in an attractive way. Everyone will have some faults in these areas, but there should be growth in bringing them under control over time. The new nature of righteousness within a Christian is always trying to overcome those "old nature" tendencies. It requires daily, even minute-by-minute, renewal as a Christian confesses each time he or she falls back into those old habits and then makes a fresh commitment to live in God's power. That is done as each one comes to know Jesus more closely and trust Him more dearly. Obviously, the opposite of the negative characteristics of the old man is all that Jesus is—He is who the "new man" ought to be. Becoming more like Him is what renewal is about.

The spiritual concept of "renewal" is a common one in the Bible and should give us hope: We don't have to be perfect immediately

. . . or even eventually. We are growing closer to Jesus's image, but we will never reach it completely.

Areas of Renewal

Scripture	Jesus Renews . . .
Isaiah 40:31	our strength
2 Corinthians 4:16	our inner being
Romans 12:2	our minds
Ephesians 4:23	our attitudes

go to

put off
Romans 13:12

metaphor
Psalm 35:26

destructive
James 3:6–12;
Proverbs 8:36

The Greek word *rid* (*apothesthe*) means "to put off," like taking off a suit of clothes. Because Paul is using it to refer to removing something disgusting, it means "throw it off like a dirty shirt." This isn't the first time the writers of the Bible have used the metaphor of removing a garment. Job 29:14 says, "I put on righteousness, and it clothed me; My justice was like a robe and a turban" (NKJV).

Commentators say that Paul's metaphor of "taking off and putting on clothes" is a reference to the common practice of that day when a new believer was baptized. When he went under the water he was wearing his old clothes. He took those clothes off and put on a white robe after coming up out of the water—signifying a new life and new nature.

Paul makes two lists of different sins. The first is back in verse 5 and deals with sexual immorality. The second list in verse 8 deals with sins toward others. Some people think sexual sin is more important or worse than the sins named in verse 8, but with God all sin is equal. We can't excuse our wrong verbal reactions toward others because we think such a "mistake" isn't the same as sexual sin. Actually, they are equally wrong in God's sight. So let's be careful to look at sin like God does: as destructive.

key point

what others say

Jan Johnson

The power of accountability comes from breaking my isolation and joining a team, not from fear that if I don't shape up, my friends will be disappointed in me. As I walk through the day and meet my problems, I have a strong sense that others are present with me. Because of their strength, I don't become entangled again.[4]

Lying can seem fairly harmless at times, especially when we think of the famous—or should I say, *infamous*—"little white lie." We try to rationalize, "After all, what can it hurt?" Actually, it can hurt lots of people. Lying tears down trust and brings disunity. When we don't trust someone, we're more likely to gossip about them and not choose to be selfless toward them.

A part of not lying to each other is being honest about our sins so that others can hold us accountable and keep us going in the right direction. This involves risk—we fear that we'll lose friends if we're vulnerable. But it's only in sharing our struggles that we find the power we need through the prayer support of others.

apply it

Created Equal

COLOSSIANS 3:11 *where there is neither Greek nor Jew, circumcised nor uncircumcised, barbarian, Scythian, slave nor free, but Christ is all and in all. (NKJV)*

Paul may have anticipated one of his readers wondering if anyone—and everyone—could take part in this "new creature" business. He wanted to reassure each one—especially if that person was wondering if he or she could be excluded from such great news—that each and every person could participate, no matter their:

- National heritage (Greek or Jew)
- Past religious affiliation (circumcised or uncircumcised)
- Cultural background (barbarian or **Scythian**)
- Economic or social history (slave or free)

Paul made sure that everyone could know that there were no such distinctions within the body of Christ. Jesus wants to be a part of every single person's life that inhabits this world; if they do accept Him as Savior, they are the same in God's eyes as everyone else in the kingdom. With Him, there are none of the distinctions like in the world.

If we truly believe that everyone is equal in the body of Christ, we won't have as much of the "old nature" tendencies that Paul is telling us to "take off." We won't become as angry because everyone has value. We won't want to make someone else impure by having immoral sexual relations with them. By seeing everyone as valuable

go to

lying
Proverbs 6:12–19

hurt
Proverbs 15:4

trust
Proverbs 11:9

disunity
Proverbs 16:28

gossip
2 Corinthians 12:20

support
James 5:16

Scythian
wild, savage nomad

and important—equal with us—we will want the best for them and we won't give in to our selfish ambition or tell lies about them. It's all wrapped up together.

go to

free
John 8:36

Since everyone has the same "new nature" in Christ, no one can use their old background as fodder for saying, "I can't live up to the standards Paul is speaking about. After all, I was formerly a barbarian out in the wilderness. Anger and lying were a part of our culture. That's just the way I am, so don't expect me to change." *No!* Paul says. Every single person who knows Christ, regardless of their heritage or past environment, can rid themselves of the bad stuff and choose the good stuff. No one is exempt.

You shouldn't use diverse heritage or different culture as an excuse for not telling others about the saving gift of Jesus. Everyone can qualify, and every single person needs His wonderful grace.

Clothe Yourselves with Love

COLOSSIANS 3:12–14 *Therefore, as the elect of God, holy and beloved, put on tender mercies, kindness, humility, meekness, longsuffering; bearing with one another, and forgiving one another, if anyone has a complaint against another; even as Christ forgave you, so you also must do. But above all these things put on love, which is the bond of perfection.* (NKJV)

Paul must still be thinking of those analytical types who need a specific list to spell out exactly what it means to have new life in Christ. He continues his discussion of the attributes that characterize Christians who are made new in Jesus. It wasn't immorality, anger, or poor use of the tongue, that's for sure. So he now gives the

love
1 Corinthians 13:13

positive side of what it is, and it all boils down to one thing: love. When a Christian is operating in God's love, he or she will naturally have:

- *Tender mercies.* This is compassion—the ability to see someone's predicament from their perspective. Christians were one of the few groups of people known for helping those who were considered inferior by others or who were inadequate because of some circumstances like disability.

- *Kindness.* Serving others as if they are important. It includes being good to others.

- *Humility.* Having a correct assessment of oneself. In the classical Greek, humility was disparaged as only referring to a servant. It was not a positive term. Christians used it in a positive way for the first time—as something to be admired and sought after.

- *Meekness.* The ability to have righteous anger about the right things. It comes from being God-controlled, not controlled by an anger that wants its own way.

- *Longsuffering.* This is a patience that doesn't expect more than a person is able to give.

- *Bearing with one another.* Being willing to stay friends with someone who isn't always friendly or being willing to continue to put faith in someone who has disappointed you.

- *Forgiving one another.* Releasing a person from your need to punish or get revenge.

When these wonderful attributes adorn a Christian like a rich robe of elegant silk and attached gemstones and pearls, it builds up the body of Christ in unity. For then there is no jealousy, envy, hate, anger, impatience, or selfishness. There is only the selfless desire to see another person built up and have their needs met as much as possible.

Many of these qualities that Paul mentions are the fruit of the Holy Spirit that he describes in another letter, Galatians 5:22–23: "But the fruit of the Spirit is love, joy, peace, longsuffering, kindness, goodness, faithfulness, gentleness, self-control. Against such there is no law" (NKJV). When a person is filled with the Holy Spirit, his reactions and behavior are in line with the same way that God would respond.

go to

can't
Matthew 6:14–15

what others say

Stuart Briscoe

The problem, quite frankly, is that the church of Jesus Christ is made up exclusively of redeemed sinners. And these wretched sinners—I'm one of them—have an awful habit of showing their true colors. If we're going to come down like a ton of bricks on everybody who shows his true colors, then there is going to be an awful pile of bricks around the place.[6]

Philip Yancey

At last I understood: in the final analysis, forgiveness is an act of faith. By forgiving another, I am trusting that God is a better justice-maker than I am. By forgiving, I release my own right to get even and leave all issues of fairness for God to work out.[7]

J. I. Packer

Holiness is actually the true health of the person. Anything else is ugliness and deformity at character level, a malfunctioning of the individual, a crippled state of soul. The various forms of bodily sickness and impairment that Jesus healed are so many illustrations of this deeper, inward deformity.[8]

For example, how can we not forgive others when God has forgiven us so much? The hurt and pain other people cause us does feel huge at the time. But that hurt isn't anything compared to the horrible pattern of sin for which God has forgiven each of us. And if we can't forgive others, God can't forgive us.

Do you want to know how to be able to love and forgive others more and more? It's by truly soaking in the fact that each of us is unconditionally loved by God—a love that will never end. The more insecure we are—not taking hold of God's unconditional love—the more we respond with hurt and an inability to forgive others. So whenever you feel like you can't forgive someone or choose to love them, think about God's great love for you, even though you don't deserve it.

apply it

Have That Attitude of Gratitude

Colossians 3:15 *And let the peace of God rule in your hearts, to which also you were called in one body; and be thankful. (NKJV)*

go to

worry
Philippians 4:6

blessings
Colossians 1:12

members
Romans 15:5

focus
2 Corinthians 10:5

lovely
Philippians 4:8

Worry, fear, and complaining could be considered some of the most unattractive "clothes" that any Christian can wear. When we are <u>worried</u> and fearful, we demonstrate loudly—as if we were wearing a bright yellow jacket with ostrich feathers sprouting from the neckline—that we really don't trust God. And when we're complaining, we prove that not only are we ungrateful for God's rich <u>blessings</u>, we're so focused on ourselves that we disregard everyone else's needs. Worst of all is when there is no peace between <u>members</u> of a church or several churches. Talk about horrible clothes! That's not the way God wants Christians to behave. Paul exhorts his readers to put on the beautiful and attractive rich robes of peace and gratitude. This peace comes from a lack of giving in to worry and also the peace that means we are "at peace" with others.

This peace must "rule" in our hearts. The word *rule* is an athletic term for being an umpire or referee. An umpire or referee determines whether the game is being played according to the rules and calls "foul" or throws out a flag when the wrong thing is done. Peace can call foul when we begin to <u>focus</u> on the things God doesn't want us to. When we begin to worry, peace throws out a flag that says, "Trust God; He is capable." When we begin to feel at odds with others, peace raises its arms and shouts, "Choose to forgive. You've been forgiven so much, even more than that." And when we focus on everything that's going wrong and feel like nothing is going our way, peace whistles and exclaims, "Stop grumbling. You have too many blessings to count. Focus on those."

We should be grateful for whatever people can offer us as their service and performance. When we are upset because they don't measure up to our expectations, we aren't practicing that "attitude of gratitude."

what others say

Luci Swindoll

Should you encounter bad news today, look within yourself. You'll find God's Spirit, which will enable you to accept graciously that which has been handed to you. Think on those parts of life that are <u>lovely</u>. For even in our saddest days, God is under the sorrow, holding us up.[9]

Jesus was never without peace. He responded with grace and poise in every situation. That's because He was always doing what He knew His heavenly Father wanted Him to do—He walked completely in harmony with God's plans and desires. Even when people tried to take His life, He knew it wasn't God's will. He knew He could peacefully <u>walk</u> through a group of angry people without their hurting Him, even if they intended to kill Him.

<u>Gratitude Grows from the Word of God</u>

COLOSSIANS 3:16 *Let the word of Christ dwell in you richly in all wisdom, teaching and admonishing one another in psalms and hymns and spiritual songs, singing with grace in your hearts to the Lord. (NKJV)*

Paul thinks that the peace and gratitude that should adorn Christians comes from a concentration on the Bible, which contains God's words. God's Word isn't supposed to just sit like a dull boy with a dunce's cap on in the corner of our minds. It's supposed to be actively involved in every corner of our minds. It's supposed to have rich dividends. It builds us up so that we can teach and encourage others with God's wisdom; then it flows out of us singing praise to God, acknowledging Him as the source of everything good.

Only as we know the Bible and apply it to our lives are we able to respond supernaturally to the situations that challenge us. <u>Meditating</u> and memorizing the Bible enable it to become such a <u>part</u> of us that our reactions are <u>affected</u> by it, sometimes even without our consciously choosing. That is exactly what God wants to happen. That's why we may find ourselves humming a hymn without even realizing it.

This verse reveals that the early Christian church was a singing group of people. Government documents from that time describing the Christians' habits say that they met at dawn to sing and worship and often spent the whole night singing their praise to God. They knew the truth: The fastest way to build up your spirit is to sing a song! Even if you feel down in the dumps and singing is the farthest thing from your mind. Singing, then, is even more reason to lift your voice in song—especially if it's a praise song for the Lord. For then you'll concentrate on who God is and your faith in Him will grow. Just watch your spirit soar! No wonder God gave us singing voices—even if some of us can only make a <u>joyful</u> *noise*.

walk
Luke 4:29–30

meditating
Proverbs 4:20–23

part
2 Peter 1:4

affected
Joshua 1:8

joyful
Psalm 100:2

go to

inspired
2 Timothy 3:16–17

Holy Spirit
John 16:13

everything
1 Corinthians 10:31

something to ponder

what others say

Joyce Meyer

If we wait until everything is perfect before rejoicing and giving thanks, we won't have much fun. Learning to enjoy life even in the midst of trying circumstances is one way we develop spiritual maturity.[10]

The Bible is God's thoughts and desires for His creation, which He directly <u>inspired</u> people to write on His behalf. He did that through the <u>Holy Spirit</u>, which indwelled the apostles and disciples, who penned the words contained in the Bible. Jesus said that would happen by stating, "But the Helper, the Holy Spirit, whom the Father will send in My name, He will teach you all things, and bring to your remembrance all things that I said to you" (John 14:26 NKJV).

Although the Bible was written by many people over a long period of time, it has a recurring theme and a consistency that could never have occurred without God's direct guidance. After all, if you pulled sixty people together and told each one separately to write on one topic, what kind of homework do you think you would get back? Most likely an inconsistent jumble of opinions with different, often opposing, ideas. But the Bible is consistent—and it was written by sixty people over several ages.

God Helps Those Who Help Themselves— NOT!

COLOSSIANS 3:17 *And whatever you do in word or deed, do all in the name of the Lord Jesus, giving thanks to God the Father through Him. (NKJV)*

Some people think, *Well, this part of my life or this particular activity isn't really of interest to God. I don't need to bother Him about that. But when I do something for Him that is religious, then I'll be sure to seek the Lord and His help.* NOT! Paul says specifically that <u>everything</u> we do, whether it's spoken or acted, is to be done in God's power and for His glory. Can you believe that even includes sex with your husband or wife? Yes, I mean everything! There isn't anything we do that isn't of interest to God. Likewise, there isn't anything we do that He doesn't want to be a part of. He wants to empower us for everything in our lives. Because He is such a great God, He is strong enough to be involved. Isn't that the most wonderful thing to thank God for? That's what Paul thinks too!

Since God wants to be a part of every area of our lives and everything we do, we can use that critera to evaluate whether something we're considering doing is something we want God to be part of. God doesn't want any part in sinful behavior, so we can make a wise choice when we remember He wants to be a part of our holy living.

Someone once quipped, "God helps those who help themselves." If that were true, Paul couldn't have written verse 17 to the Colossians. Instead, he would have said something like, "After you've tried your hardest, do it all in the name of the Lord Jesus." But that's not what he said. He said, "Whatever you do . . . do *all* . . .". Satan has tried to convince Christians through that common phrase to believe that we should go as far as we can in our own power and then seek God. Thank God that He wants to help us from the very beginning. God doesn't want us to try harder—He wants us to depend upon Him.

key point

There is no secular work versus sacred work in God's eyes. He wants us to work at our jobs or clean the toilet or teach a child his manners all in God's power, and all with giving thanks for every part of life. Don't buy into that secular-versus-sacred-activity junk! It's *all* sacred.

Giving thanks and being grateful must be important for Christians because Paul mentions it so often and so much of the Bible encourages God's people to concentrate on what is wonderful and enjoyable.

Chapter Wrap-Up

- Living like a Christian with a heavenly citizenship means looking at life from God's perspective. Paul wants his readers to remember that they are new creatures in Christ and to learn how to live like it. (Colossians 3:1–4)

- Paul wants his readers to take off the sinful things of their old nature like one would remove an old piece of clothing—things like immorality and abusive speech. (Colossians 3:5–11)

- Paul contrasts the old garments of the old man with the new garments of the new man that the Christians are supposed to choose. They will know when they are allowing their new nature to be in control because they will love others and have only positive things to say. Plus, they will do everything for God's glory. (Colossians 3:12–17)

Study Questions

1. What did Paul want his readers to do when he told them, "Set your hearts on things above"? *We belong to Christ.*
   Live like it.

2. What is it that Paul wants the Colossians to put to death, and how are they supposed to do that? *Self - sin*

3. What kind of clothing does Paul want his readers to put on?
   New nature garments.
   (creature)

Colossians 3:18–4:18
Living Out the Inner Holiness

Chapter Highlights:
- **The New Garments**
- **How's Your SQ**
- **Keep Your Prayer Antennae Up**
- **Everybody Says "Hi!"**

Let's Get Started

If you saw someone walking down Main Street wearing ugly, dirty, stinking clothes, you'd most likely think they couldn't afford better clothes—or were too ignorant to buy new ones. Well, we each wear spiritual clothes too, and Paul wants his readers to show everyone that they are wearing the new-creature garments of Jesus in their hearts. That was the theme of our last chapter. Now, in this portion of Colossians 3 and 4, Paul is going to describe in great detail how the new clothing should look when we are empowered by the Holy Spirit. Since relationships are the most telling—and difficult—way to do that, Paul focuses in on marriage, family, and the workplace. Then he addresses how to respond to unbelievers. In his closing remarks, Paul sends some encouraging greetings from those who surround him.

key point

The New Garments

Paul has some specific instructions for how wives, husbands, and children can represent the Lord by wearing their "new-creature" clothing. Wives are to be submissive, husbands are to love their wives, and children are to be obedient to their parents. Plus, fathers are to be kind and understanding. Paul is preaching mutual responsibility, a response to everyone's belonging to Jesus and surrendering their own personal rights to Him. Let's see how that is lived out.

You Need Not Be a Doormat

COLOSSIANS 3:18 *Wives, submit to your own husbands, as is fitting in the Lord.* (NKJV)

As Paul continues, perhaps he wonders if wives might be a little hesitant to apply this "glorifying God in everything" to the area of relationships, and especially marriage. We don't know whether Paul

submitting
1 Peter 3:1–4

others
Ephesians 5:22

thought some wives might want to put an exception to his gratitude sermon, but maybe he thought, *I can just imagine that Sylvia isn't going to apply that to her relationship with Fred. I better address that and let everyone know it applies to every area of life—especially marriage.* So Paul tells his readers, and first the wives, how to put on the new robes of life in Christ. For wives, it's the simple, but challenging, instruction of "submitting" that he has exhorted others in various letters.

The insights Paul had, through the Holy Spirit's guidance, were totally unique for that time period. We take for granted the status of women. But in Paul's day, in Greek and Jewish customs, women were things, not people, and were owned by husbands who could do anything they wanted. Women had no legal rights. A husband could easily divorce his wife, and she had no power to do anything about it. She was definitely to be "seen and not heard," committed to a pure life devoid of outside contact. On the other hand, a husband was definitely seen and heard—he could engage in outside affairs and relationships as much as he wanted.

So at first glance Paul seems to be preaching the "party line." But for the first time in Jewish thought, he wasn't thinking of a wife being a doormat. Instead, he went on in the next verse to determine the model for husbands—which was a completely different viewpoint.

Today, submission is lived out practically as a husband and wife discuss everything and come to a mutual decision. But if they can't decide and a decision must be made, then the husband has the option of taking the step that he feels is best. This is where the wife puts on her "new creation clothing" of compassion, love, kindness, and humility—oh, and don't forget patience—and trusts God enough to surrender her own agenda. That doesn't make it easy, but believing God can do anything, even change her husband's perspective, can strengthen her to turn it all over to the Lord.

Yet, because Paul clarifies that she is to submit "as is fitting in the Lord," there can be limits to her submission. She should never submit by agreeing to something the Bible speaks against or that is immoral or wrong.

Within the Christian community, there are different viewpoints on this controversial issue of submission. Some Christians believe that if the husband and wife cannot agree, then no decision should be made until they are equally convinced. Regardless, an absence of anger, coupled with plenty of patience and gentleness (which Paul has been talking about earlier in chapter 3), should be at the core of everything a Christian husband and wife do.

what others say

Elizabeth George

Do you know the main reason why we wives don't submit to our husband? God says it's *fear*. We are afraid of what will happen if our husband does things his way instead of our way.[1]

Wellington Boone

The very suggestion of submission brings forth a series of what ifs. What if the husband is not saved? What if he does ungodly things? Such queries answer a myriad of questions because they reveal the attitude, and submission is an attitude. It is an act of the will. With one's intellect, **volition**, and affection, as we submit to God, so our very submission models Jesus's reflection of His Father. Even if one is suffering wrongly and endures, it is commendable.[2]

Charles R. Swindoll

It doesn't take a Greek scholar to see that Paul gives a command, "Wives, be subject to your own husbands . . ." and then a comparison, ". . . as to the Lord." For wives, the basic role is one of submission, and the analogy is "as to the Lord." As the Christian wife would respond to her Lord, so she is to do to her husband.[3]

In the other letters where Paul addresses the husband-wife relationship, he gives more details about how a husband and a wife are to respond to each other. When we read the Bible, we're not supposed to just latch onto one verse and make a whole theology out of it. Instad, we're supposed to review all the verses and take it as a whole.

Marriage—God's Way

Scripture	Truth About Marriage
Genesis 2:18	Husbands and wives need each other, as God designed it.
Genesis 2:24	God designed husband and wife to be one flesh, joined in every way for mutual joy.
Matthew 19:4–9	God did not want divorce, but men sinfully choose the wrong way.
1 Corinthians 6:18; Hebrews 13:4	God wants every spouse to stay true sexually and emotionally to their own mate.
1 Corinthians 7:3–5	Neither spouse should refuse sexual satisfaction except by mutual agreement for the purpose of fasting and prayer.

go to

love
Ephesians 5:25

A man needs his wife's respect and admiration. What better way could God tell a wife to meet that need than through submitting to him? It makes him feel important, and as he feels significant in her eyes, he is more open to seeing her viewpoint. Submission may seem like a destructive thing, but it actually can soften a man's heart and help him to be more sensitive.

Same Tune, Second Verse

COLOSSIANS 3:19 *Husbands, love your wives and do not be bitter toward them. (NKJV)*

This must have been the best instruction ever that the Colossian wives had heard. We can almost hear them shout, "Right on, Paul! Preach it, brother!" Love! Love is the heart's cry of every woman, whether she's a wife or not. And God was so wise in guiding Paul to admonish husbands not to be harsh with their wives. Maybe Paul had had his own struggle with harshness toward his wife—whom some commentators believe he had. We can just imagine the hard-hitting attitude of a Pharisee who thinks he has arrived and thinks everyone else should be as holy as him. Regardless of whether Paul truly was married, he must have seen that logical side of the male rise up at times and treat a wife with impatience and unrealistic expectations. Paul doesn't think that's the way a godly man who is wearing the new clothes of compassion, love, and gentleness should act. So Paul tells them so!

what others say

Kevin Leman

Being a husband and father automatically places you in a new category—that of a servant-leader who fully realizes the whole is indeed greater than any of its parts, and you must do your part to make the whole—your family—go.[4]

for your marriage

Submission and love within a marriage relationship doesn't mean someone is more valuable than their mate. It has nothing to do with inferiority; it has to do with roles. God designed the roles within the home to have a person in the top position, but every person in the family has equal value.

A husband may think that he needs to be harsh in order to make his wife submissive, but being <u>gentle</u> and loving is the fastest way to help her submit to him. So when you are tempted to force your opinion on her, back off! Chill out! Love and tenderness go a lot farther.

We're Not Leaving Children Out

Here

COLOSSIANS 3:20 *Children, obey your parents in all things, for this is well pleasing to the Lord. (NKJV)*

When children are underage, they are supposed to obey their parents in everything. When they are grown, they are to honor their parents. Obedience must be the most difficult thing for children to do because for them, especially the strong-willed child, their whole goal is, "I do it myself!" Yet, God knows that obedience is the way of peace for the child and the best thing for them to grow strong so that they can learn discipline and obedience to Him. No wonder it pleases Him—each child is learning to submit to their heavenly Father as they grow.

Disobedience to parents in the Old Testament was considered the same as resistance against God. It was severely <u>punished</u> and served as a warning to other children to obey their parents. At the time Paul wrote his letter, a father had complete domination over his children within Roman law, and he was legally able to do anything with his child that he desired, even condemning his child to death.

go to

gentle
1 Peter 3:7

punished
Exodus 21:17;
Leviticus 20:9

submitted
Luke 2:51

honored
John 19:27

everything
Mark 3:31–33

what others say

J. Vernon McGee

Children are to obey their parents. They are to honor their parents all their lives. However, the child also needs to grow up. I don't think this verse means that a twenty-four-year-old boy must stay tied to his mama's apron strings. Whether he is married or single, when he has reached maturity, he is ready to get away from his parents.[5]

Even Jesus <u>submitted</u> to His parents and obeyed them. What better example for children can there be than Jesus, who obeyed His parents when He was young and <u>honored</u> His mother when He was an adult. Yet, He had the balance as an adult of not doing <u>everything</u> His mother wanted Him to do.

something to ponder

Verbal Sticks and Stones May Hurt Your Child

COLOSSIANS 3:21 *Fathers, do not provoke your children, lest they become discouraged. (NKJV)*

Lest any father or mother reading Paul's comment to children take advantage of a child's obedience, Paul quickly gives wise instruction to parents (yes, moms are included in this!). Don't make a child become bitter and discouraged by taking unfair advantage of God's desire for them to obey.

> ### what others say
>
> **Kevin Leman**
>
> We're to train our kids without nagging, without browbeating, without exasperating them. Instead of "losing it," as so often and easily happens, we're to discipline in a way that shows them loving respect yet holds them accountable for their decisions.[6]
>
> **Steve Farrar**
>
> Your child will have plenty of critics. Just make sure that you are not one of them. Words are very important. We all remember the childhood rhyme, "Sticks and stones may hurt my bones, but words will never hurt me." Nothing could be further from the truth. Many of us have broken bones and have recovered very nicely in a month or so. But is it not true that we can still remember the critical words that were hurled at us on a playground twenty, thirty, forty, even fifty years later? Words can hurt like nothing else.
>
> Gentlemen, let's reward with our words.[7]

The word for *provoke* in the Greek is *erethize*, which means "to stir to anger." How can a child become discouraged? Here are some things to avoid:

- Expecting more than a child can accomplish.

- Expecting a child to behave perfectly.

- Expecting a child to perform perfectly and not giving them credit for their sincere efforts.

- Overreacting to the things they say and do.

- Doling out harsh punishment, such as spanking in anger, or making a consequence bigger than the disobedience.

- Not giving respect through phrases of courtesy like "thank you" and "please."
- Neglecting to acknowledge your own errors and refusing to ask for forgiveness from your child.

How's Your Service Quotient?

COLOSSIANS 3:22 *Bondservants, obey in all things your masters according to the flesh, not with eyeservice, as men-pleasers, but in sincerity of heart, fearing God. (NKJV)*

It may grate against our modern nerves to see that Paul didn't tell people not to own slaves. That seems amazing to us today, but in that day and time, slaves were acceptable and for many were like members of the family. Paul doesn't debate the lawfulness of slavery, but he is concerned about Christian slaves representing the Lord in their position. They aren't supposed to do the right thing only when their master's eye is upon them, but all the time, even if they won't get credit for it. Their behavior is to be sincere—from the heart—not because they won't get in trouble or because they'll get a reward. They are to serve their human master as if he were indeed Jesus Himself.

Paul's attention at about the time of the writing of this letter was on a situation with a slave, Onesimus. In his letter to Philemon, Paul tells Philemon to receive his wayward servant, Onesimus (who ran away), as a fellow brother in Christ. Paul helped to convert Onesimus to Christianity, and now Paul is sending the slave home and pleading with Philemon to receive him graciously. Paul writes to Philemon, "For perhaps he departed for a while for this purpose, that you might receive him forever, no longer as a slave but more than a slave—a beloved brother, especially to me but how much more to you, both in the flesh and in the Lord" (Philemon 15–16 NKJV). Paul was so concerned about Onesimus's reception that he writes, "But if he has wronged you or owes anything, put that on my account" (Philemon 18 NKJV). Paul's attitudes toward slavery are revealed: He is concerned about the individual person and his spiritual growth. Paul wants every man to grow strong in Christ, whether slave or free.

Paul's ideas and ideals refer to any working person. Regardless of their work and position, God looks at the heart—the sincerity, motives, and whether we have Him in mind when we serve. Ultimately, we're all <u>slaves</u> of Jesus—and that's a good thing.

What Better Boss Could You Have?

COLOSSIANS 3:23–24 *And whatever you do, do it heartily, as to the Lord and not to men, knowing that from the Lord you will receive the reward of the inheritance; for you serve the Lord Christ. (NKJV)*

These verses are largely directed to the slaves that Paul addressed in verse 22, but they also offer a principle about work for everyone. If you are a trash collector, you're really working for Jesus. If you are a lawyer, you're really working for God. If you are a student, you're studying for Jesus's credit. Whatever you're doing, if you are a Christian, Paul is asking you, "Whom are you working for? Are you working for another person's approval or God's?" It should be for God's approval and notice, since He is the One who gives heavenly rewards.

In referring to slaves, Paul offers them something they will most likely never experience on earth: an inheritance. As slaves, they own nothing themselves, and that, of course, applies to land. Paul is saying that they will receive their reward in heaven—an even better inheritance than anything on earth. Each one will experience the reward of a heavenly relationship with Christ.

Of course, humans can give a reward here on earth, but it's temporary and fickle. Even after they give you some credit, they could quickly change their mind and take it back or become your worst enemy. But God isn't like that. His <u>reward</u> of <u>heaven</u> for Christians is sure, and what better boss could anyone have? The reward of heaven will be more wonderful than the rewards we receive on earth.

slaves
Romans 6:22

reward
1 Corinthians 3:14

heaven
Revelation 14:13

If you receive your reward here on earth, you may not get one in heaven. We humans find it hard to do things without getting credit, but what will truly be the most beneficial? Obviously, a reward that lasts for eternity will be of greater value.

You may be filling an underappreciated position at your church or serving in the nursery every Sunday. If you aren't helping with joy, your inheritance of a reward is being eaten up. Don't serve unless you can do it cheerfully.

Where's the Beef of Justice?

> COLOSSIANS 3:25 *But he who does wrong will be repaid for what he has done, and there is no partiality.* (NKJV)

"There just isn't any justice." We make this proclamation when evil goes unpunished and bad people continue to ruin others' lives. But Paul says, as a further motivation to serve with a cheerful and faithful heart whether slave or free man, that in the end justice will occur and we will each receive what we deserve. Paul wraps up his discussion of relationships by reassuring his readers that even if they are being taken advantage of—as a wife, husband, child, or slave—God knows and will not show any favoritism toward anyone in heaven. In other words, it will all come out in the wash of eternity.

judgment
Proverbs 20:22,
Hebrews 10:30

Max Lucado

Some of you are rehashing the same hurt every chance you get with anyone who will listen. For you, I have this question: Who made you God? I don't mean to be cocky, but why are you doing His work for Him? <u>Judgment</u> is God's job. To assume otherwise is to assume God can't do it.[11]

To our shame, we can easily put our eyes on people instead of God. We do everything to justify our ungodly or lazy reactions. We rationalize, debate, and excuse. But our employer isn't our real boss. God is, and He sees everything as it truly is—without any possible excuses.

Masters: Now It's Your Turn!

COLOSSIANS 4:1 *Masters, give your bondservants what is just and fair, knowing that you also have a Master in heaven.* (NKJV)

Paul is very thorough; he doesn't leave anyone out. He doesn't want any Christians who owned slaves and were reading his letter to take advantage of the instructions he just gave the slaves. So he continues on, pointing his inked feather at those who owned slaves. They are supposed to represent the Lord by providing what is right and fair. How easy it is for those who control the lives of others to think they're at the head of the ladder. But Paul reminds them that there is someone over them—the real Supervisor! And He is judging everything they do and will hold them accountable—just like they hold their slaves accountable.

The Greek word used here means "to provide deliberate care." Therefore Paul is saying that it's not something haphazard, but rather something planned for and executed carefully. Caring for others means meeting their needs and being sensitive to how they view life. A tall order, but in God's power it can be done.

James S. Jeffers

Slaves were part of the Greek or Roman household. Not that they were members of the family, although some became

> quite close to their masters and even at times married them and became family. Ancient families did not maintain the same physical distance from slaves that modern families often do however. And yet the Romans, in legal terms, classified slaves as *instrumentum vocale* ("speaking tools"), just above the household's livestock in status. The head of the household, the *paterfamilias* in Roman terms, held great power over the slave. His power to execute slaves without just cause had diminished by the New Testament era, but he could do just about anything else.[12]

You may not be a "master" in the sense that you own slaves, but you are in the same category if you supervise people as a manager or as an owner. God is "supervising" you and desiring for you to represent Him with love by taking good care of your people. You represent the Lord in the way you talk to people, treat them, and provide for their needs. Be gracious, while expecting their best.

Keep Your Prayer Antennae Alert

COLOSSIANS 4:2 *Continue earnestly in prayer, being vigilant in it with thanksgiving;* (NKJV)

Since most of us imagine Paul as a superspiritual person, we aren't surprised to hear that he prays all the time and expects others to do the same. We can just picture him with his hands folded in front of him, head down, muttering constantly.

But wait! That's not an accurate picture. He was actually quite active—even when he was in prison. No, he didn't constantly and actively pray, because the word *continue* carries the sense of "to persist." Therefore, not every second was spent praying, but Paul was always alert to what he could pray about in each situation that came up—along with designated times of concentrated praying. And of course, he couldn't write about prayer without including thanksgiving. To him they went together.

Jesus didn't walk around with His head down always praying either. Yet He was constantly aware of how His Father might be guiding Him. He said, "Then Jesus answered and said to them, 'Most assuredly, I say to you, the Son can do nothing of Himself, but what He sees the Father do; for whatever He does, the Son also does in like manner'" (John 5:19 NKJV).

constantly
1 Thessalonians 5:17

alert
1 Corinthians 16:13

what others say

Warren Wiersbe

This does not mean that we should walk around muttering prayers under our breath. Rather, it means we should be <u>constantly</u> in fellowship with God so that prayer is as normal to us as breathing.[13]

Continuing in prayer will be lived out in how we encounter each situation. If someone responds to us in an angry tone, we'll instantly pray, "Father, how should I reply?" If we sense old resentment rising within us toward someone, we should immediately confess it and forgive again. Like spiritual antennae, we are constantly waving them around in our soul, asking God for His direction and leading.

Don't become spiritually distracted or drowsy and forget to be praying constantly. The subtle temptations of the world can cause us to become distracted from prayer. We grow "drowsy," in a sense, unaware of how the media or incorrect evil ideas are breaking through into our thinking. Let's be <u>alert</u> and watchful!

<u>Push Open Those Doors with Prayer</u>

> COLOSSIANS 4:3–4 *meanwhile praying also for us, that God would open to us a door for the word, to speak the mystery of Christ, for which I am also in chains, that I may make it manifest, as I ought to speak.* (NKJV)

Paul wasn't being selfish in asking for prayer for himself and his workers. He wanted God's glory and knew that only with the prayer support of others would he:

- Have opportunities.
- Share effectively.

Those two requests are the heart's cry of every person who wants to share the gospel with others. They want people to be open to hearing it, and then to speak it in a meaningful way. Paul could have asked them to pray many other things: for his release, his safety, his physical comfort, or that he wouldn't be convicted at his upcoming trial. But he asked them to pray for none of those things. He was so committed to reaching out to others that his own comfort was of little importance to him.

As we've heard so many times before in these three letters—Ephesians, Philippians, and Colossians—Paul reminds his readers of his limitations but won't allow them to take away his ministry.

When Paul gently but consistently <u>reminds</u> his readers of being in chains, maybe he's saying, "Hey, some of you think you can't share the gospel because you have problems. But look at me! I've got a big, huge problem and it's not stopping me! Your problem shouldn't stop you from telling others about Jesus." We need to remember that when we think our circumstances are too big and prevent us from sharing the gospel. Nothing need slow us down!

reminds
Philippians 1:7,
Philemon 1, 9–10

what others say

H. A. Ironside

How natural it would have been for him to give up in despair and settle down in utter discouragement, or simply to endure passively the long, weary months of imprisonment, taking it for granted that nothing could really be accomplished for God so far as gospel fruit was concerned until he should be free. But he was of another mind entirely. His circumstances did not indicate that God had forsaken him nor that he had set him to one side. He was eagerly looking for fresh opportunities to advance upon the enemy.[14]

Warren Wiersbe

You, as a church member, can assist your pastor in the preaching of the Word by praying for him. Never say to your pastor, "Well, the least I can do is to pray for you." The *most* you can do is to pray! Pray for your pastor as he prepares the Word, studies, and meditates.[15]

Just as Paul recognizes his need of prayer support, we need to pray for our spiritual leaders—pastors, evangelists, teachers—who lead the way. There are many people representing Christ every day whom we might not think of praying for, but they need us to do that. Teachers in secular and Christian schools need it. Businesspeople who are serving Christ in a secular setting. Missionaries around the world. People in Christian organizations. Let's pray that they also will have open doors and the effective words to make a difference in people's lives. Don't just pray for your pastor; pray for anyone who is reaching out in their own world.

Sprinkle Some Salt on Your Speech

COLOSSIANS 4:5–6 *Walk in wisdom toward those who are outside, redeeming the time. Let your speech always be with grace, seasoned with salt, that you may know how you ought to answer each one. (NKJV)*

Paul had just asked for prayer for open doors—opportunities—for himself, and now he's going to advise how his listeners can use their open doors: wisely and graciously. Since salt makes a person thirsty, Paul wants his readers to use words that will make their listeners thirsty to hear more, which means not to be turned away with words that offend and aren't sensitive to the needs of that particular person. Grace is always understanding and gentle, never overbearing or pushy.

Paul says to make the most of every opportunity, which could be a gentle way of saying, "Don't go for the spiritual jugular. See how far you can go in mentioning Jesus, but don't ram it down their throat. They can't be thirsty if you've drenched them with a fire hose of too much information or pressure."

What is wisdom like if we want to have it in our responses to other people? James explained, "The wisdom that is from above is first pure, then peaceable, gentle, willing to yield, full of mercy and good fruits, without partiality and without hypocrisy" (James 3:17 NKJV). With attitudes like those, our speech will be very salty!

> **what others say**
>
> **Malcolm O. Tolbert**
>
> Some people always have the same phrases and clichés to use on everybody they encounter. People differ; situations differ. Christians who are sensitive will try to choose their words to fit the person and the circumstances.[16]

key point

Since wisdom is God-given insights, speaking wisely could refer to being able to sense through God's direction the needs of the person we are talking to. If a person is hurting, we wouldn't want to be insensitive by being joyful in the midst of their pain. But God might direct us to share the comfort He makes available.

It's not your responsibility to convert someone to believe in Jesus. It's God's work within that person's heart. All you can do is what you can do and let God move over time. We won't try to pressure someone if we remember that it's God's job, not ours. Trust God to work in an unbeliever's heart. You don't have to force a response.

the big picture

Colossians 4:7–14

Paul continues by mentioning several of his friends who are currently with him in the area and gives their greetings to the believers in Colosse.

Everybody Here Says "Hi!"

Just picture it. Paul is writing his letter or transcribing it to someone, when suddenly Tychicus drops by. "Hey, Paul, do you have that letter ready yet for me to take back to our Colossian friends? I can't wait to see them."

Then Onesimus stops by to tell Paul about his latest experience, sharing the gospel with his friend at work: "Paul, I can really see God working in his heart."

On and on the day goes. Everybody wants to get in the act. They either want to go along to deliver the letter to Colosse, or they have some word of encouragement to offer. Let's see what each person is about.

Who Are These People?

Person and description	Something about them	Their message
Vv. 7–8 Tychicus, faithful	Will deliver the letter	Tells about how Paul is doing and will encourage hearts
V. 9 Onesimus, faithful and dear	Originally from Colosse	Will deliver message and give an update
V. 10 Aristarchus and Mark	Mark is the cousin of Barnabas	Sends greetings
V. 11 Jesus (or Justus), a comforter	A converted Jew	Sends greetings
Vv. 12–13 Epaphras, servant of Christ Jesus and hard worker also at Laodicea and Hierapolis	Originally from Colosse	Sends greetings and prays for them, desiring for them to stand firm and mature
V. 14 Luke, dear friend, and Demas	Luke is a doctor	Sends greetings

Neil T. Anderson

The pressure to conform and avoid rejection is so powerful that Christians will also compromise in order to gain some sense of acceptance. But if I know I belong to God—my heavenly Father who will never leave me nor forsake me—then I have the power to stand and not compromise to gain acceptance, even if it means standing alone.[17]

What support Paul had! It's possible that he wasn't even naming all of the people who were visiting, having prayer meetings with him, and making sure his needs were met. His success, maturity, and persistence in staying true to Jesus weren't only because of such support, but they sure must have helped!

If Paul needed that much support around him, just think how much more you and I need to have people around us to strengthen us through encouragement and prayer support. None of us are in this alone. We need each other. Let's take advantage of the love that God has supplied through others.

Turnabout Is Fair Play

COLOSSIANS 4:15–18 *Greet the brethren who are in Laodicea, and Nymphas and the church that is in his house. Now when this epistle is read among you, see that it is read also in the church of the Laodiceans, and that you likewise read the epistle from Laodicea. And say to Archippus, "Take heed to the ministry which you have received in the Lord, that you may fulfill it." This salutation by my own hand—Paul. Remember my chains. Grace be with you. Amen. (NKJV)*

Paul's letter is coming to a close, and he gives some final greetings to the believers in the nearby city of Laodicea and to the group of people meeting in Nympha's house. In those days, Christians met in people's homes. The practice of having a separate church building hadn't started yet.

Then Paul mentions a letter that he's written to the church at Laodicea. Many commentators and scholars believe that letter is the one we now call Ephesians, since Ephesus and Laodicea are in the same general area, and the letter to the Ephesians was known to be written for the area believers—not just the Ephesians. Other schol-

stylus
writing instrument

ars wonder whether the letter to the Laodiceans has been lost. Another possibility is that what we call the Epistle to Philemon is that letter. Reasons for any of these possibilities can be put forth, but we can't be sure.

Paul addresses Archippus directly, maybe because he hasn't been fulfilling the assigned work or hasn't used the gifts God gave him. We don't know for sure, but Paul is very adamant that everyone pull their weight and obey God's directions for them.

Paul completes his letter by mentioning that he is signing his signature with his own hand—since most likely someone else has been taking his dictation and actually writing the letter. As he writes, he gives his usual closing blessing: grace.

Paul mentions writing his signature in his own hand to offer clear proof that this letter is really from him. In the past, evidently, some letters written by others were attributed to him but taught false teaching. In his letter to the Thessalonians, he wrote, "Now, brethren, concerning the coming of our Lord Jesus Christ and our gathering together to Him, we ask you, not to be soon shaken in mind or troubled, either by spirit or by word or by letter, as if from us, as though the day of Christ had come" (2 Thessalonians 2:1–2 NKJV). The possibility of Paul's name being misused must have been a concern for him, yet he doesn't worry about it. He knows the Lord can handle even that.

what others say

Ralph P. Martin

Paul now takes the **stylus** from the hand of the scribe who, like Tertius in Rom. 16:22, has been wielding it, and he appends his own signature. It is a mark of authenticity and a final appeal to heed his teaching.[18]

Paul starts out his letter talking about grace and ends it mentioning grace. Like two bookends, grace should be the beginning and the end of everything we do and say. Grace reminds us that we are received into God's kingdom through God's gracious gift of Jesus, and it reminds us to respond to others with grace—understanding they are imperfect just as we are.

key point

Chapter Wrap-Up

- Family relationships can be the true test of whether we're following Jesus. Paul addresses those difficult situations by wisely giving instructions to wives to submit, husbands to love, children to obey, and fathers to nourish. (Colossians 3:18–21)

- Paul doesn't leave anyone out in wanting them to wear their new clothes, and he also addresses the workplace. He tells slaves to obey their masters and work for them as if they were serving Jesus. For masters of slaves, he warns them to be just and fair, knowing they have a superior "supervisor" overseeing them—Jesus. (Colossians 3:22–4:1)

- Paul knows it's sometimes easy to take off new clothing, so he exhorts his listeners to be strengthened by prayer and to watch their language carefully—especially when talking to unbelievers about Jesus. (Colossians 4:2–6)

- As Paul wraps up his letter, he sends along the greetings of several of the Christians around him and gives a final benediction of grace upon his readers. (Colossians 4:7–18)

Study Questions

1. How are family members supposed to show they are Spirit-controlled, according to Paul's instructions?

2. What should the attitudes of slaves and masters be in order to represent the Lord?

3. How can believers stay strong and keep their new clothing on?

4. In Paul's closing remarks, what does he say?

Appendix A - The Answers

Ephesians 1

1. The apostle Paul wrote Ephesians; he wanted the Christians in Ephesus and around it to know God's grace and peace. (Ephesians 1:1–2)

2. Paul is saying that everything he mentions in those verses is all-inclusive in God's spiritual inheritance for every Christian. (Ephesians 1:3–14)

3. God considers every Christian forgiven because Jesus died for them and redeemed them from sin's power. (Ephesians 1:7)

4. God puts His Holy Spirit into each Christian as a seal of His promise that they are truly going to heaven. (Ephesians 1:13–14)

5. Paul always says that he not only prays for his friends but gives thanks for them as well. (Ephesians 1:16)

Ephesians 2

1. Because their sin separates them from God, because God is totally holy. (Ephesians 2:1–3)

2. Being saved by grace means that a person recognizes he cannot earn God's love or a place in heaven, and asks Jesus to come into his life to forgive and cleanse him from sin. (Ephesians 2:4–10)

3. Jews considered Gentiles less valuable because they didn't worship their Jehovah God and didn't even think that God would want to have a relationship with them. (Ephesians 2:11–13)

4. Paul wanted them all to appreciate the other and not see any dividing walls between them because Jesus had reconciled them at the cross. (Ephesians 2:14–17)

5. Because everyone is saved by the same thing: grace, and it has nothing to do with their background or importance. (Ephesians 2:18–22)

Ephesians 3

1. Because he formerly didn't believe in Jesus and

he actually persecuted believers. (Ephesians 3:1–2)

2. The mystery is the formerly unrevealed revelation that God wants both Gentiles and Jews to be a part of His forever kingdom. (Ephesians 3:3–9)

3. Rulers and authorities, which are angels and other heavenly beings. (Ephesians 3:10–13)

4. That they would be strengthened, let Christ rule in their hearts, and know God's amazing love. (Ephesians 3:14–19)

5. With a doxology, which is a statement of glory to God. (Ephesians 3:20–21)

Ephesians 4

1. Humility helps Christians give God credit for using them—instead of being proud. Gentleness will help them respond in a loving manner. Patience makes us able to accept the fact that people will make mistakes. (Ephesians 4:1–6)

2. He explains that they each have been given unique gifts by the Holy Spirit to use within the body of Christ. (Ephesians 4:7–16)

3. That they were without understanding of God's gracious gift of understanding and they lived in darkness. (Ephesians 4:17–19)

4. As if they are wearing new clothes on their soul: a new self which has been renewed by the Holy Spirit. (Ephesians 4:20–28)

5. They will speak words of encouragement, not grieve the Holy Spirit, and forgive others when they are hurt. (Ephesians 4:29–32)

Ephesians 5

1. By loving as He loves and refraining from immorality. (Ephesians 5:1–5)

2. Because they each have different goals: A Christian wants to walk in the light of God's leading, but an unbeliever wants to do their own evil things. (Ephesians 5:6–17)

3. Through speaking and singing in psalms, hymns, and spiritual songs and especially by giving thanks to God. But the most difficult thing will be to submit themselves to others. (Ephesians 5:18–21)

4. By submitting to her husband's leadership just as if she were submitting to Jesus. (Ephesians 5:22–24)

5. By loving his wife as much as Jesus loved the church by sacrificing himself for her. (Ephesians 5:25–33).

Ephesians 6

1. That they should obey their parents and enjoy a better life on earth. (Ephesians 6:1–3)

2. They should serve them with enthusiasm and joy, just as if they were serving Christ. (Ephesians 6:5–8)

3. Christians have the armor of God available to them and it consists of belt, breastplate, shoes, shield, helmet, and sword. (Ephesians 6:10–17)

4. Christians always need the prayer support of others. To think otherwise is to be proud. Even the apostle Paul recognized his need of prayer support. (Ephesians 6:18–24)

Philippians 1

1. He was confident that God would continue to work in them, and he prayed that their love would grow and that they would be sincere and blameless. (Philippians 1:1–11)

2. Because he didn't care how Jesus was exalted, as long as the gospel message was made known. (Philippians 1:12–18)

3. Because he knew it would be best for believers like the Philippians if he stayed on earth to encourage them. (Philippians 1:19–26)

4. By every Christian working together in unity for the advancement of the gospel. (Philippians 1:27–30)

Philippians 2

1. Doing nothing from selfishness, but rather acting in humility because then they won't have to compete with each other for getting their needs met. (Philippians 2:1–4)

2. Jesus, because He humbled himself by leaving the glories of heaven and was willing to downgrade into a human body—even while retaining His Godhood. (Philippians 2:5–11)

3. That they are supposed to show their changed nature by being careful to live in a godly way, but it doesn't mean they are working for their salvation. (Philippians 2:12–18)

4. Timothy, because Timothy was interested in the work of the gospel and not his own interests. (Philippians 2:19–24)

5. Epaphroditus almost died in his service for Jesus and was humble because he served Paul through taking messages back and forth. (Philippians 2:25–30)

Philippians 3

1. To rejoice, regardless of circumstances or problems. (Philippians 3:1)

2. He warned them about those who wanted them to get circumcised in order to be saved. Paul wanted them to know that wasn't necessary—only faith in Christ was necessary. (Philippians 3:2–3)

3. He had done everything right as a Jew: circumcision, following the laws, correct pedigree, and complete zealousness. Yet he realized after meeting Christ that all that was worthless in God's sight. Only faith in Jesus was needed. (Philippians 3:4–11)

4. For Paul, the past is not worth much. He would rather focus on the future and completing God's call upon his life. (Philippians 3:12–19)

5. Their future life in heaven where they have their heavenly citizenship. (Philippians 3:20–21)

Philippians 4

1. By calling them his joy and crown because he's so proud of them. (Philippians 4:1)

2. Euodia and Syntyche have an unsolved disagreement between them and Paul urges a mediator to step in and help them resolve their conflict. (Philippians 4:2–5)

3. Believers should pray and give thanks instead of worrying. And they should concentrate on the things that bring peace, like the truth, honor, purity, loveliness, and a good report. (Philippians 4:6–9)

4. He tells his readers that he is grateful for their financial and emotional support, but that he is content regardless of whether he has their money or not. (Philippians 4:10–23)

Colossians 1

1. Because there were false teachers who were trying to convince the believers in Colosse that they didn't need salvation through Jesus. Other things like special knowledge and the worship of angels were needed instead. (Colossians 1:1–8)

2. It was knowledge of God and knowing His will. (Colossians 1:9–14)

3. The false teachers taught that although Jesus

was a good person, He wasn't actually God in human form and the only way to know God and become saved—which is what Paul preached. (Colossians 1:15–20)

4. He says that they have been forgiven and cleansed from sin—which separated them from God—and are considered holy in God's sight. (Colossians 1:21–23)

5. To explain the "mystery" of how these Colossians—who were Gentiles—could be reconciled with the God of the Jews. (Colossians 1:24–29)

Colossians 2

1. Because they have never met him, therefore they can't completely understand his deep love for them. (Colossians 2:1–3)

2. Because then they won't have an awareness of the full life they can experience in Christ—and only in Christ. (Colossians 2:8–10)

3. Paul says that the circumcision of the heart through belief and then baptism brings a change in the heart—something circumcision had brought upon the body. (Colossians 2:11–14)

4. Christ's death and resurrection give a Christian victory over spiritual demons and evil angels and provided the way for Christians to be free from judgment and asceticism. (Colossians 2:15–19)

5. Because misusing the body to show faith in God doesn't please God—He's interested in the heart of a person. (Colossians 2:20–23)

Colossians 3:1–17

1. He wanted them to live like heavenly citizens on earth. (Colossians 3:1–4)

2. They are to put to death their desire for wrong things and give up practicing immoral and immature behavior. (Colossians 3:5–11)

3. The garments of their new personhood: things like compassion, kindness, humility, gentleness, and patience. (Colossians 3:12–17)

Colossians 3:18–4:18

1. Wives are to submit to their husbands, husbands are to love their wives, children are to be obedient to their parents, and fathers are to love and nourish their children. (Colossians 3:18–21)

2. Servants should obey their masters, and masters should treat their slaves with justice and fairness. (Colossians 3:22–4:1)

3. By staying alert in prayer and thanksgiving and by being careful to talk to unbelievers with salt-seasoned speech. (Colossians 4:2–6)

4. He gives the greetings of the Christians around him, and he blesses his readers with a benediction of grace. (Colossians 4:7–18)

Appendix B - The Experts

Anders, Max is senior pastor of Castleview Baptist Church in Indianapolis, Indiana. He is also an adjunct seminary professor, conference speaker, and author of over twenty books.

Anderson, Neil T. is the founder and president of Freedom in Christ Ministries and was formerly chairman of the Practical Theology Department at Talbot School of Theology. His books include the best-selling *Victory Over the Darkness* and *The Bondage Breaker.*

Arthur, Kay is the founder of Precept Ministries and the author of many books including *Lord, I Need Grace to Make It.*

Barclay, William is a New Testament expositor who was minister of Trinity Church in Renfrew, Scotland, for many years.

Blackaby, Henry T. is special assistant to the president, Prayer and Spiritual Awakening at the North American Mission Board for the Southern Baptist Convention and an author of several books including *Experiencing God.*

Boone, Pat is a singer, author, and actor.

Boone, Wellington is an author and speaker who has been instrumental in the development of numerous national ministries, including New Generation Campus Ministries.

Briscoe, Jill is known worldwide for her Bible-study and speaking engagements before women's seminar and campus fellowship groups. She directs Telling the Truth, a multimedia ministry. She is the author of many books including *There's a Snake in My Garden.*

Briscoe, Stuart has pastored Elmbrook Church in Wisconsin since 1970, and has worked with youth, pastors, missionaries, and lay leaders in more than one hundred countries. His many books include *The Fruit of the Spirit* and *The Ten Commandments: Playing by the Rules.*

Chambers, Oswald is the beloved author of *My Utmost for His Highest,* which has been continuously in print since 1935.

Christenson, Evelyn is the author of the best-selling books *What Happens When Women Pray* and *Lord, Change Me!* She is also a gifted seminar and conference speaker and chairman of United Prayer Ministries.

Clairmont, Patsy is a popular speaker and writer, an engaging humorist, and author of many books including *God Uses Cracked Pots.*

Colson, Charles is the founder and president of Prison Fellowship Ministries and an author and speaker of many books including *Born Again.*

Elliot, Elizabeth has been a writer-in-residence at Gordon College, Wenham, Massachusetts, and is the author of many books including *Shadow of the Almighty* and *Through Gates of Splendor.*

Epp, Theodore H. was director of the Back to the Bible Broadcast for many years. He also authored many books about the Bible.

Evans, Tony is senior pastor of Oak Cliff Bible Fellowship Church and the author of several books including *America's Only Hope.*

Farrar, Steve is the president of Point Man Leadership Ministries and author of several books including *Standing Tall: How a Man Can Protect His Family.*

Farrel, Pam is a pastor's wife, popular women's conference speaker, and author of many books including *Woman of Influence.* She and her husband, Bill, are founders of Masterful Living.

Frank, Jan is a professional Christian counselor, speaker, and author of several books including *A Graceful Waiting.*

Graham, Billy has led millions of people to Christ through his crusades on every continent and through his radio and television messages. He is also the author of many best-selling books, including *World Aflame.*

Hybels, Bill is pastor of Willow Creek Community Church and has authored several books including *The God You're Looking For.*

Hybels, Lynne is a pastor's wife who is also a writer and speaker.

Ironside, H. A. was the pastor of Moody Memorial Church in Chicago, Illinois, for many years.

Johnson, Barbara is a popular conference speaker and author of many books including *Boomerang Joy*.

Johnson, Jan is a popular women's conference speaker and the author of several books, including *Enjoying the Presence of God*.

Jeffers, James S. is associate professor in the Torrey Honors Institute at Biola University and the author of several books.

Kent, Carol is a popular speaker, writer, and president of Speak Up Speaker Services. Her many books include *Mothers Have Angel Wings*.

Leman, Kevin is an internationally known family psychologist, best-selling author, and radio and television personality.

Lewis, C. S. was a beloved author of many books. He taught English literature and language at Magdalen College, Oxford, from 1924 to 1954 and also at Cambridge University from 1954 to shortly before his death in 1963.

Libby, Larry is a freelance writer and editor and has collaborated on many books.

Lucado, Max is the pastor of Oak Hills Church of Christ in San Antonio, Texas. He is the author of several best-selling books and speaks at Promise Keepers stadium events.

King, Claude V. is a consultant of the Office of Prayer and Spiritual Awakening for the Southern Baptist Convention. He is also a discipleship training leader and author.

Martin, Ralph P. is retired from Fuller Theological Seminary in Pasadena, California, and has an appointment as Professor of Biblical Studies at the University of Sheffield, England.

McGee, J. Vernon is best known as a radio broadcaster, having used the medium of radio since 1941. His program, *Thru the Bible Radio*, has aired for many years and continues on even after his death.

Meberg, Marilyn is a captivating speaker and the author of *I'd Rather Be Laughing*.

Meyer, F. B. is a pastor and the author of over seventy books.

Moore, Beth is a writer and teacher of best-selling Bible studies whose public speaking engagements carry her all over the world. She has written *Things Pondered*, *A Heart like His*, and *Praying God's Word*.

Morley, Patrick M. is the best-selling author of *The Man in the Mirror* and is the founder of Morley Properties, Inc.

Needham, David C. has taught Bible and Theology at Multnomah School of the Bible in Portland, Oregon, for more than twenty-five years. He is a speaker and author of several books including *Close to His Majesty*.

Nystrom, Carolyn is a writer who has authored more than fifty books and Bible study guides.

Ogilvie, Lloyd is the senior pastor of the First Presbyterian Church of Hollywood, California, and founder of and speaker on the TV and radio ministry *Let God Love You*.

Packer, J. I. is professor of Systematic and Historical Theology at Regent College in Vancouver, British Columbia. He is the author of many best-selling books including *Knowing God* and *Keep in Step with the Spirit*.

Palmer, Earl is an author and the pastor of University Presbyterian Church in Seattle.

Sproul, R. C. is chairman of the board of Ligonier Ministries. He is also a theologian, pastor, and teacher, and has written many books including *The Holiness of God*.

Stanley, Charles is senior pastor of the twelve-thousand-member First Baptist Church of Atlanta and a prolific author.

Stowell, Joseph M. is president of Moody Institute and the author of several books, including *Eternity*.

Swindoll, Charles R. is former pastor of the First Evangelical Free Church in Fullerton, California, and president of the Dallas Theological Seminary in Dallas, Texas. He is the author of many best-selling books.

Swindoll, Luci, Charles Swindoll's sister, is a popular women's conference speaker and the author of several books including *Celebrating Life*.

Tada, Joni Eareckson is the founder and president of JAF (Joni and Friends) Ministries, an organization that accelerates Christian outreach in the disability community. She has authored many books including *Joni*.

Talbot, Louis served as the pastor of the Church of the Open Door in Los Angeles for seventeen years, beginning in 1932. He is an author, radio pastor, and Bible teacher.

Tchividjian, Gigi Graham, the daughter of Billy Graham, is a wife, mother, and grandmother who has also authored several books, including *A Search for Serenity*. She is a popular speaker at women's conferences.

Ten Boom, Corrie was an internationally known author and speaker and the subject of the best-selling book and popular movie *The Hiding Place*.

Tolbert, Malcolm O. is professor of New Testament at Southeastern Baptist Theological Seminary in Wake Forest, North Carolina. He has also served as pastor of First Baptist Church of Gainesville, Georgia.

Unger, Merrill F. was a biblical scholar and researcher, and the author of *Unger's Bible Dictionary*.

Vaughn, Ellen Santilli is vice president of executive communications for Prison Fellowship and has collaborated with Charles Colson on five books.

Wall, Robert W. is professor of biblical studies at Seattle Pacific University in Seattle, Washington, and the author of *Revelation* in the NIV Commentary Series.

Walsh, Sheila is a well-known author, singer, and speaker who wrote *Honestly*.

Walvoord, John F. is chancellor and professor of Systematic Theology, Dallas (Texas) Theological Seminary, and is the author of more than eighteen books.

Wells, Thelma is an internationally known corporate speaker and author of *God Will Make a Way*.

White, John is a counselor and associate professor of psychiatry at the University of Manitoba and the author of several books, including *The Fight*.

Wiersbe, Warren hosts the Back to the Bible Broadcast, speaks at conferences, and authors many books, including the "Be" book series.

Wilkinson, Bruce H. is the founder and president of Walk Thru the Bible Ministries, an international ministry dedicated to providing the very finest biblical teaching, tools, and training.

Willard, Dallas is a theologian and scholar who has written the books *In Search of Guidance* and *The Spirit of the Disciplines*. He is a professor at the University of Southern California's School of Philosophy.

Wright, N. T. is a theologian, teacher, and author of several books, including the commentary *Colossians and Philemon*.

Wuest, Kenneth S. is a theologian who was on the faculty of the Moody Bible Institute of Chicago for many years and has written many commentaries.

Yancey, Philip serves as editor-at-large for *Christianity Today* magazine. He is the best-selling author of many books, including *The Jesus I Never Knew*.

Zuck, Roy B. is academic dean and professor of Bible Exposition at Dallas Theological Seminary. He has also held editorial and administrative positions at Scripture Press.

Endnotes

Introduction

1. Charles R. Swindoll, *The Living Insights Study Bible* (Grand Rapids, MI: Zondervan, 1996), 1253.

Ephesians 1

1. John White, *Daring to Draw Near* (Downers Grove, IL: IVP, 1977), 127.

2. Swindoll, *The Living Insights Study Bible*, 1255.

3. J. Vernon McGee, *Ephesians* (Pasadena, CA: Thru the Bible Books, 1977), 19.

4. Lloyd Ogilvie, *Enjoying God* (Dallas, TX: Word, 1989), 22.

5. Philip Yancey, *What's So Amazing About Grace?* (Grand Rapids, MI: Zondervan, 1997), 66–67.

6. Theodore H. Epp, *Living Abundantly,* v. 1. (Lincoln, NE: Back to the Bible, 1973), 18.

7. Bill Hybels, *Too Busy Not To Pray* (Downers Grove, IL: IVP, 1988), 64.

8. William Barclay, *The Letters to the Galatians and Ephesians* (Louisville, KY: Westminster John Knox, 1954), 87–88.

9. Charles Stanley, *A Touch of His Freedom* (Grand Rapids, MI: Zondervan, 1991), 35.

10. H. A. Ironside, *In the Heavenlies* (New York: Loizeaux Brothers, 1946), 29.

11. J. I. Packer and Carolyn Nystrom, *Never Beyond Hope* (Downers Grove, IL: IVP, 2000), 76–77.

12. Billy Graham, *How to Be Born Again* (Waco, TX: Word, 1977), 128.

13. Joni Eareckson Tada, *Seeking God* (Brentwood, TN: Wolgemuth & Hyatt, 1991), 106.

14. Kay Arthur, *His Imprint, My Expression* (Eugene, OR: Harvest House, 1997), 18.

15. McGee, *Ephesians*, 53–54.

16. White, *Daring to Draw Near*, 131–32.

17. James I. Packer: *Knowing God* (Downers Grove, IL: IVP, 1973), 37.

18. Beth Moore, *Breaking Free* (Nashville, TN: Broadman & Holman, 2000), 256.

19. Rick Warren, *The Purpose Driven Life* (Grand Rapids, MI: Zondervan, 2002), 237.

Ephesians 2

1. Patsy Clairmont, *It's About Home* (Ann Arbor, MI: Vine, 1998), 21–22.

2. David C. Needham with Larry Libby, *Close to His Majesty* (Portland, OR: Multnomah, 1987), 90.

3. Patrick M. Morley, *I Surrender* (Brentwood, TN: Wolgemuth & Hyatt, 1990), 85.

4. Joni Eareckson Tada, *Heaven, Your Real Home* (Grand Rapids, MI: Zondervan, 1995), 80.

5. Elisabeth Elliot, *Discipline, the Glad Surrender* (Old Tappan, NJ: Fleming H. Revell, 1982), 28.

6. Charles Stanley, *The Source of My Strength* (Nashville, TN: Thomas Nelson, 1994), 97.

7. Pam Farrel, *A Woman God Can Use* (Eugene, OR: Harvest House, 1999), 133.

8. Ogilvie, *Enjoying God*, 78.

9. Packer and Nystrom, *Never Beyond Hope,* 76.

Ephesians 3

1. Max Anders, *Holman New Testament Commentary: Galatians, Ephesians, Philippians & Colossians* (Nashville, TN: Holman Reference, 1999), 128.

2. William Barclay, *The Letters to the Galatians and Ephesians,* 140.

3. Ogilvie, *Enjoying God*, 87.

4. Wellington Boone, *Breaking Through* (Nashville, TN: Broadman & Holman, 1996), 68.

5. Ogilvie, *Enjoying God*, 86.

6. McGee, *Ephesians*, 96.

7. Swindoll, *The Living Insights Study Bible*, 1258.

8. Warren, *The Purpose Driven Life*, 119.

9. Anders, *Holman New Testament Commentary: Galatians, Ephesians, Philippians & Colossians*, 1

10. H. A. Ironside, *In the Heavenlies*, 157–164.

11. Quoted in Anders, *Holman New Testament Commentary: Galatians, Ephesians, Philippians & Colossians*, 126.

12. Ogilvie, *Enjoying God*, 94.

13. Patsy Clairmont, *Under His Wings* (Colorado Springs, CO: Focus on the Family, 1994), 108.

14. Dallas Willard, *The Divine Conspiracy* (New York: Harper SanFrancisco, 1998), 64.

15. White, *Daring to Draw Near*, 139.

16. Bruce H. Wilkinson, *First Hand Faith* (Gresham, OR: Vision House, 1996), 113.

17. Merrill F. Unger, *Unger's Bible Dictionary* (Chicago, IL: Moody, 1957), 409.

18. Needham with Libby, *Close to His Majesty*, 24.

19. Stanley, *The Source of My Strength*, 99.

Ephesians 4

1. Ogilvie, *Enjoying God*, 46.

2. Packer and Nystrom, *Never Beyond Hope*, 17.

3. Ralph P. Martin, *Ephesians, Colossians, and Philemon, A Bible Commentary for Teaching and Preaching* (Atlanta, GA: John Knox, 1991), 47.

4. Stanley, *A Touch of His Freedom*, 95.

5. Louis T. Talbot, *Lectures on Ephesians* (Wheaton, IL: Van Kampen Press, 1937), 124–125.

6. Robert W. Wall, *Colossians & Philemon* (Downers Grove, IL: IVP, 1993), 45.

7. Gigi Graham Tchividjian, *Weather of the Heart* (Portland, OR: Multnomah, 1991), 21.

8. Louis T. Talbot, *Lectures on Ephesians*, 131.

9. Charles Colson with Ellen Santilli Vaughn, *The Body* (Dallas, TX: Word, 1992), 285.

10. Charles R. Swindoll, *Growing Deep in the Christian Life* (Portland, OR: Multnomah, 1986), 344.

11. Sproul, *The Soul's Quest for God*, (Wheaton, IL: Tyndale, 1992), 64.

12. Barclay, *The Letters to the Galatians and Ephesians*, 174.

13. Talbot, *Lectures on Ephesians*, 142.

14. Sproul, *The Soul's Quest for God*, 140.

15. F. B. Meyer, *The Heavenlies* (Westchester, IL: Good News Publications, 1960), 54.

16. Talbot, *Lectures on Ephesians*, 146.

17. Tada, *Seeking God*, 57.

18. Clairmont, *Under His Wings*, 73.

19. Charles R. Swindoll, *Strike the Original Match* (Portland, OR: Multnomah, 1980), 108.

20. Carol Kent, *Becoming a Woman of Influence* (Colorado Springs, CO: NavPress, 1999), 154.

21. Anne Graham Lotz, *Just Give Me Jesus* (Nashville, TN: W Publishing, 2000), 166.

22. Stanley, *A Touch of His Freedom*, 51.

Ephesians 5

1. Nancy Leigh DeMoss, *Holiness: The Heart God Purifies* (Chicago, IL: Moody, 2004), 103.

2. J. I. Packer, *Rediscovering Holiness* (Ann Arbor, MI: Vine, 1992), 19.

3. Sproul, *The Soul's Quest for God*, 144.

4. McGee, *Ephesians*, 138–39.

5. Farrel, *A Woman God Can Use*, 219.

6. Steve Farrar, *Point Man* (Sisters, OR: Multnomah, 1990), 70.

7. Oswald Chambers, *My Utmost for His Highest* (Grand Rapids, MI: Discovery House, 1992), February 16.

8. Meyer, *The Heavenlies*, 60.

9. Swindoll, *Strike the Original Match*, 89.

10. Joyce Meyer, *Be Anxious for Nothing* (Tulsa, OK: Harrison House, 1998), 97–98.

11. Neil T. Anderson, *Living Free in Christ* (Ventura, CA: Regal, 1993), 99.

12. Anders, *Holman New Testament Commentary: Galatians, Ephesians, Philippians & Colossians*, 173.

13. Kevin Leman, *Keeping Your Family Together When the World Is Falling Apart* (Colorado Springs, CO: Focus on the Family, 1983), 76.

14. Elizabeth George, *A Wife After God's Own Heart* (Eugene, OR: Harvest House, 2004), 31.

15. Elliot, *Discipline, the Glad Surrender*, 89.

16. Wilkinson, *First Hand Faith*, 203.

17. Swindoll, *The Living Insights Study Bible*, 1260.

18. Bill & Lynne Hybels, *Fit to Be Tied* (Grand Rapids, MI: Zondervan, 1991), 38.

Ephesians 6

1. Anders, *Holman New Testament Commentary: Galatians, Ephesians, Philippians & Colossians*, 1881.

2. William Hendriksen, *New Testament Commentary: Ephesians* (Grand Rapids, MI: Baker, 1967), 261.

3. Farrar, *Point Man*, 206.

4. Martin, *Ephesians, Colossians, and Philemon, A Bible Commentary for Teaching and Preaching*, 73.

5. Jeffers, *The Greco-Roman World of the New Testament Era*, 229.

6. Evelyn Christenson, *Battling the Prince of Darkness* (Wheaton, IL: Victor, 1990), 32.

7. Clairmont, *Under His Wings*, 43.

8. Anderson, *Living Free in Christ*, 164.

9. Christenson, *Battling the Prince of Darkness*, 62.

10. Ibid., 68.

11. Wilkinson, *First Hand Faith*, 81.

12. John F. Walvoord, Roy B. Zuck, Eds., *The Bible Knowledge Commentary* (Wheaton, IL: Victor, 1983), 643.

13. Christenson, *Battling the Prince of Darkness*, 70.

14. Meyer, *The Heavenlies*, 35.

15. Farrar, *Point Man*, 138.

16. Warren W. Wiersbe, *Be Complete* (Wheaton, IL: Victor, 1981), 136.

17. Hybels, *Too Busy Not To Pray*, 58.

18. Kent, *Becoming a Woman of Influence*, 132–33.

Philippians 1

1. J. Vernon McGee, *Probing Through Philippians* (Pasadena, CA: Thru the Bible, 1972), 10.

2. Corrie ten Boom, *Clippings from My Notebook* (Nashville, TN: Thomas Nelson, 1982), 22.

3. Jan Frank, *A Graceful Waiting* (Ann Arbor, MI: Servant, 1996), 128.

4. Morley, *I Surrender*, 114.

5. Arthur, *His Imprint, My Expression*, 102.

6. Oswald Chambers, *In the Presence of His Majesty* (Sisters, OR: Multnomah, 1996), no page number, hope section.

7. Graham, *How to Be Born Again*, 130.

8. Swindoll, *Growing Deep in the Christian Life*, 359.

9. Arthur, *His Imprint, My Expression*, 101.

10. Earl Palmer, *Integrity in a World of Pretense* (Downers Grove, IL: IVP, 1992), 65.

11. Lloyd Ogilvie, *Let God Love You* (Dallas, TX: Word, 1974), 46–47.

12. Patsy Clairmont, Barbara Johnson, Marilyn Meberg, Luci Swindoll, Sheila Walsh, and Thelma Wells, *Overjoyed!* (Grand Rapids, MI: Zondervan, 1999), 48.

13. Palmer, *Integrity in a World of Pretense*, 82.

14. Joseph M. Stowell, *Eternity* (Chicago, IL: Moody, 1995), 58.

Philippians 2

1. Henry T. Blackaby and Claude V. King, *Experiencing God* (Nashville, TN: Broadman & Holman, 1994), 39.

2. McGee, *Probing Through Philippians*, 32.

3. C. S. Lewis, *The Joyful Christian* (New York: Macmillan, 1977), 141.

4. Jill Briscoe, *How to Fail Successfully* (Old Tappan, NJ: Fleming H. Revell, 1982), 187.

5. Kenneth S. Wuest, *Philippians in the Greek New Testament* (Grand Rapids, MI: Eerdmans, 1942), 61.

6. Ogilvie, *Let God Love You*, 61.

7. Lewis, *The Joyful Christian*, 51.

8. Christenson, *Battling the Prince of Darkness*, 38.

9. Anne Graham Lotz, *Just Give Me Jesus* (Nashville, TN: W Publishing, 2000), 232.

10. Warren W. Wiersbe, *Be Joyful* (Wheaton, IL: Victor, 1974), 61.

11. William Barclay, *The Letters to the Philippians, Colossians, and Thessalonians*, rev. ed. (Louisville, KY: Westminster, 1975), 42–43.

12. "Obey God: We Must!" *Charisma* magazine, February 1987, n.p.

13. John F. Walvoord, *Philippians, Triumph in Christ* (Chicago, IL: Moody, 1971), 65.

14. Gigi Graham Tchividjian, *Weather of the Heart* (Portland, OR: Multnomah, 1991), 64–65.

15. Jan Johnson, *Living a Purpose-Full Life* (Colorado Springs, CO: WaterBrook, 1999), 112.

16. Chambers, *My Utmost for His Highest*, Feb. 5.

17. Morley, *I Surrender*, 126.

18. Barclay, *The Letters to the Philippians, Colossians, and Thessalonians*, 50.

Philippians 3

1. J. Vernon McGee, *Philippians and Colossians* (Pasadena, CA: Thru the Bible, 1972, 1977), 63.

2. Swindoll, *Laugh Again* (Dallas, TX: Word, 1991), 131.

3. Meyer, *Be Anxious for Nothing*, 61–62.

4. Wiersbe, *Be Joyful*, 90–91.

5. Wuest, *Philippians in the Greek New Testament*, 90.

6. Packer, *Knowing God*, 30.

7. William Hendriksen, *New Testament Commentary, Exposition of Philippians* (Grand Rapids, MI: Baker, 1962), 167.

8. McGee, *Probing Through Philippians*, 11.

9. Wuest, *Philippians in the Greek New Testament*, 93–94.

10. Tada, *Heaven, Your Real Home*, 126.

11. Frank, *A Graceful Waiting*, 167.

12. Moore, *Breaking Free*, 101.

13. Briscoe, *How to Fail Successfully*, 172.

14. Malcolm O. Tolbert, *Layman's Bible Book Commentary Volume 22* (Nashville, TN, Broadman, 1980), 32.

15. Tony Evans, *Returning to Your First Love* (Chicago, IL: Moody, 1995), 65.

16. Max Lucado, *He Still Moves Stones* (Dallas, TX: Word, 1993), 78.

17. Tada, *Heaven, Your Real Home*, 16.

18. Stowell, *Eternity*, 110.

19. Graham, *How to Be Born Again*, 139.

20. Lucado, *When God Whispers Your Name*, 188.

Philippians 4

1. Kent, *Becoming a Woman of Influence*, 152–53.

2. Swindoll, *Laugh Again*, 184.

3. McGee, *Probing Through Philippians*, 75.

4. Warren, *The Purpose Driven Life*, 198–199.

5. Arthur, *His Imprint, My Expression*, 114.

6. Elliot, *Discipline, the Glad Surrender*, 106.

7. Lucado, *When God Whispers Your Name*, 134.

8. Swindoll, *Laugh Again*, 204.

9. Howard G. Hendricks, *Say It with Love* (Wheaton, IL: Victor Books, 1972), 55.

10. Swindoll, *Laugh Again*, 215.

11. Warren, *The Purpose Driven Life*, 83.

12. Stanley, *The Source of My Strength*, 46.

13. Tolbert, *Layman's Bible Book Commentary Volume 22*, 36.

14. Ibid., 37.

15. Moore, *Breaking Free*, 196.

16. Lotz, *Just Give Me Jesus*, 14.

17. Walvoord, *Philippians, Triumph in Christ*, 119.

Colossians 1

1. *Life Application Bible* (Grand Rapids, MI: co-published by Tyndale House Publishers, Wheaton, IL, and Zondervan Publishing House, 1991), 2159.

2. Charles R. Swindoll, *Growing Deep in the Christian Life* (Portland, OR: Multnomah, 1986), 29

3. Stuart Briscoe, *Secrets of Spiritual Stamina* (Wheaton, IL: Harold Shaw, 1994), 34–35.

4. Robert W. Wall, *Colossians & Philemon* (Downers Grove, IL: IVP, 1993), 43.

5. Walvoord, Roy B. Zuck, Editors, *The Bible Knowledge Commentary*, 669.

6. Wall, *Colossians & Philemon*, 49.

7. McGee, *Philippians and Colossians*, 128.

8. Hybels, *Too Busy Not to Pray*, 70.

9. Yancey, *What's So Amazing About Grace?*, 70.

10. N. T. Wright, *Colossians and Philemon, Tyndale New Testament Commentaries* (Grand Rapids, MI: Eerdmans, 1986), 69.

11. Stuart Briscoe, *Secrets of Spiritual Stamina* (Wheaton, IL: Harold Shaw, 1994), 4

12. McGee, *Philippians and Colossians*, 135.

13. Willard, *The Divine Conspiracy*, 94.

14. Lotz, *Just Give Me Jesus*, 11.

15. Wright, *Colossians and Philemon, Tyndale New Testament Commentaries*, 75.

16. Wiersbe, *Be Complete*, 52.

17. Willard, *The Divine Conspiracy*, 64.

18. Ten Boom, *Clippings from My Notebook*, 12.

19. H. A. Ironside, *Lectures on the Epistle to the Colossians* (New York: Loizeaux, 1928), 53.

20. Johnson, *Living a Purpose-Full Life*, 150.

21. Chambers, *My Utmost for His Highest*, September 30.

22. Meyer, *Be Anxious for Nothing*, 161.

23. Lucado, *When God Whispers Your Name*, 150.

Colossians 2

1. Moore, *Breaking Free*, 188.

2. Graham, *How to Be Born Again*, 104.

3. Ironside, *Lectures on the Epistle to the Colossians*, 65.

4. Charles R. Swindoll, *Growing Strong in the Seasons of Life* (Portland, OR: Multnomah, 1983), 116.

5. Evans, *Returning to Your First Love*, 41.

6. Ironside, *Lectures on the Epistle to the Colossians*, 71.

7. McGee, *Philippians and Colossians*, 160.

8. Wiersbe, *Be Complete*, 79.

9. Tolbert, *Layman's Bible Book Commentary Volume 22*, 50.

10. Briscoe, *Secrets of Spiritual Stamina*, 53.

11. Blackaby and King, *Experiencing God*, 83.

12. Max Lucado, *He Chose the Nails* (Nashville, TN: Word, 2000), 34.

13. Chambers, *In the Presence of His Majesty*, n.p., love section.

14. Evans, *Returning to Your First Love*, 65.

15. Blackaby & King, *Experiencing God*, 22.

16. Wiersbe, *Be Complete*, 95.

Colossians 3:1–17

1. Elliot, *Discipline, the Glad Surrender*, 60.

2. Wright, *Colossians and Philemon, Tyndale New Testament Commentaries*, 132–33.

3. Anderson, *Living Free in Christ*, 145.

4. Johnson, *Living a Purpose-Full Life*, 138.

5. Boone, *Breaking Through*, 24.

6. Briscoe, *Secrets of Spiritual Stamina*, 118.

7. Yancey, *What's So Amazing About Grace?*, 93.

8. J. I. Packer, *Rediscovering Holiness* (Ann Arbor, MI: Vine, 1992), 36.

9. Clairmont, Johnson, Meberg, Swindoll, Walsh, and Wells, *Overjoyed!* 26.

10. Meyer, *Be Anxious for Nothing*, 21.

11. Warren, *The Purpose Driven Life*, 177.

Colossians 3.18–4.18

1. Elizabeth George, *A Woman After God's Own Heart* (Eugene, OR: Harvest House, 1997), 70.

2. Boone, *Breaking Through*, 21.

3. Swindoll, *Strike the Original Match*, 41.

4. Leman, *Keeping Your Family Together When the World Is Falling Apart*, 71.

5. McGee, *Philippians and Colossians*, 184.

6. Leman, *Keeping Your Family Together When the World Is Falling Apart*, 36.

7. Steve Farrar, *Standing Tall* (Sisters, OR: Multnomah Press, 1994), 203.

8. Boone, *Breaking Through*, 23.

9. Clairmont, Johnson, Meberg, Swindoll, Walsh, and Wells, *Overjoyed!*, 70.

10. Swindoll, *Growing Strong in the Seasons of Life*, 308.

11. Lucado, *When God Whispers Your Name*, 92.

12. Jeffers, *The Greco-Roman world of the New Testament Era*, 229.

13. Wiersbe, *Be Complete*, 136.

14. Ironside, *Lectures on the Epistle to the Colossians*, 169.

15. Wiersbe, *Be Complete*, 140.

16. Tolbert, *Layman's Bible Book Commentary Volume 22*, 60.

17. Anderson, *Living Free in Christ*, 58.

18. Martin, *Ephesians, Colossians, and Philemon, a Bible Commentary for Teaching and Preaching*, 132.

Index

A

Abraham, 266
  Abrahamic Covenant, 40
  Abraham's bosom, 72
access, 54
administrations (gift), 74
adoption, in Roman law, 15
adultery, 89–91
afar off, 40–41
affection, 143–44, 159–61
agape, 67
  in marriage, 106
ages to come, 35
alienation, 77, 249–51
ambassador, 9
  ambassador in chains,
    128–29
Anders, Max
  on importance of chil-
    dren's obedience, 110
  on mutual subjection to
    other Christians, 99
  on Paul as prisoner only of
    Christ, 48
  on Paul's rejoicing in
    suffering, 56
Anderson, Neil T.
  on avoiding pressure to
    conform, 308
  on folly of fearing Satan, 120
  on need for Holy Spirit's
    power, 98
  on putting sin to death,
    281
angel, angels
  angel ranks, 245
  angel worship, 232, 245,
    272
  and God's wisdom, 52, 53
  and Jesus, 27
  and salvation, 185
  See also fallen angels
anger, 84–85, 282

anger without sin, 80–81
antinomians, 197–98
anxiety
  overcoming anxiety, 53–54
  peace of God, 287–90
  vs. concern, 216
apostles, 44, 73, 74
  meaning of term, 6–7
Archippus, 308–9
Aristarchus, 307
Arminianism, 14
Arminius, Jacobus, 14
armor of God, 117–29
aroma, 87
Artemis, 89
Arthur, Kay
  on consciousness of Jesus
    as observer, 214
  on joy despite suffering,
    148
  on worth of every human
    being, 20
ascended, 70–72
asceticism, 273–75
assurance of heaven, 78
atonement, 16–17, 247–49
  See also salvation
authority, 27
  See also apostles

B

Bacchus, 98
baptism, 69, 267
Barclay, William
  on closeness to Jesus, 76
  on Epaphroditus's sacrifice
    for church, 178
  on fear and trembling, 168
  on Paul as prisoner of
    Christ only, 48
  on Paul's wonder at God's
    grace, 13
Barnabas, 210

believers
  as body of Christ, 6
  meeting in homes, 50
  in Old Testament, 72
  See also Christians
belt of truth, 122–23
benefits of belief, 16–18
Bible
  as inspired, 290
  as 66 books, iii
  and spiritual growth, 26
*Bible Knowledge
  Commentary*
  on faith, hope, and charity,
    238
  on surefootedness of
    believers, 124
Bible memorization, 76,
  289–90
Bible reading, study, 76,
  123, 262
Bible translations, iv–v
bishops, 138, 139
bitterness, 80, 84–85
Blackaby, Henry T.
  on God as omniscient, 274
  on God's initiating love
    relationship, 269
  on God's working through
    his servants, 160
blasphemy, 282
blessed, giving as blessed, 82
blessing, blessings, 6, 11–23
  meaning in Ephesians,
    11–12
blood
  and atonement, 248
  blood of Christ, 16–17
body
  as all believers, 69
  resurrection body, 203–4
  See also body of Christ
body of Christ, 6, 76, 104,
  161, 257, 259

not disclosed in Old
Testament, 50
Pentecost, 50
reconciling Jews, Gentiles,
52–53
representing Christ, 65–70
See also churches
churches
church at Colosse, iv, 5
church at Ephesus, 3, 5
church at Laodicea, 5
church at Philippi, 136–38
See also Colossians,
congregation;
Philippians, congregation
circumcision, 7, 183–86
circumcised without hands,
266–67
heart circumcision, 184,
186
original purpose, 185–86
Circumcision (name), 38, 39
citizen of heaven, 35
citizenship in heaven, 44,
201
Clairmont, Patsy
on accepting God's peace,
59
on danger of focus on
anger, 81
on merciful love, 33
on Satan's tempting us, 118
clay, 37
coarse language, 89–91
Colossae, iv, 5
See also Colosse
Colosse
how named, 231
location, 231
Colossians, book
its primary focus, iv
Paul's tact when addressing
heresy, 235–36
purpose, 233
when written, 231
why study Colossians, iii–iv
See also Colossians,
congregation
Colossians, congregation
heresy, 237
influenced by incorrect
teaching, 231–33

Colson, Charles
on pastor as equipping
saints, 74
comfort, 159–61
commandment with promise,
110
common grace, 12
compassion, 286
complaining, 169–72, 171–72
completeness, 142
comprehend, 60
concern, 216
See also anxiety
confession, 93–96
confidence, 36
conflict, 207
conflict resolution, 211–12
contentment, 221–23
vs. happiness, 100
contributing to others' needs,
74
conversation, 82–84, 306–7
Corinth, 89
cornerstone, 43
corrupt words, 82–84
counting all things loss,
rubbish, 188–89
Court of the Gentiles, 39
covenants with God, 39
four covenants, 40
covetousness, 89–91, 281
and sex, 90
creation renewed in Christ,
247–49
cross and forgiveness, 268–70
cults, 275
Cyprian, 178

D

Damascus road vision, 7–8
Daniel, 120
dark, darkness, 77, 92–93
David, 91
Davidic Covenant, 40
deacons, 138, 139
dead in sins, 268
See also death
death
and life in Christ, 279–80
not to be feared, 151–54
as punishment for sin,

16–17
putting sin to death,
280–82
spiritual death, 33–34
as viewed in Bible, 32
See also salvation
deliverance, 241–43
Demas, 307
Demetrius (Ephesus), 4
demon, demons, 3, 27
See also devil; Satan
DeMoss, Nancy Leigh
on call to follow Christ, 88
depth, 61
descended, 70–72
desires
of the flesh, 32
of the mind, 32
devil
as slanderer, 80
as spiritual father, 12
See also demon, demons;
Satan
Diana, 4, 89
different, 7
Dionysus, 98
dirty talk, 89–91
disagreements, 162
discernment, 144
dispensation, 48, 49
diversity, diverse gifts, 72–74
in church, 70–72
unity in diversity, 161–62
See also unity
divorce, 102
doctrine, 6, 69
false doctrine, 75
dogs, 184
false teachers as dogs, 183,
184
doxology, 62–63
drink, 271–72
drunkenness, 97–98

E

edifying body of Christ, 72, 73
elders, 139
elect of God, 285–87
Elliot, Elisabeth
on focusing on today's
concerns, 216

giving
  as blessed, 82
  and God's blessing, 224–26
glory
  Christ as hope of glory,
    251–52
  giving glory to God,
    150–51
Gnosticism, 199–200
  at Colosse, 231–33
  Gnostics vs. Christians on
    Jesus, 247–51
  good works' role, 259–61
  salvation in Gnosticism, 253
God, actions
  dealing with out-of-control
    lives, 18
  saving Gentiles, Jews, 50
  working in us, 141–43
  See also God, attributes
God, attributes
  all-knowing, 13–14
  always existing
  concerned with everything,
    290–91
  Creator, 12
  Father, 56–58, 69, 88
  glory, 150–51
  greatness, 62–63
  in control, 100
  infinite, 13–14
  known yet unknowable,
    61–62
  love, 88
  master potter, 37
  not impatient, 93
  owner of our souls, 21–22
  rich in mercy, 34
  spiritual Father, 12
  Trinity, 43, 44
  unconditional love, 287
  wisdom, 24–25, 52, 53–54
  See also Holy Spirit; Jesus
God's Word, v
  See also Bible
good report, 218
good works
  and salvation, 33–34,
    259–61
  their role, 37–38
goodness, 92–93
gospel, 237

gospel of peace, 123–24
grace, 9, 167–69
  common grace, 12
  gifts as grace, 70–72
  grace and peace salutation,
    138, 233, 234–35
  grace and salvation, 37
  grace of God, 11, 25
  grace salutation, 10
  in Paul's letter to
    Colossians, 309
  in Paul's letters, 130
  salvation by grace, 183–94
  See also salvation
Graham, Billy
  on committing past mistakes
    to God, 146
  on guilt as an excuse, 17–18
  on the resurrected body,
    204
  on who Jesus is, 259
gratitude, 52, 287–91
greed, 281
grounded, 60
grumbling, 169–72
guilt, 18

H

hagios, meaning of word, 7
hall of Tyrannus, 3
happiness, 100
healings (gift), 74
heart, 26
  heart circumcision, 186
  See also circumcision
heaven, 69
  assurance of heaven, 78
  citizenship in heaven, 201
  and fear of death, 151–54
  rewards in heaven, 272
  seeking heaven, 277–80
heavenly places, 11, 35, 52,
  54, 117
Hebrew, 186–88
height, 61
helmet of salvation, 126–28
helps (gift), 74
Hendricks, Howard G.
  on fathers' embittering
    children, 112–13
  on knowing Christ as total

experience, 190
  on leaders' following Christ,
    220
heresies, 231–33
hidden life in Christ, 279–80
Hierapolis, 231
holiness, and good works,
  33–34
holy, 13
  meaning of word, 7
Holy Spirit
  children and Holy Spirit,
    109–11
  fellowship of the Holy
    Spirit, 160
  fruit of the Spirit, 286
  grieving Holy Spirit, 82–84
  as seal of redemption,
    20–22
  signs of indwelling, 97–98
  sin and Holy Spirit, 22–23
  See also Holy Spirit, actions
Holy Spirit, actions
  assurances, 21–23
  bringing our concerns to
    God, 44
  empowers us to live for
    God, 87
  enlightening believers,
    25–26
  giving wisdom, 24
  indwelling believers, 31–32
  inspiring Bible, 290
  sealing Gentile believers,
    20–22
  strengthening persecuted
    Christians, 150
  See also God; Jesus
homes, meeting in homes, 50
honor, for parents, 110–11
hope, 236–38
  of Christian believers, 69
  of his calling, 25–26
  of salvation, 126
hostility, 41
household of God, 43
humble, humility, 52, 66–68,
  162–67, 286
  false humility, 272–73
  how acquired, 163
  Jesus as model, 164–67
humor, 90

husbands
  command to love wives,
    296–97
  listening to wives, 105
  sacrificing for wives, 102–7
  wives' submission, 100–102
Hybels, Bill
  on asking God's help in
    praying, 241
  on praising God, 12
  on writing out prayers, 129
Hybels, Bill and Lynne
  on marriage as lifetime
    challenge, 106
hymns, 289–90
hypostatic union, 248

I

imitation, 87–89
imitators of God, 87
immorality, 77, 89–91
imperfection, 171
in Christ, 16
incarnation of Jesus, 164–67
indwelling by Holy Spirit,
  97–98
inheritance, 19
  inheritance in Christ, 22–23
inner clothing, 78–85
inner man, 58
insults, 84
Ironside, H. A.
  on assurance of salvation,
    250
  on divine revelation as final
    answer, 260
  on outline of Paul's
    Ephesians 3 prayer, 56
  on Paul's view of
    imprisonment, 305
  on predestination to
    salvation, 16
  on Scripture not condemn-
    ing knowledge, 264

J

jailer, 135–36, 162
James, 50
Jeffers, James
  on master's power over

slaves, 302–3
  on New Testament view of
    slavery, 116
Jehovah, and Gentiles, 39
  See also God, actions
Jesus
  and angels, 27
  benefits of believing in him,
    16–18
  and demons, 27
  his resurrection's benefits,
    35–37
  his resurrection's
    significance, 27–28
  his teachings on Christian
    unity, 211
  See also Jesus, actions
Jesus, actions
  always acts in peace, 288–89
  appears to Paul, 7–8
  breaks down barriers, 44
  brings in Gentiles, 38–39
  creates "new man," 40–42
  demonstrates deity, 265–66
  disarms Satan, 270
  enables Christians' access to
    God, 54
  enthroned in hearts, 58–59
  his burial, 72
  holds all things together,
    245–46
  makes peace, 247–49
  makes salvation available, 37
  reconciles all things, 247–52
  submits to parents, 297
  tempted but without sin,
    281
  unique works listed, 43
  See also Jesus, his attributes
Jesus, his attributes
  all things under his feet, 27
  ascending, 70–72
  attributes in Colossians,
    243–47
  attributes in Philippians,
    152
  authority, 27
  chief cornerstone, 43
  church as his body, 27
  co-creator, 51
  cornerstone, 45

Creator, 15, 244–46
  descending, 70–72
  exalted, 166–67
  far above all, 27
  fills all in all, 27
  firstborn from dead, 246
  firstborn of all creation,
    243–44
  forgiving, 239
  fullness of God in him,
    264–66
  gentleness, 214
  head of body, 76, 246
  head of church, 7, 69, 246
  head of principality, power,
    264–66
  humble, 164–67
  image of invisible God,
    243–44
  intermediary, 54
  knowing our weaknesses, 55
  lamb of God, 248
  Lord, 69
  Lord and Master, 18
  mystery, 51
  not created, 244
  offering to God, 87
  peace, 42
  preeminence, 246
  preexisting, 243–44
  Prince of Peace, 42
  raised, 27
  sacrificed, 88
  sacrifice to God, 87
  Savior, 69
  seated in heaven, 27
  Son of God, 15
  struggling with suffering,
    147
  sustainer, 245–46
  without sin, 17
  See also God; Holy Spirit
Jesus or Justus, 307
Jews
  and circumcision, 183–86
  as first believers, 19
  and Gentiles, 38–39,
    251–52
Jezebel, 48
John Mark, 210
John the Baptist, 3

Palmer, Earl
  on how Holy Spirit uses our
    prayers, 150
  on Satan's "spooking"
    Christians, 155
parents
  behavior to children,
    111–13
  children to honor, obey,
    109–11
  not provoking children,
    298–99
pastors, 73, 138, 139
path of good works, 37
patience, 67–68
Paul, iv
  accused of bringing Gentile
    to temple, 41
  chained to soldier, 121–22,
    145–47
  conversion, 7–8, 188
  developed ministry, 251–54
  early life as Pharisee,
    persecutor, 186–88
  and Epaphroditus, 176–78
  events at Ephesus, 3–4
  friends in Rome, 307–8
  handwriting, 308–9
  healings at Ephesus, 3
  imprisoned at Rome, 3,
    47–48, 55–56
  maligned by some, 147–49
  ministered from prison,
    258–59
  possibly married, 296
  received gift from
    Philippians, 220–21
  refused Corinthians' gift,
    221
  relations with Colossian
    church, 231, 234
  released after house arrest,
    149
  reminded readers of his
    bondage, 304–5
  risks on first imprisonment,
    149
  second missionary journey, 3
  third missionary journey, 3
  and Timothy, 173–76
  See also Paul, as author
Paul, as author, 4

grace and peace salutation,
  233, 234–35
his letters passed around, 5
his prison epistles iii–iv
lost letters, 182
main goal in Ephesians, 6
See also Paul, characteristics
Paul, characteristics
  affection for congregation,
    143–44
  ambassador in chains,
    128–29
  apostle, 233–35
  apostle to the Gentiles, 52
  boldness, 149–50
  confidence in God, 141–43
  contentment, 221–23
  death not feared, 37,
    151–54
  encouraging, 235–36
  former persecutor, 51
  gratitude, 139–41
  Hebrew (Jew), 186–88
  humble, 51, 159
  imprisonment for gospel a
    privilege, 55–56,
  joy despite suffering,
    149–51
  least of all saints, 51
  man of prayer, 3, 15–25,
    56, 62–63
  persecutor, 187
  Pharisee, 186–88
  prisoner of Christ Jesus,
    47–48
  recipient of grace, 48–49
  striving for upward call of
    God, 194–96
  trust while in prison, 37
  unlikely convert, 7
  view of suffering, 145–47
  See also Paul, teachings
Paul, teachings
  on alertness, 96–97
  on anxiety, 215–17
  on asceticism, 273–75
  on Christian behavior,
    65–117
  on Christian masters'
    conduct, 115–17
  on Christian servants'
    conduct, 113–17

on Christ's position,
  actions, 241–51
on circumcision, 183–88
on complaining, 169–72
on contentment, 221–23
on cross and forgiveness,
  268–70
on equality in Christ,
  284–85
on false teachers, 197–98
on gentleness, 213–15
on glorifying Christ in life,
  death, 149–51
on Gnosticism, 232–33
on God's working in us,
  141–43
on good works, 259–61
on growing up in Christ,
  75–80
on heresies, 231–33
on imitating mature
  Christians, 198–201
on Jesus as God, 264–66
on Jesus's incarnation,
  164–67
on joy amid suffering,
  172–73
on knowing God, 191–94
on legalism, 270–71
on maturity in Christ,
  197–98
on metaphors, 196
on new life in Christ,
  277–80
on not fearing death,
  151–54
on oneness, 68–70
on parents and children,
  109–13
on perfection, 194–96
on prayer for leaders, 303–5
on referring everything to
  God, 290–91
on resisting Satan, 117–29
on resurrection body, 203–4
on righteousness, 190–91
on salvation by faith,
  261–64
on salvation for Gentiles,
  38–39
on salvation through grace,
  167–69

on meaning of "heart" in Bible, 26
on thanking God for fulfilling purposes, 213
on what born-again Christian receives, 54
water baptism, 69
wax. *See* seal
Wells, Thelma
on joy amid suffering, 154
whatsoever things, 217–19
White, John
on awareness of God's love, 60
on importance of giving thanks, 24
on structure of Paul's letter to Ephesians, 6
width, length, depth, height of Christ's love, 59, 60–61
Wiersbe, Warren
on firstborn from dead, 247
on God's delays not denials, 129
on growing spiritually from inside out, 266
on importance of prayer for pastor, 305
on Paul's priorities, 189
on prayer and fellowship with God, 304
on responding to God's grace, 168

on rules not creating spirituality, 274
Wilkinson, Bruce H.
on choosing to love one's spouse, 104
on confidence in God's love, 61
on lies as instruments of bondage, 123
Willard, Dallas
on Jesus as creator, 245
on Jesus as joyous, creative person, 248
on nature of God's love, 60
wind of doctrine, 75
wisdom, 24, 258
Christian gains wisdom, 17
as God's gift, 127–28
manifold wisdom of God, 52, 53–54
wisdom of God, 24–25
See also knowledge
without blame, 13
witnessing, 97
wives
justice for wives, 301–2
submitting to husbands, 100–102, 293–96
women in early church, 103–4
status of women, 211–12, 294
word of God, v, 126–28
See also Bible

work, 81–82
works, 167–69
and salvation, 37
worry, 36, 207
See also anxiety
worthy, 65, 66
wrath, 84, 282
wrath of God, 32
See also sin
Wright, N. T.
on God's revealing our true selves, 280
on Jesus's defeating sin and death, 246
on Jesus's preexistence, 244
Wuest, Kenneth S.
on conformity to Christ's death, 192
on imitating Jesus's virtues, 165
on losing all for Christ, 189

Y

Yancey, Philip
on forgiveness as act of faith, 287
on God of grace, not judgment, 243
on importance of grace, 10–11

Melissa Foley 2-4
2713 W. Koenig 68803
Phone# 224-1963